OXFORD MODERN LANGUAGES
AND LITERATURE MONOGRAPHS

Editorial Committee

*Oxford Modern Languages and
Literature Monographs*

VOLTAIRE: Historian. By J. H. BRUMFITT. 1958

THE PETRARCHAN SOURCES OF *LA CELESTINA*
By A. D. DEYERMOND. 1961

THE TRAGEDIES OF GIAMBATTISTA CINTHIO GIRALDI
By P. R. HORNE. 1962

PONTUS DE TYARD

AND HIS

DISCOURS PHILOSOPHIQUES

BY

KATHLEEN M. HALL

OXFORD UNIVERSITY PRESS

1963

Oxford University Press, Amen House, London E.C.4

GLASGOW NEW YORK TORONTO MELBOURNE WELLINGTON
BOMBAY CALCUTTA MADRAS KARACHI LAHORE DACCA
CAPE TOWN SALISBURY NAIROBI IBADAN ACCRA
KUALA LUMPUR HONG KONG

PRINTED IN GREAT BRITAIN

5/72

ACKNOWLEDGEMENTS

IN publishing this revised and shortened version of a doctoral thesis accepted by the University of Oxford, I should like to express my warm gratitude for the stimulating teaching of Dr. K. Chesney, Dr. M. Gerard Davis, Mrs. D. R. Sutherland, and Dr. W. G. Moore; for the ready help of Professor V.-L. Saulnier, Dr. M. L. M. Young, Mr. C. W. Whitaker, Mr. A. E. Douglas, Mrs. J. R. Lyle, and Miss P. M. Hurst; for the patient encouragement of Professor C. A. Hackett and of my relatives; and to St. Hilda's College, Oxford, the British Federation of University Women, and the University of Southampton, for help in financing my researches, and to the staff of the libraries where I pursued them, in Paris, Troyes, London, and Oxford. Finally I would offer sincere thanks to those whose works I mention cursorily or critically, but from whom I have learnt much.

KATHLEEN M. HALL

Southampton
Christmas 1961

CONTENTS

NOTE ON QUOTATIONS

In quoting I have reproduced Jean de Tournes's acute accent on inverted first-person verbs, but expanded contractions, and regularized the use of *i* and *j*, *u* and *v*, and the spelling of Baïf and Peletier. The paragraphing in quotations from Tyard's Discourses is mine, and so are all italics unless otherwise indicated. In footnotes some works are referred to by short titles, to which Bibliography II will supply the key, while Tyard's works are referred to by the following abbreviations:

CE, 1551	*Continuation des erreurs* (No. 3 of Bibliography I)
DD, 1578	*Deux discours* (No. 19)
DP, 1587	*Discours philosophiques* (No. 27)
DT, 1556	*Discours du temps* (No. 11)
DT, 1578	*Discours du temps* (No. 20)
M, 1558	*Mantice* (No. 13)
M, 1573	*Mantice* (No. 16)
RNOP, 1573	*Recueil de nouvelles œuvres poëtiques* (No. 17)
SP, 1552	*Solitaire premier* (No. 5)
SP, 1575	*Solitaire premier* (No. 18)
SS, 1555	*Solitaire second* (No. 9)
TLE, 1555	*Troisieme livre des erreurs* (No. 8)
U, 1557	*L'Univers* (No. 12)

I · LIFE

THE *Erreurs amoureuses* and the other poetical works of Pontus de Tyard are known perhaps as well as they deserve; twentieth-century attention has turned to his prose works, and chiefly his *Discours philosophiques*. These cannot be called really great, any more than Tyard himself; they have often been called unreadable; but they were highly esteemed in their time, and offer a revealing glimpse into the mind of a man growing up in the most fruitful period of the Renaissance, alive to the exciting impacts of broadened knowledge and use of the classics, scientific and geographical discovery, and religious and political speculation.

Yet critical estimates of Tyard differ widely. Chamard finds it possible to ignore him almost completely in the concluding chapters of his *Histoire de la Pléiade*, and indeed never seems quite sure why he was ever included in that body. Busson classes him as one of the 'disciples des Padouans avant Montaigne', 'épris de rationalisme';[1] J. C. Lapp is impressed first of all by the 'forthrightness and originality of certain of his views on science and philosophy';[2] while for Frances Yates he is a musical and mystical humanist, 'the philosophical theorist of the sixteenth-century French academies'.[3] Perhaps it is S. F. Baridon who brings his reader nearest to a sympathetic understanding of Tyard's 'amore dell'indagine autonoma, seria, serena'.[4]

A review of what is known of Tyard's life, his own pronouncements about his work, and his use of his sources contributes to a modified but perhaps consistent picture of what he was like and what he was trying to do. He was certainly not a member of the 'Brigade', he may even have seldom met the Pléiade till late in his life, and it can have been only a minor part of his time and energy that he devoted to Baïf's Academy and its exploration of esoteric truths. To the implications of rationalism in particular he was sometimes blind, sometimes definitely hostile, and he found a fideistic way of escape from them more comparable with Giorgio's

[1] Busson, *Rationalisme*, 1922, p. 314; 1957, p. 295.
[2] Lapp, *Universe*, 1950, p. vii.   [3] Yates, *Academies*, 1947, p. 77.
[4] Baridon, *Pontus de Tyard*, 1950, p. 186.

or La Primaudaye's than with Tahureau's or even Montaigne's. He was above all a popularizer of the lower and middle ranges of Renaissance and especially Neoplatonic learning, alive to the need to open them in simple French to the young men and women of the provincial *cénacles* and *salons*, struggling to keep up with the intellectual pace of the Parisian ones.

Detailed study of Tyard's works, and chiefly of the different strata of the *Discours philosophiques*, has another value. It seems possible to trace, in part at least, the chronological order in which the influences of the Renaissance played upon Tyard, the gradual development of his attitude towards them and especially towards Neoplatonism, and his gradual discovery of his vocation. One can, in short, detect something of the working and growing of a 'second-rate sensitive mind' at that bewildering time.

1 · Provincial Student

One has to guess at Tyard's early life, and even his date of birth; the latest guess is 1522, the only date which reconciles the demands of five contemporary testimonies.[1] That would make him the same age as Du Bellay, a few years older than most of the rest of the Pléiade, nearly twenty years younger than Scève, and some seven years older than Guillaume des Autelz, his friend and second cousin. Both came of a family of Burgundian nobles, important in their province if not outside it, who could trace their descent back to the beginning of the fourteenth century. Tyard's father, Jehan de Tyart of Bissy-sur-Fley, was lieutenant-general of Mâcon, and married Jeanne de Ganay, of the family of the Chancellor of France. Besides a daughter, they had three sons, Nicolas, Claude, and Pontus; it was the last who preferred to spell his surname with a *d*. His romantic baptismal name, though it became a family one after he reached fame, was nothing but that of the knight of the Round Table whose adventures were still popular.

Born at Bissy, Tyard presumably passed his early years there; but little is known about them. His family were good Catholics and cultured, and his young cousin, whose home was within sight of Bissy, must have grown into a stimulating companion. His education, according to his nineteenth-century biographer Jeandet,[2] was

---

[1] K. M. Hall, in *Revue des sci. hum.*, 1958.
[2] Jeandet, *Pontus de Tyard*, 1860, p. 80.

directed by his father and included Latin, Greek, Italian, and Hebrew; but this needs some qualification. Certainly by 1552 at latest he could read Latin fluently, while from 1560 onwards he showed that he could also write it elegantly and forcefully. In most instances of his use of Greek sources, however, a Latin version was available when he wrote, and until 1578 his use of Hebrew proves little more than an acquaintance with the Hebrew alphabet and with Latin compendia. Finally Saulnier has discovered Tyard's copy of Petrarch, in the Lyons edition of August 1545, and has shown from an examination of Tyard's marginal notes that when he made them his Italian was elementary.[1] The disappearance of such jottings after the first few sonnets may indeed indicate rapid improvement; Tyard knew Italian well by 1551, when he translated Leo Hebraeus's *Dialoghi d'amore*. But the legend that he travelled to Italy in his youth has no basis other than a reference in the *Solitaire second* to 'meints lieus d'Italie . . . principalement en la Pouille, ou je me suis rencontré quelquefois',[2] a remark attributed not to the 'Solitaire', more or less representing Tyard, but to the 'Curieux', more or less representing Des Autelz.

A letter of protection[3] in the Côte d'Or archives shows that Tyard was an 'escollier juré' at the University of Paris in 1537; but we do not know his college, his associates, the course of his studies, the length of his residence, or whether he resided at all. Claude Perry saw the remains of student prejudice in his 1591 *Fragmentum Epistolae* against the Jesuits:

Il les y traitte assez mal, soit qu'il ne les conneût pas, ou qu'il eût aversion de leur institut, qui n'agréeoit pas à beaucoup de gens de l'Université de Paris, où il avoit fait ses estudes. . . .[4]

But this may be the mere guesswork of one who was anxious to defend his own Order without seriously attacking a past bishop. In any case it would seem that Tyard cannot have attended the lectures of Dorat, a revelation to so many of the Pléiade. Dorat did not move to Coqueret before 1545—according to Chamard, not before 1547; by 1549 a liaison in Burgundy had drawn from Tyard nearly a hundred love-poems, some of which suggest his presence there in 1545 or earlier.

He himself dates the beginning of his poetic career around 1543,

[1] Saulnier, in *Revue de litt. comp.*, 1948.   [2] SS, 1555, p. 117.
[3] Baridon, *Pontus de Tyard*, 1950, p. 235.
[4] Perry, *Chalon-sur-Saône*, 1659, p. 356.

in the preface to the 1573 collection of his complete poetical works, 'ceste longue continuation, commencée il y a trente ans'. This may be an approximation, but clearly amounts to a claim that his first poems preceded those of Du Bellay and Ronsard, and were therefore the first to introduce the style now known as that of the Pléiade:

> N'ayant aucun devant moy, qui en François eust publié Poëmes respondans à l'elevation de mes passionnées conceptions ... je mis peine d'embellir et hausser le stile de mes vers, plus que n'estoit celuy des rimeurs qui m'avoient precedé. . . . Mais au mesme temps que je fiz prendre l'air à mes Poësies, sortirent en lumiere les œuvres de Ronsard Vandomois, et du Bellay Angevin. . . .

The claim has led to much confused argument. The question of Tyard's independence of the rest of the Pléiade was complicated as long as the date of the *Olive* was uncertain. It is now agreed that the *Olive* was published at Easter 1549 (new style), and the first volume of the *Erreurs amoureuses* not till November; but Tyard's poems would surely be more than six months in preparation, and perhaps even be 'taking the air' in private circulation before Easter. Even Ronsard implied this in the 1578 version of the *Elegie à Jean de la Peruse*, when a reference to Du Bellay's priority was replaced by the couplet:

> Longtemps avant d'un ton plus haut que luy
> Tyard chanta son amoureux ennuy. . . .

Sonnet 19 of Tyard's *Continuation des erreurs*, written in 1550 or 1551, describes his attachment as having lasted for two years and six months:

> Le demi lustre est desja revolu,
> Et l'œil du Ciel ha sa veuë tournee
> A l'opposite et contraire journee,
> Que je fu tout à liberté tollu.

This would suggest that he fell in love and started his sonnet-sequence in late 1547 or early 1548.

The style of his first two volumes strongly indicates that he read the work of the 'Brigade' in the interval between them, and not before. The *Erreurs amoureuses* of 1549 are noticeably bare of the characteristic devices of the Pléiade, which so richly adorn the *Continuation* of 1551. This overflows with classical and mythological allusions, imitations of Latin phrases and turns of thought, compound epithets, and the motifs of the transience of beauty and the immortality of the poet:

> Je n'ay encor de la sainte eau sceu boire
> Dessouz le pied du prompt cheval des cieux:
> Ni le doux songe ha repeu mes deux yeux
> Au double mont, des filles de Memoire.
> Mais j'ose bien, soit ma honte, ou ma gloire,
> Me confesser du grand vainqueur des Dieux
> (Des jeunes cœurs le soucy gracieux)
> Estre vaincu en superbe victoire.
> C'est donq d'Amour la poizon aigredouce,
> Qui en fureur poëtique me pousse,
> Pour consacrer mes vers sus son autel.
> Pourróy-je aussi sus un aelle plus forte,
> Que celle la que le petit Dieu porte,
> Hausser mon vol louable et immortel?[1]

It is natural to conclude that the *Continuation* is a swift reaction to a new stimulus; possibly the first *Erreurs* had called out a response from the Brigade; almost certainly Tyard had been deeply impressed by the *Olive* and Ronsard's *Odes*, published so soon before and after the *Erreurs*. He evidently had enough imagination to produce fluent and even distinctive work in the new style as soon as it attracted his attention, but not enough to have directed him independently along the same lines.

Pasquier understood Ronsard to be claiming for Tyard the glory of introducing the sonnet into France:

> Celuy qui premier nous apporta les Odes fut Ronsard; et du Bellay les Sonnets . . . Ronsard en une Elegie qu'il escrit à Jean de la Peruse, l'attribue à Pontus de Thiart: mais il s'abuse. . . .[2]

At the beginning of this century the claim was thought worth examining, and sometimes admitted in part. But it seems to be a red herring; neither Ronsard's 'Elegie' nor Tyard's dedication refers specially to the sonnet form. Tyard's fancy did run as far as reviving the sestina in French, in a rhymed form still harder to write than the unrhymed. He need not be credited with the much greater discovery of the possibilities of the sonnet. If he did not know Marot's and Mellin de Saint-Gelais's exercises in the form, he must surely have known those of Scève.

---

[1] CE, 1551, concluding sonnet.   [2] Pasquier, *Recherches*, 1596, IV. xxxi.

The influence of the School of Lyons, to be seen in greater
or less degree in all Tyard's poetry after the *Erreurs* of 1549, is to be
seen there in an almost pure state. It includes the idealization of
women in general and of the poet's beloved in particular, a Petrarchist attitude in the lover, a Neoplatonic conception of love, scientific and philosophical imagery, and the subtly refined style of Scève.
As an undergraduate in Paris, Tyard may have sat at the feet of
Héroet, whom he ranks immediately after Scève in a 'Chant en
faveur de quelques excellens poetes de ce temps' in his *Livre de vers
liriques*. But Scève was his most honoured master; the first sonnet of
the *Erreurs* is addressed to him, and virtually admits to imitating him:

> Si en toy luyt le flambeau gracieux,
>> Flambeau d'Amour, qui tout gent cœur allume,
>> Comme il faisoit lors, qu'à ta docte plume
> Tu fis haulser le vol jusques aux cieux:
> Donne, sans plus une heure à tes deux yeux
>> Pour voir l'ardeur, qui me brule, et consume
>> En ces erreurs, qu'Amour sur son enclume
> Me fait forger, de travail ocieux.
> Tu y pourras recongnoitre la flame,
>> Qui enflama si hautement ton ame,
>> Mais non les traits de ta divine veine.
> Aussi je prens le blasme en patience,
>> Prest d'endurer honteuse penitence,
>> Pour les erreurs de ma jeunesse vaine.

So, if the genesis of the *Erreurs* was similar to that of the *Continuation*, it would seem also to have been a reaction to a stimulus
received not long before: a reading of the *Parfaicte amye* of 1542,
the *Délie* of 1544 and the 1545 edition of Petrarch, and an introduction to Scève and his circle. This must have been obtained in
the period of these publications, very likely in the latter part of it;
Saulnier thinks Tyard may have been first drawn to Scève by Jean
de Tournes's eulogy of him, printed in the Petrarch. Scève would
have been living in semi-retirement from about 1542 to 1545, and
a Mâconnais student little more than twenty could hardly have
penetrated that retirement, still less seen Scève's unpublished
manuscripts. But Saulnier has evidence[1] suggesting that Tyard
already knew Pernette du Guillet, who died a month before the
Petrarch appeared.

---

[1] Saulnier, in *Bibl. d'Hum. et Ren.*, 1943.

The *Erreurs* of 1549 contain not only sonnets and a sestina, but 'chansons' and 'epigrammes', really dixains closely imitating those of the *Délie* in content and style. Saulnier derives one of them, however, from a sixain in the *Fleur de poésie françoise*, a well-known collection of 1542:

C'est ung grand mal que d'ung refus,
Et si n'est-on jamais plainct d'ame. . . .

He thinks Tyard elaborated from that piece the 'epigramme' which follows his eleventh sonnet:

Ce m'est un mal, que je n'eusse pensé,
De ne pouvoir, ou je pretens atteindre:
Ce m'est grand mal, quand tu m'as offensé,
De ne m'oser, et moins me savoir plaindre. . . .

A dixain by Pernette would be a reply:

C'est un grand mal se sentir offensé,
Et ne s'oser, ou sçavoir a qui plaindre:
C'est un grand mal, voire trop insensé,
Que d'aspirer, ou l'on ne peult attaindre. . . .

This seems closer to the anonymous original than does Tyard's, and the truth may be merely that he read the dixain in her posthumous *Rymes* and worked out a variant on it. But one inclines to agree with Saulnier that 'c'est l'épigramme de Pernette qui rend le son d'une "réponse", d'un "corrigé"', and that she and Tyard were playing the game of *complainte et réponse* which her circle had revived from the days of the Grands Rhétoriqueurs.

This applies even more to the manifest relationship between her sixth 'Chant' and the 'Chant non mesuré' which follows Tyard's fourteenth sonnet. His song opens:

J'ay passé plusieurs ans du temps de ma jeunesse,
Sans congnoissance avoir de dueil, ou de tristesse:
Lors estoit ma pensée
De toute affection delivre et dispensee.
Sans passion d'esprit en ce temps là j'estois:
Mon regard franchement en tout lieu je jettois:
Et moins de liberté
N'avoit, que mes deux yeux, ma franche volunté.
Mais les Dieux envieux de mon aise et repos,
M'attiltrerent un jour un archer à propos:
Qui descochant sa flesche,
Et tirant à mon cœur, luy fit piteuse bresche. . . .

Pernette begins:

> Sans congnoissance aucune en mon Printemps j'estois:
> Alors aucun souspir encor point ne gectois,
> Libre sans liberté: car rien ne regrectois
> En ma vague pensee
> De molz, et vains desirs follement dispensee.
>
> Mais Amour tout jaloux du commun bien des Dieux,
> Se voulant rendre a moi, comme a maintz odieux,
> Me vint escarmoucher par faulx alarmes d'yeux,
> Mais je veis sa fallace:
> Parquoy me retiray, et lui quictay la place. . . .
>
> A la fin congnoissant, qu'il n'avoit la puissance
> De me contraindre en rien luy faire obeissance,
> Tascha le plus, qu'il peust, d'avoir la congnoissance
> Des Archiers de Vertu,
> Par qui mon cueur forcé fut soubdain abattu. . . .

In his 'Étude sur Pernette du Guillet' Saulnier only mentioned
the parallel as an example of imitation by Tyard; but it reads more
as if Pernette is rewriting his poem from a greater poetic maturity,
and refusing his plea for 'guérison' on the ground that she is
already 'chastement' bound to Scève:

> . . . es mains, ou heureuse devins,
> D'un qui est haultement en ses escriptz divins,
> Comme Caton severe,
> Et chaste tellement que chacun l'en revere. . . .

This literary correspondence need not be dated back to the high
summer of Scève's relationship with Pernette, but rather to its
exquisite autumn, dated by Saulnier[1] from 1542 to 1545, when
Lyons knew it to be a pure relationship of poet and Muse. As an
admirer of it, Tyard might well have presented himself to Pernette
with his dixain and song as letters of introduction, and, in face of
her discouragement of him and her death soon after, transferred
his allegiance to her lover, and his literary exercises to the sequence
he was soon to begin to a lady of his own.

A little more can be deduced about what Tyard must have been
before the coming of either the stimulus of Lyons or that of the
Brigade. One sees him as a man still young in artistic development;
with a sound general education, a passion for learning, and an

---

[1] *Maurice Scève*, 1948, i. 163.

inclination towards literature; but with talents that had not yet found the task naturally suited to them, with latent powers that waited for something or someone to render them active. It seems necessary to believe, however, that he had undergone some preparation, conscious or not, for the inspiration that was to come; and three possibilities suggest themselves.

Firstly, he must have passed through an apprentice stage in versifying; the first book of the *Erreurs amoureuses* is the work of a man who was at least expert in his medium, who could compose technically correct sonnets, and songs with a certain amount of musical charm. Where the poems are bad it is due not to inexperience but to a constitutional lack of genius. Tyard may have learnt in the school of Marot; Saulnier calls his borrowing from the *Fleur de poésie françoise* 'une sorte de développement pétrarquiste d'une pièce marotique'. He may have learnt from Mellin de Saint-Gelais, admiration for whom is expressed in the 1555 'Chant en faveur de quelques excellens poetes'. But if he destroyed all his earlier efforts it may well indicate that he was dissatisfied with his models as well as with his achievements.

Next, it was surely not during a period of intoxication by the productions of either Lyons or the Brigade, but through study for its own sake, that he acquired the accurate scientific and metaphysical knowledge shown in the imagery of even his first volume of poems, for example in his exercise in *terza rima*, 'Disgrace':

> La haulte idee à mon univers mere,
>   Si haultement de nul jamais comprise,
>   M'est à present tenebreuse Chimere . . .
> L'ame, qui fit long temps en moy demeure,
>   Iniquement d'autre corps s'associe:
>   Et s'eslongnant de moy, veult que je meure,
>   Pour s'exercer en palingenesie.

And thirdly, Tyard's life was so crowded from about 1545 to 1558 that one inclines to attribute to the period before 1545 the unorthodox studies described in *Mantice*:

ce mesme desir . . . pour la science des choses avenir, m'a tellement entretenu, et je puis dire trompé les premiers ans, que je n'ay espargné ny l'estude, ny la peine, ny ce que j'ay peu du bien, pour acquerir ce don, qui me sembloit le plus souhaitable, que ce Monde peust clorre: voire que les Cieux nous peussent departir. J'ay esté en queste des Daimons et Esprits avec les armes requises en telle entreprinse, mais je n'y sceuz onques voir ny ouïr que la finale moquerie de ma folle superstition. J'en ay autrefois recueilli et experimenté infinies receptes, et formé cent et cent characteres monstreux: mais tout cela me succedoit comme l'espoir fumeux de l'Elixir aux Alchimistes. . . .[1]

This reminds one of the development of two of Tyard's contemporaries. Henri Estienne recounts his own:

contigit . . . ut genethlialogos quoque evadere summopere cuperem . . . acrior vehementiorque cupiditas illius scientiae mihi excitabatur. . . . Adimus igitur quendam . . . petit ille a nobis pretium mirum quantum. . . . At ecce quod in Graeco proverbio est, Thesaurus, carbones. . . . Postea vero hoc etiam certo cognovimus, ipsum nihil certi, nihil veri solitum praedicere. . . .[2]

Sherrington traces a similar interest in astrology, followed by a similar reaction against it, in Jean Fernel, who was connected with Estienne's circle.[3] He and Estienne did not go as far as Tyard in occult studies, nor did Tyard go as far as they in giving up belief in judicial astrology. But it is interesting that both Estienne's and Fernel's investigations were in the years around 1540, which they spent in Paris as Tyard may have done.

11 · Platonic Lover

Pernette du Guillet can only have been a Rosaline for Tyard; in 1547 or 1548 he found his Juliet. He gave her the name of Pasithée, made her a speaker in his first two Discours philosophiques, the Solitaire premier and Solitaire second, and clearly addressed to her the three books of his translation of Leo Hebraeus and the love-poems of his four early volumes, though in those he rarely permitted himself to use even his own name for her. It was the Homeric name of the Grace usually known as Aglaia; it may have meant rather more to Tyard on account of the etymology and charming description given by Giraldi in his encyclopædia De Deis Gentium:

Hesiodus autem eam Nereidum unam facit, dictam quod omnibus esset admirabilis, vel quod ad eam omnes properarent. . . . Scribunt nonnulli Pasitheam unam Gratiarum, quae tres sunt: Aglaia una, quae

[1] M, 1558, p. 89.
[2] H. Estienne, Noctes Atticae . . . Henrici Stephani noctes aliquot parisinae, atticis A. Gellii noctibus seu vigiliis invigilatae . . ., Paris, 1585, p. 150.
[3] C. Sherrington, The Endeavour of Jean Fernel, Cambridge, 1946, p. 18.

nobis dici potest Maiestas, seu venustas, honestasve: Euphrosyna alia, quae hilaritas, iucunditas, laetitiaque: Thalia tertia, festivitas, lepiditasve, ac concinnitas. . . . Sed hanc aliqui Pasitheam, quasi dixeris undique divinam, quae scilicet maiestatem, hilaritatemque ac lepiditatem in sese, et alias quoque complicet.

Tyard seems to have been the first Renaissance poet to consider Pasithea along these lines, as a unique Grace equivalent to Charis, and to give her name to his lady, 'l'unique simulachre'[1] of the three Graces; though Vaganay showed how many poets, including Du Bellay and Ronsard, followed his example.[2]

After 1555 Tyard's works do not mention Pasithée, except for an 'Elegie à Pierre de Ronsard', published in the *Recueil de nouvelles œuvres poëtiques* of 1573 but evidently composed much earlier. Most of the new poems, and certain introductory paragraphs added in 1578 to the *Second Curieux*, again sing the praises of a 'belle et honneste Dame . . . ornee de toutes les vertus qui peuvent embellir l'humain entendement . . .'.[3] Undoubtedly this was the attractive and accomplished leader of society whom her friends called Pasithée, Claude-Catherine de Retz. One cannot be sure that Tyard contributed to her famous album; but his 1573 poems contained enough puns on the *rets* of his lady's hair and the *rais* of her eyes to make his allegiance clear, even before the 1575 edition of the *Solitaire premier* was explicitly dedicated 'à non moins docte et prudente, que genereuse et vertueuse dame, Dame Catherine de Cleremont, Contesse de Raiz, &c.' But she was not the Pasithée of Tyard's youth, the only woman to whom he himself ever gives the name. She was born only in 1544.

Yet the original Pasithée was not 'une Iris en l'air'. Unless Tyard was perpetrating an elaborate mystification, he himself disproved this when he prefixed his lady's portrait to the first two books of *Erreurs*, stated in dedicating his translation of Leo that she was eighteen in 1551, and explained to both Louise Labé in 1555 and Catherine in 1573 that his heart had already been engaged elsewhere:

> Ah! de quel feu brule un cœur ja en cendre?[4]

> Comment souz nouveau Joug me suis-je encor jecté?[5]

---

[1] SP, 1552, p. 61. [2] Vaganay, in *Revue de litt. comp.*, 1935.
[3] DD, 1578, p. 87.
[4] 'En contemplacion de D. Louïze Labé', *Euvres de Louïze Labé Lionnoize*, Lyons, 1555. [5] RNOP, 1573, Sonnet 1.

Several of his friends, including his cousin, write of Pasithée as if she really existed; on one occasion, not recorded in Tyard's own works, she would appear to have been teasing Des Autelz about his own relations with his 'Sainte':

> Vous voulez donc, Dame trois fois tresgrande,
> Me déroler de l'amoureuse bande . . .
> Je suis tout seul, qui ne puis (ce vous semble)
> Estre eloigné et Amoureux ensemble. . . .[1]

It is doubtful whether Tyard was even capable of conceiving and completing a long series of works dedicated to a creature of mere imagination. The evolution of his poetic style and of the *Discours philosophiques* shows how far he depended for inspiration on concrete sources and personal contacts. But he would have been quite capable of weaving round a real person, as previously round Pernette du Guillet, a set of unreal fancies.

The first book of the *Erreurs amoureuses* leaves only the vague impression common to Petrarchist sequences, while the second and third books seem to retell the same story rather than to carry it much farther. Tyard fell in love suddenly and incurably with Pasithée's 'beauté', 'esprit', and 'gent cœur revestu de vertu'. After an initial coldness, she began to show a certain tendency to flirt with her adorer, and to permit a slightly closer intimacy, withdrawn when he spoke too freely of his love. Sonnet 44 records a day when she promised:

> Je mettray fin à tes jours langoureux,
> Pour commencer tes bienheureuses nuits.

But this promise, as Vianey puts it, 'n'eut point de suite, Pasithée s'étant vite aperçue, je pense, qu'en la faisant elle avait simplement cédé au désir, irrésistible chez une lectrice de Tebaldeo, d'aiguiser une pointe'.[2]

Though Tyard speaks in Sonnet 52 of

> Le grand plaisir, que j'euz de toy jouir,

the line by itself has an unconvincing baldness, and in its context turns out to mean rather less than it leads one to expect. The most that is described, before the influence of Ronsard becomes unmistakable in the later *Erreurs*, is one kiss on Pasithée's hand in

---

[1] G. des Autelz, 'Elegie à la toute divine de Pontus de Tyard', *Amoureux repos*, Lyons, 1553.   [2] Vianey, *Pétrarquisme*, 1909, p. 127.

Sonnet 51, and one on her lips in Sonnet 54. Sonnets 53 and 54 suggest that after Sonnet 51 she was confined at home with a feverish cold, and Sonnet 52 recounts no more than that

> Fortune en fin piteuse à mon torment,
> Me fit revoir le Soleil de mes yeux,
> Alors qu'Amour me traittant encor mieux,
> Me fit jouir de mon contentement.
> O jour heureux esclarci clairement,
> De mon Soleil! ô Soleil gracieux
> Saint, et luisant plus que celuy des cieux,
> Digne de luire en tout le firmament.
> Le grand plaisir, que j'euz de toy jouir,
> Fit tellement mes deux yeux esblouir,
> Au flamboier de tes vives ardeurs,
> Que prenant peur de trop me contenter,
> Content je fuz loing de toy m'absenter,
> Dont maintenant, helas, helas je meurs.

According to Schmidt's interpretation, 'ces bagatelles dès qu'elles excitent en lui certains mouvements irrépressibles, symptômes d'un plaisir menaçant, lui causent une terreur panique';[1] alternatively, the hackneyed metaphors, subtle scruples, and facile 'contentment' may betray a literary exercise, based on book-learning rather than either imagination or experience. The youthful sins of which Tyard repented on his death-bed comprised only 'quelques poësies un peu trop amoureuses'.[2] It would seem that the sonnet of the promise came less near to Tyard's real feelings than the poem *De chaste amour* which concludes the first *Erreurs*:

> ... J'ay des faveurs ce que j'en vueil avoir,
> Car je ne veux que ce, qu'il fault vouloir,
> Et sçay si bien conduire,
> Suyvant honneur, tout ce que je demande,
> Qu'elle ne sceut onques d'une demande
> Seulement m'esconduire.

> Noz deux esprits d'une complexion,
> Sont eslongnez de toute passion,
> Passion qui tormente:
> Vivans ainsi en ce mortel sejour
> Avec espoir, qu'au ciel leur grande amour
> Sera du tout contente. ...

---

[1] Schmidt, in *La Table ronde*, 1956, p. 84.
[2] Perry, *Chalon-sur-Saône*, 1659, p. 414.

More definite details about Pasithée can be gathered from the *Solitaire premier* and *Solitaire second*; for the attainments of the Solitaire's pupil are so consistent and well defined, and the first treatise at least so well adapted to her level, as to suggest that Tyard had in mind a particular girl, by then aged nineteen, perhaps combining the qualities of the three Graces and the nine Muses, but also human. 'Je ne puys n'admirer', he writes,

en si jeune aage, en si delicate personne moins propre pour endurer le labeur de l'estude, à laquelle encor (autant à mon regret, qu'au vostre) vous ne pouvez despendre que le tems desrobé: je ne puis, dí je, non admirer en vous l'abondance de tant de gentilz discours, la congnoissance de tant de diverses choses. . . .[1]

She was familiar with philosophical and musical terms, and accomplished at calculating, versifying, performing on various instruments, and casting horoscopes.[2] One can also discern in her a little coquetry, much tact, a pretty wit, and a sense of humour: the Solitaire finds her 'embesongnee en la consideracion de quelques figures Astronomiques':

En bonne foy (ajouta elle, avec un serenement de face qui ne peut s'escrire qu'en mon cœur) je voulois former une figure du Ciel, pour rechercher de quel aspect fut sur vous cete continuelle solitude descochee, et comme elle pourra, ou quand, estre allegree.[3]

However, her questions to him show the limits of her education. Like the Aristotelian schoolboy, she has been 'trained in music so as actually to take part in its performance', but not trained in the theory behind it; it is the Solitaire who leads her on to the next stage foreseen by Aristotle for his pupils: 'when they get older they should be released from performing, but be able to judge what is beautiful and enjoy it rightly. . . .'[4] Her opinions, such as her admiration for the Pléiade, are sensitive and well formed; but her contributions are mostly from personal experience or practical knowledge, as of the Parisian lisp, 'R. et S. tousjours au rebours, l'un pour l'autre'.[5] Tyard represents her as unfamiliar with the Greek language, Neoplatonic philosophy, and elementary classical

---

[1] SP, 1552, pp. 92–93.
[2] Ibid., pp. 17 and 29; SS, 1555, pp. 9, 14, 154, and 156.
[3] SS, 1555, p. 9.
[4] Aristotle, *Politics*, VIII. vi. 1–2, in Rackham's translation.
[5] SP, 1552, p. 112.

mythology, while she is 'jealous' of the poetesses of France, and finds some difficulty in her studies: 'je sentois en mon esprit une confusion de choses ....'[1] Finally, she tends to concentrate on the material side of any subject and the literal sense of any remark, as when the Solitaire hints at his liability to divine and particularly erotic frenzy:

l'indisposition, laquelle vous pensez avoir congnue en moy, se doit plustot nommer fureur, qui vexe, et agite mon esprit. . . .

Haa, Solitaire, ostez ces paroles de facheux presage. . . . Fureur ne me semble estre autre chose (poursuivit elle) qu'une alienation d'entende-ment procedante d'un vice de cerveau, que vulgairement lon appelle folie. . . .[2]

Some of this artlessness Tyard may have lent her for his own pur-poses, to show what he is prepared to find among the readers of the Discourses; but, had he loved a lady of Scève's circle, she might not have been pleased at being cast for such a role.

Lapp argues from Des Autelz' poem that Pasithée was of 'high rank';[3] but 'greatness' is not necessarily social. It seems just as likely that she was the daughter of some country gentleman: the *Solitaires* represent her house as within easy reach of her admirer's, and 'à la ville' where he dealt with his 'domestiques, et privez affaires'.[4] If she came from a quiet home it would account for Tyard's apparently having only one rival throughout the *Erreurs*, and for the continual fear of scandal evinced there. Such a young girl can have had little influence over Tyard as a literary artist; but one must acknowledge her importance in inspiring the *Erreurs* and the first project of the Discourses. Nominally in her honour, Tyard produced in quick succession the first two volumes of *Erreurs*, examples of the newest fashions in verse composition; the translation of Leo's *Dialoghi d'amore*, that most important manual for a Renaissance Platonist; the *Solitaire premier*, intended as a work of literary elucidation and appreciation, 'pour servir de fueille aux escrits de tant de bons esprits, qui embellissent nostre France';[5] the third volume of *Erreurs . . . plus un livre de vers liriques*; and the *Solitaire second*, on music.

This is often stated to have appeared in 1552, like the *Solitaire premier*. But the 1555 copies give the impression of a first edition:

[1] SP, 1552, pp. 34, 50, 73, 106, and 92.   [2] Ibid., pp. 19–22.
[3] Lapp, *Universe*, 1950, p. xv.
[4] SP, 1552, p. 17.   [5] Ibid., p. 16.

there is an inaccuracy in some of the diagrams which necessitated an apology from the printer; a number of other serious mistakes remained uncorrected till 1587; and the privilege describes the work as a 'premiere impression'. It is a highly technical treatise, expensive to print, and the only one of the Discourses not thought worth republishing in the seventies; it would be surprising if it had been the only one thought worth republishing in the fifties. No copies of a 1552 edition are now known, and only two twentieth-century writers hint that they have seen one: L. Torri, who alone made the unlikely allegation that the 1555 edition reprinted it without change, mistakes and all—'l'edizione del 1555 non è l'edizione principe, ma semplicemente una ristampa di quella del 1552'[1]—and whose article contains one evident mistake, a reference to an imaginary edition of 1573; and Yvonne Rokseth, who told Chamard 'que l'édition princeps de 1552 se trouve à Milan'.[2] But it is untraceable there; perhaps Madame Rokseth misread as M.D.LII. the M.D.LV. of the edition in the Biblioteca di Brera. All other references to a 1552 edition appear to stem from one, present-day ones[3] from Marty-Laveaux's and Jeandet's, theirs from Papillon's and Niceron's, theirs from Du Verdier's; and Du Verdier's describes it as

Solitaire second, ou Prose des Muses, et de la Fureur poétique; avec quelques vers Lyriques sur la fin; imp. à Lyon, in-8°, par Jean de Tournes, 1552.

Surely this merely repeats, by a printer's error, the subtitle and other details given just before in respect of the *Solitaire premier*.

The works of the early fifties, accompanied by occasional pieces, were followed by the *Discours du temps* of 1556, *L'Univers* of 1557, and *Mantice* of 1558, works of popularization at the same level as the *Solitaires*, the first on the measurement of time, the next 'des Parties, et de la Nature du Monde', and the last on astrology. None of these three works mentions Pasithée, and we can only guess at what became of her. But it is clear that in these years Tyard had

---

[1] Torri, in *Rivista musicale italiana*, 1901.
[2] Chamard, *Histoire de la Pléiade*, 1939, iii. 147.
[3] The latest is in A. Cioranesco, *Bibliographie de la littérature française du seizième siècle*, Paris, 1959; but Professor Saulnier, who contributed the reference, has authorized me in a private conversation to say that he no longer believes in an edition of 1552. Further details of my argument are given in my thesis, *An Introduction to the* Discours philosophiques *of Pontus de Tyard*, in the Bodleian Library, Oxford.

acquired enthusiastic disciples and a willing if limited public. Sonnets like those of Philibert Bugnyon referred to Pasithée as 'immortelle',[1] sequences like the *Amoureuses occupations* of Guillaume de la Taissonière and the *Odes de Jean Tagaut, Pasithéophile,* imitated the *Erreurs*; Olivier de Magny asserted that the *Solitaire premier* 'fauche au vulgaire L'herbe sous le pié',[2] and Guillaume des Autelz went so far as to assure his cousin:

> Et des grands, et du vulgaire,
> Les cœurs tu vas conquestant.[3]

Though the last testimony is not unbiased, it cannot have been entirely baseless. Tyard's renown not only as a lover but as a teacher, commentator, and critic must have been established in Burgundy at least.

III · *Provincial Noble*

Tyard is known, even when by no other title, as a 'member of the Pléiade'. The curious truth seems to be that there is no authentic record that he met Ronsard before the formation of the Palace Academy, in or about 1575, and no direct evidence that he even visited Paris from his matriculation in 1537 until the decade of 1560–70, perhaps even the last years of the decade. This is not evidence that he did not do so; but in his century meetings of poets usually left literary traces. The absence of such traces indicates at least that his relationship with Ronsard's group may have been much less close than has been thought. To him, if not to them, the Pléiade may well have been a mere literary expression, 'un groupe poétique purement idéal'.[4]

This is surely how Pasquier considered it when reminding Tyard of their part in 'cette belle brigade, que produisit le regne du Roy Henry II'. But the legend of Tyard's presence in reunions of the Pléiade appears to have sprung from a literal interpretation of this, and of the word 'compagnie' in the 1597 edition of Binet's life of Ronsard:

... Jan Antoine de Baïf, Joachin du Bellay, Pontus de Tyard, Estienne

---

[1] P. Bugnyon, *Erotasmes*, Lyons, 1557, Sonnet 1.

[2] O. de Magny, *Hymne sur la naissance de Madame Marguerite de France ... avec quelques autres vers liriques . . .*, Paris, 1553, 'Ode au seigneur Gabriel le Seneux'.

[3] G. des Autelz, *Amoureux repos*, Lyons, 1553, 'A Pontus de Tyard Troisieme Façon par dizains'.

[4] Chamard, *Histoire de la Pléiade*, 1939, I. ix.

Jodelle, Remy Belleau . . . la compagnie desquels avec luy et Dorat à imitation des septs excellens Poëtes Grecs qui florissoient presque d'un mesme temps il appella la Pléiade. . . .

On this Sauval seems to have based his remark that 'chés Baïf, Ronsard, Dorat, du Bellay, Jodelle, Tyard, et Belleau s'assembloient au commencement . . .'.[1] The myth grew until Roy-Chevrier, giving no source for any of his details, was able to follow a glowing account of the 'folastrissime voyage d'Hercueil' by a description of Tyard as a 'gai compagnon, gambadant volontiers dans leurs joyeuses sorties'.[2] Laumonier is more cautious:

J'en conclus que Ronsard et Tyard ne se sont pas connus au collège de Coqueret; que c'est Tyard qui a fait les premières avances en 1551 (ou même en 1550, car la dédicace de son second recueil est de 1550); que Ronsard répondit à son éloge dans le sonnet des Amours de 1552; qu'à partir de 1553 Tyard fut admis dans la Brigade . . .,[3]

and Chamard can only say of Tyard's life from 1555 onwards: 'S'il allait quelquefois à Lyon, il ne venait guère à Paris.'[4]

If this is true of the six or seven years after 1555, it must be equally so of the six or seven before. Tyard's attachment to Pasithée, so far as it was real, would keep him in Burgundy during much of those years; the Erreurs amoureuses tend generally to imply that their author was within reach of his lady even when in temporary disgrace. Three sonnets of the Continuation and one of the Troisieme livre des erreurs describe him as 'lointain', but they are the only ones on this theme, so dear to Petrarchists, and Sonnet 31 of the Troisieme livre explicitly laments his exile from Paris amid the 'Crasse Maconnoise'. From 1549 to 1558 he published a work at Lyons in every year except two; another appeared there in 1562, yet only one reprint at Paris before 1573. Events and circumstances at home would also draw him or hold him there.

Tyard had apparently been destined to the Church by his father, and had received a canonry at Mâcon, supplemented after 1553 by an archidiaconate at Chalon-sur-Saône. But when Jehan de Tyart died in 1552 or early 1553 he had already lost his eldest son Nicolas,

[1] H. Sauval, Histoire et recherches des antiquités de la ville de Paris, Paris, 1724, ii. 490.

[2] Roy-Chevrier, 'Les Amours de Pontus de Tyard', 1924, p. 171.

[3] P. Laumonier, Vie de Pierre de Ronsard de Claude Binet, 1586, édition critique, Paris, 1909, p. 211.

[4] Chamard, Histoire de la Pléiade, 1939, iii. 144.

and left his estates to his two remaining sons jointly. The result seems to have been that Pontus de Tyard felt no need to hasten beyond preliminary orders; Baridon[1] shows that he did not trouble till 1566 to make the donation expected of a new canon, and, as Roy-Chevrier discovered, even when Gregory XIII approved his appointment as a bishop, on 17 March 1578, it was 'cum decreto quod antequam adipiscatur Ecclesiae possessionem sacrum etiam presbyteratus ordinem suscipiat'. His brother Claude, who married in 1553 and acquired as his wife's dowry the estates of Bragny and Charney, evidently raised no objection to Pontus's considering himself a master in the castle of Bissy. His independence would be increased by his mother's death in 1562, still more by Claude's the year before, which left him trustee for two small nephews, the elder of whom, Heliodore, inherited his father's half-title to the Bissy estate. Pontus de Tyard would be only the more inclined to settle down, not indeed as a 'solitaire' but as a provincial *seigneur*, administering the estate, journeying little farther than to Lyons for business or change of scene, keeping in touch with Paris by correspondence or rare excursions, and finding society among his books and his friends at home.

Not a single passage in all the works of Ronsard and Tyard states or implies that they ever actually met, cordially though they esteemed each other. As Laumonier indicated, Tyard made the first approach, saluting Ronsard in Sonnet 1 of the *Continuation des erreurs* as 'cest autre Terpandre', and partially transferring his allegiance to the style of the Pléiade. Ronsard replied courteously and briefly in Sonnet 73 of the 1552 *Amours*:

> Il me fauldroyt non l'ardeur de ma rime,
> Mais la fureur du Masconnoys Pontus.

In the same year Tyard's *Solitaire premier* completed his illustrated exposition of the way in which the Pléiade's aesthetic might be fused with that of Lyons, and in 1553 Ronsard showed his approval by references which marked the formal inclusion of Tyard in the Pléiade. The 'Elegie à Jean de la Peruse' ranked him next after Ronsard himself and Du Bellay. The 1553 *Amours* included a 'Sonnet sur les Erreurs amoureuses de Pontus de Tiard Mâconnois', closing with a polite imitation of Tyard's own style:

> Pour contr'errer tu fais errer mes pas
> Apres l'erreur de ton erreur si sainte.

[1] Baridon, *Pontus de Tyard*, 1950, p. 40.

In May, Tyard was invited to join the voyage to the 'Isles Fortunées', a project which might or might not appeal to one whose tastes were 'solitary', sedentary, and not wholly dissatisfied with the Old World. Later, in 1555, Ronsard included Tyard in the list of his six colleagues in the 'Hymne de Henry II', and in the *Amours de Marie* confided to him his embarrassment in the face of his public:

> Quand j'escri haultement, il ne veut pas me lire,
> Quand j'escri bassement, il ne fait qu'en medire . . .
> Paix, paix, je t'entends bien: il le faut laisser dire,
> Et nous rire de lui, comme il se rit de nous.

Here again he was recasting a passage by Tyard himself:

> . . . l'intention du bon Poëte n'est de non estre entendu, ni aussi de se baisser, et accommoder à la vilté du vulgaire . . . aussi se soucioit bien peu le Seigneur Maurice que sa Delie fust veüe, ni maniee des veaux.[1]

It will be observed, however, that it is always as a writer that Ronsard is commending Tyard,

> Toi, de qui la labeur enfante doctement
> Des livres immortels . . .

> car tu sçais tout . . .

as he is described in later versions of the 1555 sonnet. There is no hint of any more informal relations, any personal acquaintance; and the same can be said of Tyard's dozen references to Ronsard.[2] Tyard's name never appears in the 'Bacchanales', the 'Dithyrambes', or the anecdotes told by other members of the Brigade. Finally, though after 1555 Ronsard did not delete any mentions of Tyard, he did not make any new ones; and his poems to or about Guillaume des Autelz show a silence about his cousin which would have been almost rude had Tyard enjoyed any prominence in Ronsard's intimate circle. A striking example is the attack on the churchmen in the 'Elegie à Guillaume des Autels', where etiquette should have suggested Ronsard's excepting Tyard by name, as Vauquelin de la Fresnaye was to do in his fifth Satire.

---

[1] SP, 1552, p. 110.

[2] CE, 1551, 1 and 9; TLE, 1555, 22; 'Chant en faveur de quelques excellens poetes'; 'Elegie à Pierre de Ronsard'; U, 1557, p. 12, and M, 1558, p. 60, which quote two of Ronsard's 'Hymnes'; *De Coelestibus Asterismis Poematium*, 1573 and additions of 1586.

Tyard's relations with others of the Pléiade appear to have been equally formal. Dorat left only a Latin poem in the final edition of the *Discours philosophiques*, and perhaps two anagrams on Tyard's name, and Tyard never mentions him. Baïf, despite their common interest in the 'marriage' of music and poetry, only referred to Tyard thrice, in his capacity as author: 'Tiard vagant d'amoureuses erreurs', 'Tyard si bien errant',

> Toi, grand Tiart,
> Qui Saône fais bruire: et premier en nos pays
> D'amour les erreurs en Sonnets hauts depliant,
> En prose eclaircis sagement les trois fureurs
> Divines, au ciel enlevant les esperis. . . .[1]

He received no published acknowledgement except a mention in Sonnet 9 of the *Troisieme livre des erreurs*:

> Melline, estreinte en l'amoureus lien,
> Rend plus mielleus l'esprit Catulien
> Au vers mignard de son heureus Baïf. . . .

Sonnet 31 of that volume refers to Jodelle and Magny in a way implying that in 1555 Tyard still hardly knew them:

> Encor m'assaut la Crasse Maconnoise . . .
> Pendant, Chandon, qu'une vie sans peine
> Tu viz heureus au rivage de Seine,
> Ou la chanson, en Helicon choisie,
> De ton Magni, tous les soucis te ront:
> Et ou Jodelle engrave sur son front
> L'honneur plus cher de notre Poesie.

Magny had been in Italy since the end of 1553.

There is a more personal note in Du Bellay's sonnet, 'Divin Thyard . . .':

> Priez pour moy l'oyseau Cylenien
> Guyder mes pas, jusqu'à tant que j'arrive
> Dessus le bord du Tybre Ausonien.

We know from Des Autelz that it was written to commemorate a meeting of the three as Du Bellay passed through Lyons in May 1553 on his way to Italy, and indeed only such a meeting could

[1] 'A Monseigneur le Duc d'Anjou', *Les Amours*, Paris, 1572; 1552 version of a sonnet in that collection, 'Que n'ay-je l'arc de Ronsard . . .'; 'Aus Poêtes François', *Étrenes de poésie françoise*, Paris, 1574.

give point to the request that Tyard should invoke for him the aid of the bird of Mercury, patron of both conversations and journeys. The acquaintance so formed may have led to the yet more familiar tone of Sonnet 155 of the *Regrets*:

> Contemplons donc (Thiard) ceste grand' voulte ronde,
> Puis que nous sommes faits a l'exemple du monde:
> Mais ne tenons les yeux si attachés en hault,
> Que pour ne les baisser quelquefois vers la terre,
> Nous soyons en danger par le hurt d'une pierre
> De nous blesser le pied ou de prendre le sault.

But this acquaintance, too, ripened into little more than an exchange of literary compliments; even here Du Bellay, like Ronsard, is recalling not a private joke but passages from Tyard's published work. *L'Univers*, which appeared a few months before the *Regrets*, opens with an embroidery on the theme 'l'homme est nay pour contempler le monde', and later devotes many pages to the conception of man as a microcosm.

Frances Yates[1] suggests that 'this poet-philosopher of the Pléiade must have been a person of no small importance in the whole undertaking' of the decoration of Anet, that magnificent château presented to Diane de Poitiers by Henri II. This is deduced from Tyard's composition of the *Douze fables de fleuves et fontaines*, a series of prose designs and verse inscriptions for mythological pictures. Estienne Tabourot, Tyard's lawyer, took the responsibility for publishing the booklet in 1586, and declared in a dedication to Tyard that the latter had produced the designs for Diane some thirty years earlier:

Vous les fistes . . . y a environ trente ans, lors que l'on accommodoit cette superbe maison d'Anet, qui a pris son plus grand lustre de vos belles inventions, dont aucuns se sont emparez, et en ont emporté la gloire à bon marché.

It is an attractive fancy that a journey which Tyard recorded in 1558 that he made 'passant à Diepes sont environ deux ans'[2] included a detour to Anet.

But Tyard need not have been introduced to Diane by the Brigade, who were never high in her favour, while Ronsard was on distinctly bad terms with her architect Philibert Delorme. The recommendation may equally well have been that of Mellin de

---

[1] Yates, *Academies*, 1947, pp. 135–8.   [2] M, 1558, p. 91.

Saint-Gelais, who must have known and may have reciprocated Tyard's esteem; or that of Jacques de Vintimille, who had earlier furnished designs for Anet, and, as Pasithée says in both editions of the *Solitaire second*, 'duquel la frequente memoire votre, Solitaire, descouvre assez, combien vous est chere son amitié'.[1] It may even be that Tyard merely drafted the scheme and aired it at Bissy for his own satisfaction and that of his *salon*, some unscrupulous members of which worked out his ideas. Otherwise, it is difficult to see why the 'humanist expert . . . at Anet' obtained no credit, nor any acknowledgement like that bestowed on the more obscure Vintimille, appointed *conseiller* to the Parlement of Dijon in 1550.

Tyard's only warm friendship within the Pléiade seems to have been with Jacques Peletier du Mans, who spent most of the years from 1553 to 1557 in Lyons. Tyard refers to him in his treatise on music with a diffidence which suggests some ignorance of Peletier's prestige:

plût à Dieu qu'un signeur Jaques Peletier voulut se travailler en cete partie, comme il fait aus autres Matematiques: car de lui en devroit on atendre (à mon jugement) ce que notre aage peut.[2]

However, by May 1557 their relations were close enough for Peletier to make a stay at Bissy—as Tyard puts it,

pour, en m'honorant de sa gracieuse familiarité, se refreschir, apres le travail qu'il avoit presté à son Euclide, partie revoyant son Algebre, pour la donner aus Latins, partie se recreant avec moy, selon qu'infiniz sugetz se presentoient à nous pour filozofer ensemble.[3]

Tyard offered to translate the Euclid into French, and Peletier enthusiastically accepted the offer in the letter of thanks printed at the end of the Latin volume. The project came to nothing, but the friendship continued to Peletier's death; in 1579 he dedicated to Tyard his *In Clavium de Contactu Linearum Apologia*.

One other friendship was with Estienne Pasquier. The only remaining evidence of it is in Pasquier's works, and in the *Recherches de la France* Tyard is treated somewhat stiffly:

ses Erreurs amoureuses furent du commencement fort bien recueillies; mais je ne voy point que la suitte des ans luy ait depuis porté telle faveur: Aussi semble-il que luy mesmes avecq' le temps les condemna....[4]

[1] SS, 1555, p. 114. [2] Ibid., p. 86; deleted from DP, 1587.
[3] U, 1557, p. 35. [4] Pasquier, *Recherches*, 1596, IV. xxxi.

Four surviving letters, however, give a different impression, though the first two once again suggest an acquaintanceship literary rather than personal. The first letter, the third in Pasquier's own first volume, is dated 1554 and addressed to a common friend, Denis Sauvage; it reveals a curious incident:

Vous me mandez qu'entre autres propos que Monsieur de Tiart vous a tenus de mon Monophile, il trouvoit mauvais l'endroit où faisant mention de luy, je soustiens que lors que noz Poëtes discourent le mieux de l'amour, c'est lors qu'ils sont moins attaints de maladie. Au moyen dequoy pour le contenter estiez d'advis qu'à la seconde impression je corrigeasse ce passage. . . .

Pasquier disclaims any intention of offending Tyard:

Quant à ce que me mandez que sa maistresse luy a par exprés cotté ce passage, pour luy en faire reproche, je ne la pense pas de si pauvre esprit, que l'authorité de celuy qui s'est voüé à elle, ne luy soit de plus grand effect que celle d'un homme estranger. . . . Ne pensez point que sur vostre advis je change jamais ce passage . . . à pis prendre, j'en serois quitte pour effacer le nom de Tiart: mais je le cognois homme de si bon entendement, qu'il en seroit grandement marry. Je vous prie me recommander à luy. . . .

This confirms one's impression that Pasithée really existed and possessed a sense of humour, perhaps more than Tyard himself.

Letter 8 of Book III offers Tyard, in an easy colloquial style which suggests that some preceding letters have not been preserved, a comparison of Commines's life of Louis XI and other lives of him recently read by Pasquier, with moral reflections; and by the time of the last two letters Pasquier has passed to subjects showing a yet more intimate knowledge of Tyard's tastes and probable opinions. Letter 7 of Book X, written while Tyard was working on his 'belles et sainctes homelies', about 1585, entertains him with a spirited caricature of 'je ne sçay quel Sarlatan de Cour [qui] nous vouloit enseigner les moyens de se faire paroistre fort sçavant, à peu de peine'. Letter 3 of Book XVI, composed after Tyard's resignation of his bishopric, is the famous 'cartel de deffi' uttered in the face of Death:

Si je ne m'abuse, vous et moy restons presque seuls en cette France de cette belle brigade, que produisit le regne du Roy Henry II. . . . Employons, je vous prie, ce qui reste de nos jours à nous entretenir, non du corps, ains de la plus belle et noble partie de nous, des yeux de l'esprit. . . . Il faut tromper la mort, qui est aux aguets pour nous surprendre.

If such a varied choice of subjects and approaches is typical of Tyard's conversations and correspondence with others, we can build up a pleasant picture of the way of life that prompted him to sign his prose works with the Ciceronian motto, 'Solitudo mihi provincia est'.

iv · Courtier and Bishop

One of the greatest changes in Tyard's life, if these contentions are valid, will have been brought about at a date not yet determined exactly, that of his acceptance of an appointment involving attendance at Court. Henri II made him *aumonier du roi* according to Roy-Chevrier, *conseiller du roi* according to Baridon; but the honour may have been merely formal, and it is not stated whether François II confirmed it. Sainct-Julien de Balleure mentions another king as taking a more personal interest in Tyard:

> Charles IX . . . en ayant eu advis, ne cessa de le solliciter par personnes à ce choisies, qu'il ne l'eust attiré à sa suyte et service. . . .[1]

This cannot have been before 1560, hardly before 1563, judging from Tyard's busy life in Burgundy until then, and from the behaviour ascribed to Charles, uncharacteristic of a boy not yet in his teens. A more credible date would be after Charles's return, at the end of 1565, from his tour of France, which included a progress through Burgundy in the summer of 1564.

But there is another possibility, that Tyard did not go to Court till 1570. He was certainly there from that year onwards; the proof is his attachment to the second Pasithée, Madame de Retz. Sonnet 20 of the *Recueil de nouvelles œuvres poëtiques*, published in 1573, indicates that his 'doux feu' had lasted for 'quatre ans continuels', that is, since the beginning of 1570 at latest. The merely literary character of the attachment is clear; in the *Recueil* Tyard asserts that he is more in love than ever before, but asks only for the sight of his lady and spiritual support for his enterprise of immortalizing her. Yet something happened to Tyard in 1570, memorable enough to cause the striking of a mysterious medal, bearing a design of a moon, nine stars, and a ship at sea, and the motto 'Me Pontus sequitur'.

---

[1] Sainct-Julien de Balleure, *Antiquitez de Chalon-sur-Saône*, 1581, p. 490; cf. Perry, *Chalon-sur-Saône*, 1659, p. 353.

Jeandet considered this as symbolizing jointly Tyard's allegiance to Pasithée, astronomy, the Church, and Baïf's Academy; to this list Roy-Chevrier added the Muses, one for each star, while Guégan[1] proposed Scève's moon-goddess, Délie. But a medal, especially a dated one, is usually struck to commemorate not the loyalties of a lifetime but a single momentous event. Tyard's attachment to Madame de Retz was hardly such; he was not even her most favoured admirer. The *Académie de poésie et de musique* was certainly founded in 1570, and designed a medallion for members to show at the door; but Frances Yates[2] has shown how unlikely it is that Tyard's medal, with its personal device, was the official one. Nor, in fact, is it clear how great a part Tyard played in that Academy at all. The surviving records make no mention of him, there are no enlightening references in his works or in Baïf's, and his interest in music was by 1570 losing ground to his other interests; the *Solitaire second* was not republished between 1555 and 1587.

The conjecture of Jeandet and Roy-Chevrier, that the moon on the medal represented the Church, has been rendered much more interesting by Marcel Françon.[3] He shows convincingly that the moon was a traditional symbol of the Roman Catholic Church, and argues persuasively that it was so regarded by several of Tyard's contemporaries, including Marot and Saint-Gelais. For them Luna wore something of a hostile aspect, which was not the case for Tyard, as Françon suggests. But, instead, one might well consider the possibility that his decision in 1570 to 'follow the moon' was a decision to take more seriously his ecclesiastical career, in which the King was offering him advancement.

If Perry[4] is to be believed, at the death of Charles IX Tyard 'se retira de la Cour', or at least made a gesture in that direction. He withdrew to Burgundy, as is seen from his dating the dedication of the 1575 *Solitaire premier* from Bissy; and thence, as the accounts of the royal treasury show, he had to be recalled.

Henri III qui avoit eu connoissance de son merite le fit retourner à la Cour, l'attacha près de sa personne, et luy donna les mesmes emplois qu'il avoit eus sous le Roy son frere . . .,

says Perry. These duties rapidly became both more honourable and

---

[1] Guégan, *Œuvres de Scève*, 1928, p. lxxii.
[2] Yates, *Academies*, 1947, p. 22.   [3] Françon, 'Luna', 1945, p. 59.
[4] Perry, *Chalon-sur-Saône*, 1659, p. 353.

more arduous; among the first was that of escorting the Swiss am-
bassadors, who had come to congratulate Henri on his accession
and marriage, during their stay in Paris and their return journey
as far as the frontier. Tyard also became a member of Henri's
'Palace Academy'.
There we can at last be certain that he must frequently have
met Ronsard, Baïf, and Desportes. Other congenial companions
would be Jacques Amyot, *grand aumônier* and former tutor to the
King, and Jacques Davy du Perron, who was to pronounce Ronsard's funeral oration and die a cardinal. It was Du Perron who
wrote a long introduction to the second edition of *L'Univers*, explaining Tyard's aims and extolling his style:

Elisant le devis entre les stiles autant, que laborieux à tracer aisément,
agreable à suyvre, où ses disputes esclairantes à la verité sçavam-
ment debatue, et s'esgayantes en leurs diversitez applanissent mille
achoppemens. . . .

Meanwhile a letter written by Amyot to Tyard on 12 September
1577 refers back to earlier correspondence, and probably conversations too:

Monsieur de Bissy je fus bien aise laultre jour que je receu vostre
lettre du 27 d'aoust dentendre lhoneste occupation que prent le Roy de
vous ouyr discourir de la constitution et mouvement du ciel et que vous
aiez trouvé par experience ce quaultre fois je vous en avois dit touchant
la capacite de son entendement. . . . Cest a mon advis le plus meritoire
service que lon pourroit faire a Dieu premierement a sa patrie et a tous
ceulx qui ont a vivre soubz sa puissance et protection que destudier a
enrichir ce noble esprit de toutes sciences honestes et vertueuses. . . .[1]

It is hard to tell from this letter whether Henri had become the
last and most eminent of Tyard's personal disciples, or whether
Tyard was reporting a session of the Palace Academy at which
Amyot had not been present. Less is known about their scientific
sessions than about their debates on moral philosophy, brilliantly
reconstructed by Edouard Frémy[2] and Frances Yates[3] from the
Copenhagen Manuscript. Two of the discourses preserved there
Frémy is tempted to ascribe to Tyard, on the ground of their 'style
âpre et obscur . . . incorrect et prolixe . . .'. This seems inadequate

[1] Jeandet, *Pontus de Tyard*, 1860, pp. 174–5.
[2] Frémy, *L'Académie des derniers Valois*, 1887, pp. 259 and 327. The Discourses are quoted from the text reprinted there, pp. 325, 250, and 266.
[3] Yates, *Academies*, 1947, pp. 105–30.

reasoning, especially in the case of Discourse XVI, *De l'envie*, with its pervading Aristotelianism, rather cold logic, and paradoxical contention that envy 'n'est pas méchante de soy'. But elements of Tyard's thought and style might be recognized either in Frémy's other selection, VIII, or in VI, which Frances Yates is inclined to attribute to Bartolomeo Delbene. Both discourses are on the same subject, 'Des passions humaines de la joye et de la tristesse, et quelle est la plus véhémente', and both give the primacy to joy. VI passes on to a comparison very much in the manner of the *Solitaire second*:

tout ainsi . . . qu'en la musicque l'accordance et l'armonie n'est pas à du tout en oster le hault et le bas, mais à bien faire acorder l'un avec l'autre . . . pareillement en bien acordant et bien attrempant la Joie et la Tristesse, ensemble les autres afections et passions que Dieu a mises en nous pour bonne fin, nous osterons de nous les vices et les perverses passions et planterons en nous les bonnes mœurs et les vertus.

VIII concludes with a myth in the manner of the *Solitaire premier*, a version of the story of Pandora:

entre les biens qui sortirent de la boette estoit la Joye. . . . Mais elle ne fust si tost cognue des hommes qu'oublians toutes choses ils commencèrent à la suivre et mesprisèrent tout sans plus se soucier des autres Dieux; dont Jupiter courroucé . . . envoya les Muses et Apollon qui sceurent tellement enchanter la Joye qu'ils la ramenèrent au ciel. Mais, de hâte qu'elle eust, elle laissa tomber son manteau.

La Douleur erroit cependant, misérable, fuye et déchassée de tout le monde qui lors, par fortune, vint à rencontrer ce manteau dont elle se couvrit et déguisa.

Cependant les hommes, après le partement de la Joye, ne sçachant qu'elle estoit devenue, la cherchoient partout et trouvèrent la douleur ainsi déguisée; laquelle, depuis, ils ont tousjours suivye comme la vraye joye, bien que c'en soit seullement le manteau. . . .

Certainly, in or outside the Academy, Tyard must have received in this decade enough of the intellectual stimulus that he always needed, and enough indication of public interest in his matter and manner, for him to complete and publish in Paris revised editions of almost all his works. Most were filled out with much new information; perhaps, like Montaigne, he had been noting it down for years on margins or inserted leaves in his first editions. *Mantice* was probably the first to reappear, in or shortly before 1573; there

are undated copies, but they can hardly have appeared more than
a few months before or after the dated ones, since a Parisian printer
would probably have entirely reset a reissue after a year or more. In
1573 the *Œuvres poëtiques de Pontus de Tyard* came out, containing
reprints of the *Erreurs* and *Vers liriques*, the *De Coelestibus Asterismis* which may or may not have been published already, and the
new *Recueil de nouvelles œuvres poëtiques*. In 1575 the *Solitaire
premier* was republished, and in 1578, rededicated to the King, the
Discours du temps and *L'Univers*, the latter now divided into 'Deux
discours de la nature du monde . . . le premier Curieux . . . et le
second Curieux . . . '. In January of the same year the bishopric
of Chalon-sur-Saône fell vacant, and Tyard, to quote Perry again,
'l'emporta sur tous ses competiteurs. . . . Le Roy qui vouloit luy
faire du bien, fut fort aise qu'une occasion si favorable se fût pre-
sentée . . . '.

However late he had been in taking orders, Tyard devoted himself earnestly to his episcopal duties. He remained in residence as
long as possible; he officiated and preached at cathedral services;
he maintained good relations with his clergy and officials and with
the most prominent citizens of Chalon; and he did his best to
quiet the growing troubles and dissensions in his diocese, until
at the death of Henri they became too acute for him to keep the
peace. One may even guess that it was in part due to his influence
that Chalon and its neighbourhood remained loyal when in 1585 the
Catholic League took possession of the string of fortresses including Dijon and Lyons.

It must have been these preoccupations which left Tyard time
for so few recorded activities in other fields between 1578 and
1587. Almost all we know is that he was present in October 1580
at the marriage of his nephew Heliodore to a lady of the neighbourhood, and ceded to him 'les deux tiers de ses biens presents et à
venir'; and that in the latter half of August 1583 Estienne Tabourot
spent ten or twelve days with him at Bragny. The visit culminated
in the production of Tabourot's *Touches*, one more revelation of the
tolerant atmosphere and catholic tastes reigning in Tyard's 'Musée',
as he named it in letters dated thence. The evidence seems to show
that Tyard passed most of his leisure there, in studies of increasing
profundity. It may be that, except to see his publishers, he hardly
visited Paris at all; its attractions were steadily waning as the
lights of the Pléiade went out and the political sky darkened, and

by 1585 even the two Academies had fizzled out by reason of the difficulty of maintaining their meetings.

Perhaps Tyard was moved to prepare a final edition of his *Discours philosophiques* by the feeling that an age was coming to an end, that it might be the last chance to epitomize and preserve something of what the Pléiade and the Academies had stood for, their delight in life and their quest for truth. But the edition published in 1587 was not a mere echo of past achievements: Tyard had again revised and lengthened his six treatises. Nor was this the only fruit of the last nine years, though his other prose productions, political pamphlets and devotional homilies, also reflected the more serious colour of his new way of life, and the erotic sonnets and lyrics of his younger days were replaced by epitaph after epitaph. These included the masterpiece on Ronsard, Tyard's contribution to the *Tombeau* of 1586 edited by Buon,

Petrus Ronsardus jacet hic: Si caetera nescis,
Nescis quid Phoebus, Musa, Minerva, Charis.

They were to end, with the collaboration of Philippe Robertet and some others, in a forty-page Latin and Greek *tombeau* for Heliodore and his wife, both killed during the hostilities in Burgundy in 1592–3.

Past biographers have tended to represent Tyard's part in the last War of Religion as that of an inspired Vicar of Bray, who, whichever side he favoured, was always in the right.[1] Certainly Tyard followed the course of the best *politiques* in devoting his allegiance to Henri III personally, and subsequently to Henri IV for the sake of peace, and in the hope or with the proviso that he would change his religion. Elected without opposition to the States General at Blois in 1588, the Bishop may have disconcerted some of his supporters by his slashing denunciation of the Catholic League and its alliance with Spain; according to Pasquier and Sainte-Marthe, 'luy seul se roidit pour le service du Roy, contre le demourant du Clergé . . . '.[2] When the standard of rebellion was raised in Chalon, first against Henri III and then against his ally and successor, Tyard registered his disapproval by retirement to the castle of Bragny.

---

[1] An opposite view is that of Fouqueray; moderate views are those of Drouot and Baridon.

[2] Pasquier, *Recherches*, 1607, VI. xi; cf. Scévole de Sainte-Marthe, *Elogia*.

There, however, he appears to have been considerably embarrassed, firstly by finding himself cut off in the midst of the province which formed the central stronghold of the League; secondly, by the oath taken at the States General of Blois which bound both him and his nephew to preserve the Catholic monarchy: Heliodore, temporarily seated on the fence, wrote to the Navarrists that he might have joined them had not his uncle 'fait un serment pour luy, qu'il ne pouvoit rompre'. Thirdly, this young man, something of a player for his own hand, had collected two companies of men-at-arms, and in April 1590, while actually on the pay-roll of the League, he seized their town of Verdun-sur-Doubs, and proceeded to obtain Henri IV's ratification of his governorship and to wage a guerrilla war on Chalon.

Pontus de Tyard went so far as to help in financing this; to refuse, though courteously, to meet Cardinal Caetano when at the end of 1589 he was touring Burgundy with a view to reconciling the Navarrists and the League; and to write an open *Fragmentum Epistolae* to Robertet in 1591, replying to an attack by the Jesuit Charles Sager, and combining a disclaimer of responsibility for Heliodore with a bitter parody of the Jesuits' new Article of Faith:

Credo sanctam unionem Hispanicae factionis, et coniurationis in Henricum Tertium Francorum et Poloniae Regem. . . . Quicunque vult salvus esse, opus est ut huius sanctae unionis vinculo sit ligatus. . .

For as long as possible, however, he seems to have tried to keep the peace among the various claimants to his loyalty, and on several occasions he took the role of a messenger or mediator between Heliodore, the League, and the neutrals of Chalon. When at last, in July 1593, Mayenne held Heliodore prisoner, the bishop's help was sought in connexion with a vain attempt to persuade his nephew once more to change sides. Pontus de Tyard shared the natural royalist suspicions when it was announced within the week that Heliodore had died of wounds: 'quem vi armorum non necarant, dubium quibus artibus evitarunt.'[1]

Meanwhile Tyard had been growing more and more unpopular with the League supporters in his diocese. In July 1591 he wrote to the Cathedral treasurer:

L'absence que je fais de mon église, ne vient pas par ma négligence, mais par la mauvaise volonté de ceux qui se sont opposés à moi, et m'empêchent le libre accès de Chalon.[2]

---

[1] *Tumuli Duo . . .*, p. 22.　　[2] Jeandet, *Pontus de Tyard*, 1860, p. 66.

And when in May 1593 he was invited to join the conference at Mantes to instruct Henri IV in the Catholic faith, the League headquarters, apparently from mere personal animosity, refused him a safe-conduct. Tyard had his revenge when he met the King at his triumphal entry into Dijon in June 1595; but this was one of his last official acts as a bishop. No doubt feeling his age rather than a final movement of disapproval, he had already taken the necessary steps to transfer his bishopric to the successor he recommended, his surviving nephew Cyrus, who made his episcopal entry in October 1596.

In retirement at Bragny Tyard still retained his health, occasionally assisted the new bishop, and even continued to see editions of his own works through the press, though there is no evidence of his composing any new ones after Heliodore's *tombeau*. In 1601 he made his will, providing chiefly for Heliodore's sons, Pontus and Louis. On 23 September 1605 he died, to be buried in Bragny church with a simple rite and no memorial, in accordance with his own desires. His Homilies denounce the

mondains pleins de vanité, qui estendez vos superbes et ambicieuses imaginations, jusques aux folles pompes, que lon fera pour vous apres la mort . . . .[1]

Perry's final picture of Tyard is a pleasant one:

Sa mort ne donna point d'inquiétude à son neveu pour l'estat de son ame, parce qu'elle fut fort Chrestienne et qu'il eut le bon-heur de recevoir les Sacremens avec grande devotion et beaucoup de repentir de ce qu'en sa jeunesse il avoit composé quelques poësies un peu trop amoureuses. . . . Il estoit civil discret et judicieux, mais depuis qu'il fut Evesque, il prit une façon de vie plus grave et plus serieuse que celle qu'il avoit passé à la Cour, où il parut d'une humeur enjoüee et d'un agréable entretien. Il estoit bel homme, d'une haute taille, d'un visage et d'un port fort majestueux; la vivacité de son esprit paraissoit dans ses yeux, dont le brillant éclat actif et pénétrant poussoit au dehors les belles lumières dont il estoit éclairé. Son grand divertissement estoit l'estude, et quand quelqu'un de ses amis l'alloit visiter à Bragny, si c'estoit un homme sçavant, il s'entretenoit agréablement avec luy des sciences. . . .[2]

One may note, however, Tyard's susceptibility to the influence of others. He was not a natural leader in any sphere; he lacked

---

[1] *Homilies . . . sur la Passion . . .*, 2nd ed., 1586, p. 211.
[2] Perry, *Chalon-sur-Saône*, 1659, p. 414.

initiative, developed slowly, and took little interest in public affairs until Charles IX and Henri III induced him to do so. But he became successively an enthusiastic follower of the School of Lyons, of Ronsard, and of the Parisian literary movements of the seventies. At the same time, he always remained something of a conservative: what he learnt from Scève was never jettisoned in favour of what he learnt from the Pléiade; he remained a royalist in the face of Mayenne, and a Catholic in face of both rationalists and Navarrists. Perhaps he was governed as much by a ready appreciation of the views of others, as by the possession of firm views of his own. His hospitality at home, and his ambassadorial services to Henri III and during the war of the League, show that he possessed real social and diplomatic talents. He had, above all, the gift of understanding different people and of preserving friendly relations with them.

II · THE *DISCOURS PHILOSOPHIQUES*

It appears that for Tyard, as for an increasing number of his modern readers, the *Discours philosophiques* were the most characteristic and important part of his work. They occupied his mind for thirty years, were subjected to two detailed revisions, and were collected in an impressive final edition signed with his episcopal title and dedicated to the King. It is therefore worth while asking what Tyard thought he was doing in them.

What lies behind their title, used even in 1555 in a reference to the *Solitaire premier* as 'l'un de mes discours Filozofiques',[1] is shown by a passage in the 1578 dedication of the *Second Curieux*, discussing the styles of Roman authors:

la lettre missive, ou epistre familiere, l'oraison, et le discours philosophique, avoyent chacun leur propre et peculiere mode. Aussi me semblent ceux là beaucoup estre deceuz, qui pensent le langage vulgaire des Romains estre celuy qu'ils lisent dans les livres de la nature des Dieux, les Tusculanes, ou Academiques de Ciceron. Et que telles fussent les façons de parler en leur entretien ordinaire, qu'ils voyent en une oraison escrite pour Milon. . . .[2]

Evidently Tyard is thinking especially of the three categories of the works of Cicero, and considering the works in the philosophical category as prototypes of his own. But at first glance the rambling form and heterogeneous content of Tyard's *Discours* seem to relate them rather to Montaigne's *Essais* than to the Tusculan Disputations.

The *Solitaire premier* opens on a purely Neoplatonic note, but closes with 'une grande partie de ce, que les fables Poëtiques ont touché des Muses', into which irrupts a discussion of the poetic technique of the Pléiade. The *Solitaire second*, after its introduction on 'le vrey moyen de s'alonger une vie, vreyement vie', follows step by step the standard medieval textbooks of music, till it concludes by showing 'de quelle harmonie le Monde et le corps humein sont participans de Musique'. The *Discours du temps*, third

[1] SS, 1555, p. 9.　　　　[2] DD, 1578, p. 85 v°.

to be published though placed last in the 1587 edition, links together a metaphysical disquisition on the nature of time, an historical and mythological account of ancient calendars, and an advanced scientific study of the problems involved in time-measurement. The subjects discussed in the two *Curieux* range from astronomy to zoology and from Aristotelianism to Zoroastrianism. Only *Mantice* is a formal dispute on the truth or falsity of astrology, bearing some relation to Cicero's *De Divinatione*.

From Tyard's prefatory and passing comments in each Discourse, however, may be gleaned a number of consistent pronouncements on his aims, pronouncements which are hardly ever traceable to his written sources.

1 · *The Mountain of the Knowledge of God*

Many of these pronouncements emphasize what is doubtless a platitude, but one with considerable implications for Tyard: the value and virtue of study in itself. He speaks continually of a beauty to be found in knowledge, 'toutes belles et rares sciences'.[1] He speaks, in the earliest preface of all, of an absolute pleasure to be gained from learned composition:

ceux, qui par quelque opinion de leur savoir se confient de pouvoir mettre la derniere et heureuse main à un œuvre entrepriz, quittent, voire chassent le proufit et avancement du bien, qu'on appelle temporel, desdaignent la solicitude de leurs domestiques affaires, et oublient l'entretien de la tant aymee santé, pour, en toute haleine, et non interrompue pensee, le commencer, le poursuivre, et l'achever, bien que (tant est forte l'inclination naturelle, qui les pousse à l'effect de leur puissance) ilz n'esperent aucune digne recompense de leur labeur.[2]

Study is the fulfilment of man's peculiar function, 'l'homme est nay pour contempler le Monde';[3] and the writer has the further duty to publish:

toute personne accomplie . . . doit declairer et mettre en evidence avec toute[s] les graces de bien dire, les disciplines acquises, et ce qu'avec jugement non deceu il peult eslire de bon et recevable par ses inventions. . . .[4]
duquel la trasse laissast memoire aus siecles suivans, que nous avons vescu en desir de leur porter proufit. . . .[5]

---

[1] DD, 1578, p. 86.   [2] SP, 1552, p. 3.
[3] U, 1557, p. 6.   [4] SP, 1552, p. 92.   [5] U, 1557, p. 7.

According to Febvre, this last claim was unusual for the time:

Que la verité soit le bien commun de tous les hommes: que chacun de ces hommes, s'il en possède une parcelle, si minime soit-elle, doive aussitôt la communiquer à tous . . . cette idée, les hommes du XVIᵉ siècle ne l'avaient guère, ou ne la formulaient pas. Il faut descendre, à ma connaissance, jusqu'à Palissy, c'est-à-dire jusqu'à 1580. . . .¹

But Tyard was following the much older tradition which Jessie Crosland traces back through the medieval didactic writers to St. Gregory of Tours, 'that to know a good thing and to keep it to one-self was a crime and most displeasing to God'.²

For Tyard, indeed, the virtuous man is *ipso facto* studious and the studious man *ipso facto* virtuous: 'la vertu ne peult estre separee, ou desjointe des studieux, et sinceres amateurs de sapience et doctrine',³ 'car nul sans Vertu peult estre sage, non plus que le Sage ne peult estre privé de vertu'.⁴ He talks of 'la diligente recherche, ordinaire occupacion de tous bons et vertueus esprits',⁵ and, conversely, of 'celle douceur et humanité, qu'on void reluire aux personnes bien nees avec l'institution des bonnes lettres'.⁶ At least in his earlier dialogues, Tyard is echoing a Neoplatonic theory, the one which it is most certain that he held and practised personally. The road to God is not only a moral one, but also an intellectual one:

De tous ceux (véux je dire) qui ont tasché de s'acquerir l'intelligence des choses celestes et divines, et acheminer leurs entendemens jusques au plus hault siege, ou repose l'object de l'eternelle felicité, les voyes ont esté diverses, comme les doctrines, disciplines, sciences, et arts leur ont esté devant les yeux diversement presentez. Qui fait doute que les sciences ne servent de tres propres degrez pour s'eslever à la plus haulte cime?⁷

Any such intellectual route is valid and any knowledge found by the way is valuable:

tous ceux, qui ont juré à la louable entreprinse de monter au sommet peu accessible de tant ardue montaigne, qu'est la difficile congnoissance de la divinité, cherchans l'un deçà, l'autre delà, qui un endroit, qui un

---

¹ L. Febvre, *L'Incroyance au seizième siècle: la religion de Rabelais*, Paris, 1942, p. 451.
² J. Crosland, *Medieval French Literature*, Oxford, 1956, p. 22.
³ SP, 1552, p. 81.   ⁴ *Leon Hebrieu de l'amour*, 1551, i. 69.
⁵ U, 1557, p. 56.   ⁶ SP, 1552, p. 97.   ⁷ Ibid., p. 14.

autre plus commode, et aisé, font diverses rencontres de choses, neaumoins rares, et precieuses, comme rien se peult trouver autre en lieu tant rare et precieux: à la nouveauté et plaisir desquelles la plus grand part s'est arrestee, demeurant à ceste cause sa queste non poursuivie, et son voyage interrompu.[1]

One must not halt one's mental activity and development at any point short of the 'summit'; but Tyard, with this proviso, has found the perfect defence of the magpie's miscellany into which his work sometimes degenerates.

The Neoplatonic terminology decreases in the dialogues which succeed the two *Solitaires*, but the idea remains that the learning and knowing of any true fact has a moral as well as a mental value. Tyard recommends the study of astronomy for the reason that 'si jamais les ames genereuses se sont elevees en contemplation de quelque excellence, le Ciel me semble en avoir esté le plus louable sujet'.[2] His supposedly most free-thinking character, the 'Curieux', argues that

la congnoissance certeine de la Nature des choses . . . nous fait eslever jusques en l'admiration de la Divinité: en contemplation de laquelle noz mœurs sont meilleurees au choix des vertus et des vices. . . .[3]

Even the pious 'Hieromnime', who condemns 'ceux, qui en s'acheminant aux raisons naturelles, s'esgarent du chemin de la vraye cognoissance de Dieu', offers encouragement and example to

ceus, qui d'une honneste et vertueuse diligence s'exercent aus sciences pour apprendre la verité des choses: et de ce qu'ils en ont rencontré, rendent graces à Dieu, tenant et reconnoissant tout reveremment de lui, à qui il plait par l'ayde de telle connoissance leur descouvrir sa lumiere.[4]

The intellectual approach to God is still seen as supplementing the approach through faith; the study of any of His creatures can be one way of learning more about Him.

On this theory, however, the whole of the *Discours philosophiques* might have formed no more than an encyclopædia in the loose modern sense, or, at best, in the literal classical sense. According to the introduction of the *Solitaire premier*, Tyard certainly felt 'que les lettres, tant en respect des sciences particulieres, que de la spherique Enciclopedie . . . [l'avaient] appellé à leur service',[5]

---

[1] SP, 1552, pp. 13–14.   [2] DT, 1578, dedication.
[3] M, 1558, p. 7.   [4] U, 1557, p. 44.   [5] SP, 1552, p. 15.

and, according to Du Perron's 'Avant-Discours', the aim of *L'Univers* was to show 'la nature universelle raccourcie au petit pied'. But the *Solitaire* immediately concentrates on a much more restricted subject, and the 'Avant-Discours' makes no comment on the function of the other dialogues. One still feels that there must be some more real unity in the *Discours philosophiques*, connecting the pair of *Solitaires* with the pair of *Curieux*, and accounting for the presence of the *Discours du temps* and *Mantice*. Saulnier finds this unity in a humanistic attitude:

La curiosité est immédiatement encyclopédique. Il s'agit en somme de tout savoir. Mais, en tous domaines, elle sacrifie volontiers ce qu'on pourrait appeler l'aspect des existences autonomes, à l'étude de l'intérêt humain . . . Ainsi pourrait-on présenter la suite des six *Discours* comme une manière de cycle à la gloire de l'Homme. . . .[1]

But any such impression is surely a by-product rather than a primary aim of the *Discours*. Saulnier has evident difficulty in explaining how the dialogues other than the *Curieux* fit into the 'cycle à la gloire de l'Homme: les deux premiers étudiant la Poésie et la Musique, ses créations les plus cosmiques . . . le dernier, l'homme dans le temps et devant le temps'. It is also hard to find textual support for the interpretation outside the *Curieux*, and especially hard to find it in the introductory and concluding passages, where one would expect to find Tyard's philosophy most clearly revealed, and which tend much more to stress man's dependence on God. The *Solitaires* demand an initial belief in 'une secrette puissance divine, par laquelle l'ame raisonnable est illustree';[2] *Mantice* ends by denying both man's ability to read the stars and his complete freedom from their influence; and the *Discours du temps* denounces man as 'tant inconstant et incertein, que fable (tant soit elle fabuleuse) ne me semble moins avoir de verité ou vray semblance, qu'il s'en rencontre en nous'.[3]

Where Saulnier takes the *Curieux* as the starting-point of his interpretation, Frances Yates takes the *Solitaires*:

After his long devotion to the rational disciplines . . . the Solitary has reached another stage in his 'ascent', a stage in which he knows more but knows in a different way. He has reached a region in which he begins

---

[1] *Maurice Scève*, 1948, i. 390.   [2] SP, 1552, p. 25.
[3] DT, 1556, p. 2.

to perceive a kind of coherence and unity in the whole encyclopaedia of the separate arts and sciences. . . . The vision of the union of Poetry and Music, of Pasithée, symbolises the beginning of a process of initiation into higher spheres of knowledge, for which the way was prepared by the arduous devotion to the individual disciplines. The Solitary is describing his passage from the rational to the intuitive. . . .[1]

Miss Yates claims not only that the two *Solitaires* expand this theme, but that it governs the later dialogues: at the opening of the *Second Curieux* 'we come through Pasithée to the *musica humana*', and at the close of the *Discours du temps* and of the *Premier Curieux* we hear the strains of music and singing. It is the 'fureur poétique' of the Muses, descending upon the philosophers after their long exploration of the disciplines of the natural sciences. . . .[2]

Some such symbolism may well have been in Tyard's mind, especially when he first conceived the *Solitaire premier*, which he was later to describe as 'l'un de mes discours Filozofiques, auquel j'essaye de prouver la Musique contenir toute discipline, et la Temperance toute vertu'.[3] Miss Yates's theory, however, seems to require modification at a few points.

Pasithée, as has been seen, is not the Solitaire's Muse but his pupil; 'pour le prys de ses amoureuses audiences, elle reçoit l'instruction des plus haultes et louables disciplines',[4] as Tyard says of Leo Hebraeus's Sofia before going on to draw a comparison between her and Pasithée. Miss Yates, who represents the latter as a quasi-supernatural figure, takes literally some conventional compliments where the Solitaire equates his lady with the Graces and Muses, and overlooks her numerous disclaimers. 'Gardez vous . . . ', the Solitaire has to warn her,

que le trop de modestie, qui vous fait souvent estendre au mespris de voz graces . . . n'irrite les Muses, et non seulement les esmeuve à restraindre celle prodigue liberalité, avec laquelle elles vous font ouverture de leurs cabinets, mais encor retirent et vous ostent ce, que vous avez d'elles.

Quand elles se seroient mises en colere contre moy (repliqua Pasithee, me regardant du meilleur œil) je m'asseure que vous, qui leur estes tant serviteur, travailleriez en tout devoir, pour les appaiser, et les me rendre amies: feriez pas, Solitaire?[5]

[1] Yates, *Academies*, 1947, p. 79.   [2] Ibid., p. 90.
[3] SS, 1555, p. 9.   [4] *Leon Hebrieu de l'amour*, 1551, ii, dedication.
[5] SP, 1552, p. 93.

What Muse, however virtuous, would be so modest as to deny her own rank?

Miss Yates supports her case with the passage from Baïf:

> Tiard vagant d'amoureuses erreurs
> Va celebrer du nom de Pasithee
> Celle beauté, dont son ame agitee
> Vint decouvrir en solitude, apres
> Le grand Platon, les plus divins segrets.[1]

She comments: 'Baïf himself regarded Tyard's Pasithée as containing "the divinest secrets of the great Plato".'[2] But surely one must understand, not 'son âme vint découvrir les plus divins secrets de cette beauté' but 'son âme, agitée par cette beauté, vint découvrir, d'après le platonisme, les secrets de Dieu'. It is good Neoplatonic doctrine that love of a lady should start the lover on the ascent to knowledge and love of God; in this way Peletier, in *L'Amour des amours*, is led by his lady to 'Le Parnase', but is then handed over to the care of Urania. This is the inspiration which the Solitaire receives from Pasithée, 'me confiant . . . en je ne say quelle promptitude, à laquelle l'esperon de voz divines graces me pousse'.[3] His interview with her in the *Solitaire premier* is not presented as a 'vision' after the ascent of a mountain of truth, but as a neighbourly visit, 'un deviz tel, que souvent il s'en rencontre entre celle, que je cache souz le nom de Pasithee . . . et moy', after a few days' hunting and rambling in the country.[4] And a 'deviz' in such a context is not 'a picture painted on the tablet of the mind; a "device" which holds a meaning for the author',[5] but simply a conversation.

In this conversation, based on Ficino, the Solitaire instructs Pasithée in a theory of knowledge which is certainly an 'ascent', and which, from its key position, was certainly of importance to Tyard. It is the Neoplatonic theory according to which the soul has fallen away from its original unity with God even in its use of the reason, much more in its use of the body, and has to climb the stairway back again by the help of the divine frenzies. Miss Yates appears to suggest that the 'rational disciplines' are not even the first step of the stair; they are all to be ranked below the intuition, of which prophetic, mystic, and erotic enthusiasm are all forms, as well as

---

[1] 'A Monseigneur le Duc d'Anjou', *Les Amours*, Paris, 1572.
[2] Yates, *Academies*, 1947, p. 85.   [3] SP, 1552, p. 35.
[4] Ibid., pp. 16–17.   [5] Yates, *Academies*, 1947, p. 79.

poetic inspiration. It is the last on which Miss Yates dwells particularly:

The 'art' of the individual disciplines has been welded by the divine
gift of inspiration into that 'naïve,' 'native,' or 'natural' power by which
the inspired poet can range through and over all.[1]

Indeed, for Miss Yates there seems to be a desirable state, 'Nature',
'the beginning of the imaginative life, full of confused forms,
shapes and fancies', which is both the fourth stage of the fall of the
soul according to Neoplatonism, and the inspired frenzy of the poet
according to Plato's *Ion* and Cicero's *Pro Archia*.

As 'nature' is the last stage of the descent, and poetic inspiration the
first stage of the ascent, therefore the two are on the same level and
'nature' may be used as the equivalent of *furor poëticus*.[2]

But Cicero's 'Nature' and Ficino's have nothing but the name
in common, and Tyard makes this clear by using the term and its
derivatives almost exclusively in Ficino's sense, and, when translating literally from Cicero, by substituting other definitions as soon
as possible. The poet is inspired by a

puissance de divinité, qui excede le common cours de la naturelle apprehension. . . . Aussi estce ce, que le grand disert Romain Ciceron enten-
doit, disant, en faveur du Poëte Archias, que plus souvent la nature sans
doctrine, que la doctrine sans la nature avoit servi et valu à la vertu et
louenge: appellant du nom de nature celle divine agitation. . . .[3]

But for Ficino and Tyard 'Nature, signifie celle puissance animale
consistente en l'office de nourriture, et generation, qui se respand,
et restraint dens le corps . . .'.[4] The fallen soul, in the state of
'nature', has developed a reprehensible attachment to the body:

amie de ces formes particulieres, et de la Nature, dispersant sa force à la
generation, accroissement, et nourriture des corps . . . tellement, que la
superieure partie de soy est endormie, et (comme on pourroit dire)
estonnee du coup de si lourde cheute: et l'inferieure toute agitee. . . .[5]

The poetic frenzy provides the specific treatment for this state,
pacifying the lower self and stimulating the higher:

réveillant par les tons de Musique l'Ame en ce, qu'elle est endormie,
et confortant par la suavité et douceur de la harmonie la partie per-
turbee. . . .[6]

---

[1] Ibid., p. 84.
[2] Ibid., p. 82.
[3] SP, 1552, pp. 43 and 49.
[4] Ibid., p. 31.
[5] Ibid., pp. 33 and 37.
[6] Ibid., p. 38.

However, this is by no means the end nor even the most important part of the story—'encor toutefois n'est ce rien': for the soul remains in the state of 'false opinion' condemned so often by Plato, 'l'inconstante solicitude des diverses opinions empeschees au continuel mouvement de la multitude des images, et especes corporelles'. Although the cure for this is, in strict Neoplatonic terms, the mystic frenzy, 'la sainte communication des mysteres et secretz religieux', the result is to reinstate the enlightened reason,

quand ces diverses puissances de l'Ame au paravant cà et là en divers exercices espandues sont recueillies, et r'assemblees en l'unique intention de l'Entendement raisonnable. . . .[1]

Reason is to be done away only by what are called the prophetic and erotic frenzies, but may be explained more simply as faith and love of God:

la troisieme fureur est necessaire pour eslongner les discours de tant de ratiocinations intellectuelles . . . s'eslevant haut outre toute apprehension d'humaine et naturelle raison, pour aller puiser aux plus intimes, profonds, et retirez secretz divins. . . . En fin, quand tout ce qui est en l'essence, et en la nature de l'Ame, est fait un, il faut (pour revenir à la sourse de son origine) que soudain elle se revoque en ce souverain UN, qui est sus toute essence . . . par un fervent, et incomparable desir, que l'Ame ainsi eslevee ha de jouir de la divine et eternelle beauté.[2]

No mere intuitive grasp of the encyclopædia is called for, but a true and loving contact with God, the ultimate source and object of all knowledge.

This is not to deny the value of the first frenzy; the *Solitaire premier* ends in a collection of poetic symbols, 'ce, que les fables Poëtiques ont touché des Muses, souz l'escorce de quoy le suc et la moelle se treuve de plusieurs bonnes doctrines'.[3] The art and insight of the poet are given by God, like all true learning and understanding. But clearly, even in this Discourse, Tyard's view is that the life of the divinely purified reason is far above that of poetic imagination, and the life of divinely implanted faith far above both. The later dialogues deal less and less with fiction and image, more and more with the respective roles of reason and faith;

---

[1] SP, 1552, pp. 38–39.   [4] Ibid., pp. 39–40.   [3] Ibid., p. 50.

and reason or authority is given precedence, time after time, over mere opinion or imagination:

Aucuns ont pensé la terre se mouvoir, et non le Ciel: les autres, la Terre et le Ciel se mouvoir ensemble. Mais l'opinion plus favorisee, et d'autorité et de raison, est que le Ciel se meut, et la terre demeure ferme et immuable.[1]

Frances Yates, like Saulnier, seems to have some difficulty in fitting *Mantice* and the *Discours du temps* into her theory; and it seems to be a forcing of the text when she fastens on 'the strains of music and singing' as a symbol which crowns the *Discours du temps* and the transition from the *Premier Curieux* to the *Second*. Indeed, the musical interlude does not appear at all in the 1557 edition of *L'Univers* as one continuous dialogue. Surely the references form no more than a conventional setting, or, at best, a reminder that the treasures found on the lower slopes of the mountain of truth need not be thrown away when richer ones are discovered. The real endings of the scientific dialogues are surely in their last speeches. That attributed to Scève in the *Discours du temps* is an act of submission of the will to God in faith:

j'estime la vie m'estre donnee de Dieu, comme un depost en garde: et vrayment je la garderay tant et si cherement qu'il me sera possible, atendant qu'il plaise au Signeur, duquel j'en ay la charge, de la r'avoir de moy. . . .[2]

That of the Solitaire in *L'Univers* is a similar submission of the reason:

je ne m'esmerveille si la difficulté de tant haut suget ne peut estre esclarcie aisément, connoissant bien que les esprits, qui en discourent, sont humeins, et qu'entreprendre par raison d'en descouvrir la moindre connoissance, c'est oser une chose qui ne sera jamais executee.[3]

This fideistic acceptance of whatever God communicates, or may be thought to communicate, through poetic intuition, enlightened reasoning, and direct revelation alike is the philosophy which is considered to lie behind the *Discours philosophiques*; but it is not claimed that Tyard's creative and executive powers were such as to make his work a clear expression of his attitude. It is the present writer's opinion that the real history of the *Discours* is

[1] U, 1557, p. 15.   [2] DT, 1556, p. 81.   [3] U, 1557, p. 156.

one of change of intention on Tyard's part, that the series was originally conceived on a plan very different from the final one, and that the plan underwent perhaps one alteration even while the *Solitaire premier* was being written, and certainly another alteration after the *Solitaire second* was completed. This would explain the apparent disunity of the complete volume, the difference in purpose between the earlier and later Discourses, and some of the difficulty found in interpreting them.

There is evidence in the *Solitaire premier* that the 1552 version was already intended to be a part of a longer work: the dedication refers to 'ce commencement de plus long, plaisant, et utile ouvrage'. The complete work was to cover all four of Ficino's *furores*. Pasithée demands a full account of them:

Grande (dit elle) et admirable est l'efficace de tant rare voye, et ne pourra mon esprit demeurer calme premier que vous m'en ayez fait entendre l'entier acheminement.[1]

After hearing a general account she issues the further order, 'depaingnez moy premierement la fureur Poëtique';[2] and when this has been fulfilled she insists

que vous n'espargnerez vostre peine pour faire tant qu'encores les autres trois fureurs, ne me demeurent incongnues.

Je ne say (lui respondí je) quelle congnoissance je pourray vous donner des deux suivantes. Mais quant à celle d'Amour, je n'ay autre travail en plus songneuse recommendation, que de la vous representer devant les yeux. . . .[3]

Their next conversation, recounted in the *Solitaire second*, actually concerns music. The *Solitaire premier* foreshadowed this too: Tyard spoke there of the Greek heptachord—'Mais je veux reserver à plus propre loisir le discours de telle diversité'[4]—and of the emotional impact of music, 'ce que demain (si l'opportunité le permet) je vous declaireray'.[5] The end of the *Solitaire second* reveals that he still considers it as closely linked to the *Premier*, and still does not intend it to be the last of his dialogues, though no third meeting was ever proposed 'to discuss poetic composition' as Lapp states.[6] The Solitaire explicitly refuses to write a longer work on poetic theory:

---

[1] SP, 1552, pp. 34–35.   [2] Ibid., p. 42.
[3] Ibid., p. 120.   [4] Ibid., p. 54.
[5] Ibid., p. 124.   [6] Lapp, *Universe*, 1950, p. xxxi.

pource que ce propos requiert une plus longue haleine, que je n'estime la mienne, je la laisse: pour vous prier (m'adressant à Pasithee) de joindre ce que nous avons dit de la Musique, à ce qu'hier j'avois commencé sous le nom des Muses, d'ou le Musicien-poëte, ou, Poëte-musicien, reçoit l'enthusiasme, et est épriz de celle sainte Poëtique fureur: laquelle (puis qu'à ce que j'ay dit qu'elle tempere les dissonances de l'Ame, je ne veus rien ajouter) quand il vous plaira j'acompagneray des autres.

Le Curieus ayant sù l'ocasion de notre discours, et comme le jour precedent j'avois touché brievement les noms des quatre fureurs divines, avec promesse d'en faire plus expresse description, pria Pasithee lui permettre, au jour suivant, de servir d'un tiers.

Mais (dit elle) je vous en prie . . . .[1]

This passage is accompanied by the marginal note 'Ocasion du troisieme Solitaire'; no work of Tyard's bears this title, however, nor are the three characters ever again shown together.

Now poetry and music, virtually inseparable in antiquity, are both gifts of the first divine frenzy; the next two frenzies are the mystic and the prophetic, and their gifts are religious knowledge, the final subject of *L'Univers*, and the power of divination, the subject of *Mantice*. It is suggested, therefore, that the *Discours philosophiques* were first conceived as a series of dialogues with Pasithée, to be grouped perhaps under the title of *Le Solitaire*, and to treat more or less strictly of the *fureurs*. There might have been five, covering in turn poetry, music, the mystic and prophetic frenzies, and the erotic frenzy in a final dialogue on the lines of those of Leo Hebraeus, which certainly influenced the presentation of the Discourses. There might have been four, corresponding in number though not individually with the *fureurs*, if the erotic frenzy was to have been represented only in passing, as the *Solitaire premier* seems to imply.

There might have been only three, like the three *Dialoghi d'amore*; it may be that in his purely Neoplatonic period Tyard thought of treating poetry and music in a single Discourse, as Pasithée hints in the *Solitaire premier* that he should:

Voulez vous ici fermer le pas? vrayement l'entreprinse de ceste journee n'est achevee. Oubliez vous l'acointance, laquelle (bien que tacitement) vous avez faite de la Poësie, et de la Musique, comme de deux ruisseaux, qui procedent d'une mesme sourse, et rentrent en une mesme mer?[2]

[1] SS, 1555, p. 156.   [2] SP, 1552, pp. 119–20.

The indications that music was to be the subject of the *Solitaire second* occur only in the later parts of the *Solitaire premier*, the parts penetrated and expanded by the influence of Giraldi, the antiquarian loved by the Pléiade. Meanwhile the *Solitaire second* contains hints, which may date from its earliest draft, that Tyard once intended to relegate his more technical knowledge to a separate treatise:

Combien s'estend le mot de Musique, et combien telle discipline est sutile, et estimable, je le pourray dire ailleurs. . . .[1]

La Chromatique . . . est demeuree inusitee en friche.

En bonne foy (dit elle) je desirerois que vous prinssiez peine de la cultiver en quelque sorte. . . .

Je voudrois (dí je) sous votre commandement embrasser toute charge, et ne refuse ce labeur à l'essay, si le vivre me le permet. . . .[2]

Aussi n'a rencontré l'opinion d'Aristoxene assez de faveur, pour demeurer autorisee de ceus qui lui ont succedé. . . . Laquelle toutefois je vous feray voir quand vous m'aurez commandé de recueillir en un corps tout ce qu'on peut (si ma diligence y sufit) en ce tems rencontrer des membres espars de c'est antique ouvrage. . . .[3]

De tout le discours des Modes de chanter . . . je m'ofre, Pasithee, d'en escrire en faveur de vous, et si vous me le commandez, assez pour vous en contenter.[4]

Perhaps the pages published as the two *Solitaires*, like the two *Curieux*, are the two halves of a manuscript which swelled until, like *L'Univers*, it split apart.

Certainly by 1556 the project of a series of Neoplatonic *Solitaires* must have turned out to be too rigid for Tyard's developing interests. Even in 1552 he was beginning to move away from it; the borrowings from Giraldi in the *Solitaire premier* mix oddly with those from Ficino. Tyard's musical studies expanded the *Solitaire second* to thrice the length of its predecessor, its connexion with a 'fureur . . . procedant du don des Muses' is often merely nominal, and the subsidiary technical treatise never appeared. The love affair with Pasithée, which was to illustrate the erotic frenzy, was abandoned in the *Discours du temps*, perhaps because it cramped the style, perhaps for more personal reasons. In *L'Univers* Tyard's scientific knowledge far outweighs his borrowings from Ficino and Giraldi, so that one cannot say how he would have treated the

[1] SS, 1555, p. 8.   [2] Ibid., pp. 85–86.
[3] Ibid., p. 102.   [4] Ibid., p. 125.

mystic frenzy. By the time of *Mantice* he had realized that his belief in divination was not strong enough to allow him to treat it without arguing the pros and cons; it is no longer a 'fureur prophétique' but a 'fureur impudente',

et si en quelque sorte Divination est une verité: celle me semble seulement recevable, qui, affranchie de toute superstition, s'exerce par congnoissance de quelque raison naturelle. . . . Mais autour de l'ouy et du non de sa verité, est un neud fort difficile à deslacer. . . .[1]

II · *Research, Occupation of All the Good*

That quotation from *Mantice*, and that from *L'Univers* about 'la diligente recherche, ordinaire occupacion de tous bons et vertueus esprits', point to the second interest which had come to modify Tyard's thirst for learning in general: a desire for precise information and resolution of differences of opinion. Another series of pronouncements in the *Discours philosophiques*, parallel to those on the value of knowledge, shows an increasing dissatisfaction with mere diversity of knowledge. For the Tyard of the *Solitaire premier*, 'richness' of knowledge lies in quantity, 'diverses rencontres de choses, neaumoins rares, et precieuses'. Interpretations of a symbol may be many, and all true:

Combien que grande soit la diversité des raisons, qui ont esmuz les anciens à feindre neuf Muses, si ne s'en treuve il point qui ne semble estre fondee sus assez bon respect . . .[2]

and this, besides the correspondence with the nine disciplines and the nine spheres, includes St. Augustine's story that there came to be nine Muses through a civic committee's inability to choose between three equally good sculptures of three Muses—or, the Solitaire serenely interpolates, it may have been Graces, 'car j'ay leu et l'un, et l'autre'.[3]

The *Solitaire second* still offers a 'plaisir de la diversité', but as a second best, 'pour, si nous n'en rencontrons une seure resolucion, au moins donner le plaisir de la diversité à Pasithee'.[4] The Solitaire is coming to speak with contempt of theories like that of Plato's Simmias, that the soul is a harmony, and 'autres telles nuees: qui ont plus montré de curiosité que de preuve ni aparence

---

[1] M, 1558, pp. 3–5.
[3] Ibid., p. 62.
[2] SP, 1552, p. 67.
[4] SS, 1555, p. 104.

de verité. . . .'[1] In *L'Univers* diversity has become a sign of uncertainty:

> En bonne foy (dí je) je croy que sans erreur lon ne peut se donner quelque assurance de ces mouvemens de la huitieme sphere en si grande diversité d'opinions. . . .[2]

In *Mantice* it has become even a proof of falsity; the Solitaire declares,

> Vrayment ceste discorde entre les Astrologues, est de tel poix à mon avis, que possible peu d'autres plus vives raisons suffiront pour les conveincre de mensonge et de vanité . . .;[3]

and to a conclusion by the Curieux 'qu'estans differens en avis, ceux cy, ou ceux là demeurent menteurs inexcusables' the 1587 edition adds 'ou (croy-je bien) et tous deux'.[4]

Tyard gave more and more rein to the inquiring and critical element in himself. Even in the *Solitaires* it is to some extent externalized by Pasithée, whose questions provide the framework. The progress of the *Discours du temps* is continually guided by the attempt to solve particular problems, like that of calendar-reform. The whole of *Mantice* is an inquiry into the credentials of astrology; and, before 1558, the introductory pages of *L'Univers* put in a nutshell the new direction of Tyard's studies:

> n'y ha secte de Filozofie, qui n'ayt estendue la plus belle partie de ses recherches, entour les substances et causes mondeines: en la consideracion desquelles m'estant quelquefois delecté, et en ayant remarqué certeins traiz grossiers, et (comme on diroit) monogrammes, je n'ay voulu refuser à mes François, en ce Discours que je vous donne, partie du fruit que j'y avois fait. . . .[5]

The finest part of research concerns the essences and causes of things; concerning these Tyard has picked up certain rough ideas, mere outlines as Epicurus pictured the gods, *monogrammos deos*; and the 1587 version of the passage will go so far as to say that he has 'remarqué une Ichnographie ou plant de certains traits', an *ichnographia* or architect's ground-plan, a provisional system embracing these ideas.

This is what the later *Discours philosophiques* are intended to

---

[1] SS, 1555, p. 153.   [2] U, 1557, pp. 21–22.   [3] M, 1558, p. 91.
[4] Ibid., p. 19; cf. DP, 1587, p. 144 v° and author's corrections.
[5] U, 1557, p. 7; cf. DP, 1587, p. 198 and author's corrections.

comprise, an encyclopædic survey of the universe, including the results of Tyard's search after exact knowledge, even if only as a starting-point for future students: 'partie du fruit que j'y avois fait, pour en ouvrir le chemin à quelque autre studieus et diligent . . . '. The abandonment of the series of *Solitaires* marks a change not in Tyard's interests alone but in his very way of thinking and of writing. From a specialist in Neoplatonic psychology and aesthetics, interesting and instructive only to readers prepared to accept the necessary assumptions, Tyard became, so far as the Renaissance understood the concept, a scientist. He was never to be a great scientific thinker, or to make a discovery of any importance; but he deserves perhaps a higher rank than he has been allotted in the history of one branch of education, the popularization of science. *L'Univers*, which may once have been meant to treat only of the second *fureur divine*, became the centre of his 'circle of learning', and around it gathered the dependent technical treatises, the *Discours du temps* and *Mantice*. Rarely discarding anything he had once written, Tyard let the *Solitaires* continue to stand at the beginning of the *Discours philosophiques*; but it is noteworthy how little rehandling they underwent in the later editions, compared with the discourses whose subjects still interested him.

To pursue these subjects he still used the dialogue form, which enjoyed both the prestige of its classical origins and the popularity due to its use in medieval education. He had introduced it in the *Solitaires* with an air of apology; the continual changes of speaker, he says, 'empireront l'aspre rudesse de mon stile grossier',[1] and will produce 'un entretien malgracieusement entrerompu, à cause de sa diversité'.[2] Clearly, however, he found the form well adapted to his original aim of general instruction, and still better to his later aim of inquiry and argument. Variety and humour are supplied by the Solitaire's courtship and Pasithée's badinage, though it is true that the commonplace, common-sense quality of the pupil's contributions to the discussions leaves the tutor lecturing rather dogmatically and one-sidedly. But when in the scientific discourses the dialogue became one between well-matched experts, it lent itself excellently to different approaches, sharp debate, and appropriate conclusions.

Tyard introduced three new characters in addition to the

[1] SP, 1552, p. 16.   [2] SS, 1555, p. 102.

Solitaire and the Curieux, though, in accordance with classical tradition, no dialogue featured more than three speakers. He followed Ciceronian convention too in pretending that the conversations really took place and in modelling the speakers on real people; Maurice Scève is presented by name, and research has come sufficiently near identifying some others to suggest that all had their prototypes. According to Peletier, *dialogues à clef* carry the added weight of the attainments and experience of the participants:

Je n'introduis point personnages feints ni obscurs, mais qui sont tous de connoissance chacun en son endroit pour le plus suffisant, et pour homme de plus grand esprit.[1]

But Tyard's use of pseudonyms reduces this advantage. Perhaps, as when he adopted the original Pasithée as the recipient of his sonnet-sequences, he found that his limited imagination was better sustained if he bore in mind particular acquaintances to whom to attribute utterances at will.

However, the conversations cannot be taken as faithful records either of events or of the true opinions of Tyard's friends, since single speeches may extend over many pages, and much is literally translated from written sources, or appears in re-editions only. In *Mantice* the dramatic form breaks down to such an extent that Tyard reverts to that of the *De Divinatione* and puts each complete case in turn:

furent de telle vehemence leurs paroles mises hors, que mal aisément les pourráy je rescrire au vray. Aussi me suffira il, recherchant par cy par là dens ma memoire, ce, de leurs discours, dont j'auray plus prompte souvenance. . . .[2]

Peletier claimed openly the right to rehandle conversations:

j'ay fait declairer par T. Debeze tous les arguments et raisons qu'autrefois lui ay ouÿ adduire en nos disputes . . . et encores . . . tout ce que j'ay avisé estre pertinent à sa cause, bien sachant s'il l'omettoit alors, que ce n'étoit faute de l'entendre, mais seulement de s'en souvenir.[3]

This is obviously how Tyard has proceeded. The structure of the Discourses is neither realistic nor dramatic; when Tyard wishes to say something, into the mouth of one or other of his actors it must

---

[1] *Dialogue de l'Ortografe*, Poitiers, 1550, p. 42.
[2] M, 1558, pp. 5–6; later editions correct to 'recercher'.
[3] Op. cit., p. 6.

go; when he has no wish to say it on his own account, it remains
unsaid, however typical in the mouth of one actor it might be. Yet
the detail of the execution is skilful; the personalities are touched
in sharply and humorously, and more and more clearly in later
editions. One can grow quite attached to some of Tyard's
characters.

In the first two discourses it is the Solitaire who is assisted with
well-timed questions and entertaining parentheses by Pasithée,
joined in the *Solitaire second* by the Curieux. In the scientific discussions, though the Solitaire acts as the host in 'cette maison de
Bissy',[1] the leadership passes first to Scève and then to the Curieux.
The Solitaire speaks less and less, till in what later became the
Second Curieux, as in *Mantice*, his part amounts to a few pages
only, and in 1578 even his speech on man as a microcosm is transferred to the Curieux. 'De ce nom', says the Solitaire, 'je veus
masquer un gentilhomme, mien parent, diligent amateur de toutes
disciplines',[2] and one cannot doubt that Guillaume des Autelz is
meant. Two of his many poems in honour of Tyard accompany the
Solitaire second and the earlier editions of *Mantice*; in the former he
declares,

> ja desja furieus
> Vous me rendez, de suivre votre trace
> (Mais pourneant helas) trop curieus,

and in the latter, 'En tes escrits moymesme je pren vie'. But
Margaret L. M. Young confirms that 'it is interesting to study the
opinions of *le Curieux* . . . but it would be quite unjustifiable to
presume that what he says and believes represents the sayings and
beliefs of Des Autelz'.[3]

The Curieux has gained for himself, and by implication for
Tyard, the reputation of free-thinking. Busson calls Tyard 'épris
de rationalisme' and describes how 'sceptique . . . incrédule . . . le
Curieux s'efforce de ruiner l'idée de Dieu . . . '.[4] Lapp terms the
Curieux 'the advocate of reason and the experimental method',
and goes so far as to say that 'the statements assigned to "Le
Curieux" are those of the author'.[5] It is hard to see how this can
be when the Solitaire is always referred to in the first person, is

---

[1] U, 1557, p. 36.   [2] SS, 1555, p. 103.
[3] Young, in *Bibl. d'Hum. et Ren.*, 1960, 363.
[4] Busson, *Rationalisme*, 1922, pp. 314 and 408–10; 1957, pp. 295 and 400–2.
[5] Lapp, in *P.M.L.A.*, 1949, 542.

present at all the discussions, as the Curieux is not, and is often in disagreement with the Curieux. It may be wiser to say, as Lapp does elsewhere, that the Curieux 'is the voice of the prelate's more audacious thoughts';[1] but even so it remains to consider how far Tyard internally approved and accepted those thoughts. The verdict of Du Perron's 'Avant-Discours sur l'un et l'autre Curieux' is that Tyard

fait jouër au Curieux le roule d'Euthydeme, Protagore et Thrasymaque, ramassant les opinions des Philosophes: et bien certain que la Philosophie est vassale de la Theologie, met en jeu le Theologien Hieromnime qui rabat ses coups, s'il tire un peu trop haut.

The very name of the Curieux indicates that he is not to be taken too seriously; Tyard often uses 'curiosité' in the Thomist sense of 'unprofitable subtlety', and classes the 'correspondences' alleged to exist in the universe as 'certeines plus curieuses que necessaires consideracions'.[2]

The key to the character of the Curieux is given in a remark made to him by Pasithée:

ce n'est de votre part que je puis perdre, Curieus, qui par le divers estude, avez aquis une doctrine tant meslee, que, sur le plus frivole suget, vous trouveriez un grand argument de bien dire.[3]

The remark is intended and accepted as a compliment; the Curieux represents one of the ideals of ancient, medieval, and Renaissance culture. He is the sophist or rhetorician, who can talk well on any subject at a moment's notice and who argues for argument's sake; Panurge is another, but so is Pantagruel, though a good deal more besides. Such a virtuoso is not always to be found on the same side; the Curieux is prepared to argue for the existence of God as well as against it in the *Second Curieux*, for the music of the spheres in the *Solitaire second* and against it in the *Premier Curieux*, for astrology there and against it in *Mantice*. There are strong hints in the last discourse that his position is only adopted for the occasion:

le Curieux . . . avec une naïve liberté (en laquelle il se permet tousjours de desdire(r) tout ce, qui par raison ne lui est vivement demonstré) se declairoit contraire à Mantice. . . .[4]

---

[1] Lapp, in *Romanic Review*, 1947, 18.   [2] SS, 1555, p. 12.
[3] Ibid., p. 103.   [4] M, 1558, p. 5; cf. ibid., p. 88.

His learning and views are often as traditional as those of any of Tyard's characters; Lapp is justified in saying that even his attitude in *Mantice* is theologically orthodox.[1] The Curieux gives the up-to-date survey of secular knowledge and problems, interrupted from time to time by his friends with their special interests and insights.

If there is a rationalist at Bissy, it would seem rather to be the Solitaire, as the Curieux hints:

sous ombre que vous faites profession de ne croire de leger, et de ne donner à l'autorité qu'autant de foy (dites vous) que la raison lui en pourra permettre: vous feriez peu de conscience de desdire Ptolomee et ceus qui l'ont suivi.[2]

Pasithée agrees:

si par seures demonstracions, ou argumens raisonnables, il s'en est imprimé quelque chose, mal aisément lui pourriez vous persuader le contraire par le recit de quelques nues contemplacions. . . .[3]

The Solitaire denies consistently that the spheres make music, where the Curieux varies; denies the value of the constellations' mythological names, which the Curieux would keep for convenience; combats the Curieux's assertion that the sky is solid and coloured, gives the account of recent geographical discoveries, and quotes Copernicus in support of heliocentrism, where the Curieux has quoted only ancient authorities. However, the Solitaire protests only in matters of science; the Curieux's description of him is emended in 1587 to read 'profession de ne croire de leger . . . (dites-vous parlant des choses naturelles)'. By disputes about religious doctrine, such as that about the material existence of hell, he is hardly disturbed at all, and as a result falls almost silent in the *Second Curieux*.

The name of Hieromnime is derived by Lapp 'from the Greek *hieromnemon*, a religious official whose . . . function so closely resembles that of the *archidiâcre* in the sixteenth century that Pontus, by calling the speaker "Hieromnime", may be hinting that he is the archdeacon of the cathedral of Chalon or Mâcon'.[4] It may be doubted whether Tyard could have known much about the religious functions of the ἱερομνήμων as revealed by modern study of inscriptions; he must have known the name's literal meaning,

[1] Lapp, in *P.M.L.A.*, 1949, 530.
[2] U, 1557, p. 22; cf. DP, 1587, p. 207 v⁰.
[3] SS, 1555, p. 135.   [4] Lapp, *Universe*, 1950, p. xix.

'mindful of sacred things', which sums up the role. Since Tyard did not wish to represent himself as a cleric, his creation of this role gave him a freer hand, though perhaps at first he did not see all its possibilities. In the 1556 *Discours du temps* Hieromnime is described only as 'un pie et religieus de la compagnie',[1] and utters only two speeches; his part is much longer in *L'Univers*, but it is not till the conclusion added in 1578 to what had become the *Premier Curieux* that his clerical 'profession'[2] is mentioned.

Hieromnime takes a firm stand in defence of articles of faith; yet he contributes not dogma only, but a rich assortment of learning drawn from any source, provided it be Christian as opposed to pagan, Hebrew as opposed to Gentile, lofty pagan conceptions as opposed to low ones, or, occasionally, speculative philosophy of any school as opposed to science based on observation. He does not always take this learning seriously; he is ready to laugh with the Solitaire and the Curieux at the most doubtful authorities, for example on the origin of the Milky Way:

Aussi plaisante (dit Hieromnime) est la frivole opinion de quelques Talmudistes, resvans, que Dieu à la creacion du Monde laissa ceste partie imparfaite. . . . Non (respondit il aus Anges qui s'enqueroient de la cause) à faute de puissance, ou de matiere pour l'achever: mais à fin que si quelqu'un se vouloit dire aussi grand Dieu que moy, je lui offre en parangon de noz puissances l'espreuve de l'achevement et cloture de ce lieu entr'ouvert.[3]

The Solitaire, the Curieux, and Scève are ready, for their part, to submit to Hieromnime when he speaks as the voice of the Church. It is at times like these, when the three characters who symbolize the different sides of Tyard are in harmony, that one can be certain of his real thought; and the times are more frequent, and the Bissy of the *Discours* less of a bear-garden, than is often supposed.

The champion of astrology, Mantice, remains outside the circle of agreement. Tyard introduces him only in the dialogue which bears his name, and only as 'amy mien excellent en ceste profession, le nom duquel je cele sous cetui'.[4] Clements conjectures that this may be Mellin de Saint-Gelais;[5] but the old man, who died in 1558, was hardly enough of a specialist. Lapp's suggestion is Peletier du Mans, so that there would be a double meaning in the

[1] DT, 1556, p. 10.   [2] DD, 1578, p. 83 v°.
[3] U, 1557, pp. 78–79.   [4] M, 1558, p. 5.
[5] Clements, *Critical Theory*, 1942, p. 221.

name of Mantice,[1] and an extra sting in the pun on 'Manties, ou (plus vray) menteries';[2] but Tyard is not given to aiming such sarcasms at his close friends, and Mantice does not reflect Peletier's definite views on such problems as that of constructing the twelve celestial Houses, which troubles the Solitaire. Whether or not Mantice had a prototype, he soon becomes an entirely symbolic figure.

Since he is the champion of a special cause, it is natural that he should feel more strongly than any other of Tyard's characters, and that, under his influence and without the restraining presence of Pasithée or Scève, the style of the discourse should be less polite than that of any other. It seems unjust, however, to consider him as a figure of fun whose 'endless and often absurd variations on the theme of authority and antiquity as proofs of validity serve, as the author obviously intends they should, to strengthen Le Curieux' case'.[3] Tyard is putting the standard arguments for astrology as fairly as he can; some he approves, in the person of the Solitaire— 'vous suffise que je sois d'opinion avec vous, que les Astres ne luisent là hault sans nous faire sentir çà bas quelque efficace de leur[s] vives vertus'.[4] That it is the party of the Curieux which has eventually triumphed was scarcely foreseen or perhaps even intended by Tyard.

Only in the *Discours du temps* is the name of a real person, Scève, used throughout the text and in the final version of the title. The dialogue seems to reflect some of Scève's learning, interests, and perhaps sentiments: he is shown as impressed by the Bissy garden—'il se taisoit arresté en la consideracion du lieu'[5]—sceptical of superstition and astrology, gifted with courtesy and humour and with what Saulnier calls 'une sereine soumission au destin fixé par Dieu, conciliée à l'épicurisme'.[6] But Saulnier has to confess that 'l'on démêle mal ce qui reste de Scève, dans le Scève mis en scène par Pontus'.[7] His speeches turn out to be largely from Giraldi, and in the later editions are rehandled freely, though less than the Solitaire's. Like the Curieux in *L'Univers*, he supplies the orthodox secular knowledge against which Hieromnime sets his theology, and the Solitaire his more modern or more personal

---

[1] Lapp, *Universe*, 1950, p. xix.   [2] M, 1558, p. 8.
[3] Lapp, in *P.M.L.A.*, 1949, 546.
[4] M, 1558, p. 97.   [5] DT, 1556, p. 32.
[6] Saulnier, *Maurice Scève*, 1948, i. 380.
[7] Ibid., i. 141 (though cf. his article in *Mélanges Bonnerot*, 1954).

information; and, like the Curieux, he ends in harmony with Hieromnime.

The role of Scève, therefore, is constructed in the same way as all the others; but a clue to why a pseudonym was not used for him may perhaps be found in the Solitaire's earlier mentions of 'Maurice Scæve (lequel vous savez, Pasithee, que je nomme tousjours avec honneur)',[1] 'mon extremement aymé ami, mais non jamais assez honoré de moy, le Signeur Maurice Sceve'.[2] One may guess that Tyard wished once more to give Scève the honour of explicit mention and public homage, to ascribe his own learning to his master, and, with the diffident reliance on authority that attended even his most daring thoughts, to let Scève have the last word in the *Discours du temps*, and so in the 1587 volume.

Tyard's claim to be in the service of the 'spherique Enciclopedie' may now be reconsidered in connexion with another of his claims to priority. In the *Solitaire premier* he asserted only that he was offering information not previously published in French:

j'entrepren avec des aesles nouvelles, sortant d'un Labirint Grec, et Latin, voler par cest air, et chargé de marchandises estranges, vous apporter chose[s] non jamais veües (que je sache) en vostre region Françoise.[3]

But in the 1578 dedication of the *Second Curieux* he alleged that he had dared to 'escrire le premier, n'y ayant autre que je sçache, qui m'ait precedé en ce sujet de Philosophie et de ceste façon',[4] while Du Perron's 'Avant-Discours' supported him, 'l'Autheur, ayant defermé le premier aux François les barrieres de ce parc'. If this was a claim to be the 'first to write in French about philosophy',[5] it was reckless.

But we have now seen that Tyard had a clear and rich conception of philosophy: the synthesis of knowledge, first on the Neoplatonic system, then, taking a much wider sweep, in a series of attempts of his own to reconcile the findings of scientific and religious thinkers of the past and his own time. He had also the Pléiade's definite aim in the realm of style: not simply to vulgarize thought by translating it into vulgar diction, but to elevate diction to become a fit vehicle for elevated thought: 'former un stile de plus elevee et belle façon, pour dignement representer et exprimer

[1] SP, 1552, p. 110.   [2] SS, 1555, p. 28.
[3] SP, 1552, p. 4.   [4] DD, 1578, p. 86 v°.
[5] Lapp, *Universe*, 1950, p. xxxi.

les hautes et belles conceptions des Philosophes. . . .'[1] His elegant phraseology, romantic setting, verse quotations, and dialogue form are parts of a deliberate attempt to mirror the urbane colloquies of Cicero and the evocative poetry of Plato. Writing with the scanty knowledge of literary history current among the humanists even of 1578, he need not be accused of dishonesty in saying that in the early fifties he knew of no predecessor in French and in print who shared both his encyclopædic scope and his stylistic aim.

The first presses had concentrated on making available the classic surveys of knowledge, from Plato's and Cicero's down to Boethius's and Reisch's, whose range, sense of system, and artistic form Tyard was trying to reproduce. Early in the sixteenth century some of the medieval French equivalents were printed, the *Roman de la rose* in Marot's modernization and even Gossouin's *Miroir du monde* in Buffereau's plagiarism; but it would have taken a more delicate appreciation than Tyard's to realize that Gossouin was thorough and elegant in his time, and that the *Roman de la rose* anticipated almost every aim of the *Discours philosophiques*. In any case, for Tyard they were not up to date. The first half of his century saw the humanists' rearrangement of knowledge in the light of later discoveries and insights, Giraldi's methodical analyses of all ancient mythology, or Giorgio's of all the 'correspondences' in the universe; on these Tyard pounced with joy, since they gave him the same information as the classics and yet saved him the trouble of finding and sorting it. But in that half-century arrangements of such knowledge in French seem only to have taken the form of monographs, Champier's *Nefs* or Tory's *Champ fleury*, handbooks of geography or architecture, medicine or astrology, translations of individual Platonic dialogues. Pasquier's *Monophile* of 1554 comes nearest to the *Solitaires* in style, but is less in the encyclopædic tradition than in that of Castiglione.

It is in the second half of the sixteenth century that the idea of summarizing all essential knowledge in an artistic French form reappears: in verse, as in the *Microcosme*, the *Semaines* of Du Bartas, and the *Encyclie* and *Galliade* of Guy Le Fèvre de la Boderie; and in groups of prose dialogues and essays, those of Tahureau and Le Caron, Bruès and Viret, Des Caurres and La Primaudaye. Among these Tyard does seem in point of date to have been the first. His nearest rivals would be Tahureau, whose *Dialogues* must have been

[1] DD, 1578, p. 84.

completed by 1555, but ranged less widely than Tyard's and might have remained unknown to him till their publication in 1562; and Le Caron, the list of whose *Dialogues*, published or projected in 1556, reads curiously like an attempt to outdo Tyard in every way. This is suggested even by Le Caron's description of his own style and use of dialogue:

> Recueillant donc en mon esprit infinis . . . discours je ne les ai peu mieux expliquer, qu'en une maniere de familier devis, lequel desirant embellir et decorer de toutes ses bienseances, à l'exemple des anciens . . . j'ai pensé qu'il representeroit bien sa dignité, s'il estoit discouru par les deux, qui sont au jourdhui à bon droit reputez les premiers poëtes de nostre tems, Ronsard et Jodelle. . . . Mais si aucun d'eux s'estonne, que je le fai parler de ce que paraventure il n'a jamais ne dit ne pensé, ou est entierement contraire à son opinion: je croi, que se resouvenant de la coustume des dialogues il ne trouvera estrange, que j'aie emprunté son nom et sa personne. Aussi je les congnoi estre mieux nez, qu'ilz daignassent tirer en la mauvaise part, ce qu'une bienveullance me leur fait franchement attribuer. . . .[1]

Ronsard, ou, de la poësie attacks directly the subject of the *Solitaire premier*; *Claire, ou de la beauté* and *Valton, de la tranquillité d'esprit, ou du souverain bien* cover other aspects of Platonism; *Le Courtisan premier* and *Le Courtisan second* suggest Tyard's titles. A still more pointed imitation is to be found in the promise of a further dialogue to be called *Le Solitaire, ou de la description du monde*, while others, headed by *Le Chaldéan, ou des divinations*, were to treat 'de la science', 'de l'utilité, qu'apporte la congnoissance des choses naturelles', 'de la nature de l'homme'. A knowledge of these promises, or threats, might have spurred Tyard to bring out *L'Univers* and *Mantice* before Le Caron could forestall him; but it seems clear that his interest had already been turning towards science, and that in both interest and achievement he was first in the field.

It is perhaps a pity that Le Caron, with his more original mind, never completed his rival encyclopædia; but perhaps Tyard's was a more reliable textbook for Pasithée and her contemporaries. As far as we know the average reader of the time—his culture and tastes, his capacity for sustained attention, his limitations and difficulties—the *Discours philosophiques* seem well calculated to respond to his needs. Tyard's expositions of Neoplatonism and of

[1] Louis Le Caron, *Dialogues*, Paris, 1556, pp. 128–9.

the Great Chain of Being may be incomplete, but are easier to understand than many written in his time and in ours; his expositions of musical theory and astrological controversy may be outdated, but at least illuminate the tomes from which they are drawn. His works are not storehouses for experts, but gateways for beginners; accused nowadays of verbosity, they struck their readers as short and pithy; Du Perron likened Tyard to the apothecaries who 'escrivent au plus court les noms sur le front de leurs boüettes'. Finally, they show in practice the Neoplatonic way of life, the seeking of the Supreme Good through the knowledge of the disciplines and the harmony of the virtues.

In watered and shaded gardens, in rooms furnished with scientific instruments, gracious men and women impart and receive learning in a courteous intellectual communism, submit their differences to arbitration, and sublimate their passions with the aid of lute and spinet. The meeting which opens the *Solitaire premier* shows us the etiquette of polite society, 'les ceremonies qu'on fait ordinairement aux survenues'; the song which closes it accords with all Tyard's poetic theories, in its ornate style, its Petrarchist attitude, and its effect on the singer's emotions. Even when the Curieux moves Mantice 'jusques à la colere', or when Scève and Tyard cannot agree on a definition of time, it proves easy to change the subject and preserve peace. No doubt, could Tyard have had his way, all the disputes of his age would have ended so.

III · SOURCES

I T is now well known that the *Discours philosophiques* are an anthology, a patchwork of translated passages which would nowadays be
called plagiarisms. The process of source-hunting was begun by
Du Verdier, who says of *L'Univers*, 'En ce livre y a quelques pages
prises et tournees mot à mot de Philon Juif, en son livre du monde',[1]
and it has been continued by Frances Yates, Saulnier, Lapp, and
Baridon. Tyard perhaps gives the impression that the *Discours* are
rather more original, when he quotes without acknowledgement;
but he admits frankly that

mal aisément pouvons nous rien discourir, que par redites, et imitacions
de ceus qui nous ont precedez, et desquelz les euvres sont encores entre
noz mains. Si est ce toutefois que cela ne me semble esteindre la voix
en la bouche, ny arracher le stile de la main des vivans. . . .[2]

In his time it was not thought wrong to copy, even without saying
who was being copied. The very concept of originality had hardly
yet been clearly formed.

One might say, indeed, that Tyard and his fellow thinkers had
a twofold view of words. On the one hand, they were of no importance in comparison with thoughts; so style might be careless,
clichés conventional, allusion sketchy, and the printer left surprisingly free. On the other hand, some words at least were of
immense intrinsic importance, not yet as the *mot propre*, but as
endowed with a certain eternal function and fitness: 'car selon les
Mosaïques, suivis par Platon, les noms sont substanciels, j'enten
signifians la substance de la chose nommee. . . .'[3] The name of God
was a tetragram not only in Hebrew but in almost all languages,
'soit par fortune, ou par quelque mistere plus secret',[4] and the
name of Adam signified 'de grans secretz'[5] in both Hebrew and
Greek. The principle could be extended to cover the glossing of a
sacred or classical text word by word, and the making of anagrams,
acrostics, or puns on the names of one's friends.

---

[1] Du Verdier, *Bibliothèque*, 1585, p. 1072.
[2] U, 1557, p. 6. DD and DP read 'semble pouvoir esteindre'.
[3] U, 1557, p. 127.   [4] Ibid., p. 128.   [5] Ibid., p. 116.

So one may account for the plagiarism of Tyard's time. Either, since truth is free to all and wording is of no importance, there is no reason why anyone should go to unnecessary trouble to put into his own words the ideas of another; or, since wording may be of the highest importance and the master may have taken great trouble over it, exact copying is the highest tribute which the disciple can pay. The latter view might be illustrated by Tyard's remark that 'Junon, Alecto, Venus, et quelques autres sont aucunefois appellees Dieux, aucunefois Deesses, ainsi que celui, qui en fait memoire, veult donner congnoissance de quelque secrette conception',[1] the former by his assertion of his intention to 'reciter nuement un deviz . . . non pas mettre en avant un œuvre elaboré curieusement'.[2] It has been seen how this can scarcely be a claim that the conversations at Bissy really consisted of long recitations from Ficino and Giraldi; but behind the conventional apology for imperfections of style may be Tyard's recognition of the unworked state of much of his material.

One more reason for his plagiarism may well be the fact that he simply did not have enough creative power to construct a long original work; in his poems there are few *œuvres de longue haleine*, many imitations. This may also be one more reason for his abandoning the project of illustrating the four divine frenzies; he always needed to build on a scaffolding supplied by some earlier author, and scaffoldings perfectly suited to his purpose may not always have been available. He used what came to his hand: as long as he could adapt the works of Ficino to his aim, he did so; when Ficino's *In Platonis Ionem* proved too slender a frame on which to construct a study of the poetic frenzy, he turned to Giraldi; and for his treatises on music, cosmology, and astrology he adopted the standard arrangements of his age. His works often reflect not only the order and content of a source, but its exact wording and most trivial details.

His propensity is to translate using word-for-word equivalents, even the French derivative of the Latin word to be translated. Where he changes the original syntax, such derivatives may still be seen: 'quod cantus suavitate poetas reddit gloria immortales, et posteritatis memoriae commendet' becomes 'rend d'une gloire immortelle les chants des Poëtes recommendables à la posterité'.[3]

---

[1] SP, 1552, p. 43.   [2] Ibid., p. 16.
[3] Ibid., p. 98; cf. Giraldi, *Opera omnia*, Basle, 1580, i. 539 (*De Musis*).

Even where he develops a borrowing in his own fashion, words from the source may stray into the new passage: his condemnation of those who, 'trop vivement piquez du *corporel*, se sont en lui entierement *arrestez*'[1] echoes two of the terms in what it replaces, Ficino's description of 'hanc molem *corporum*, qua Democritiorum, Cyrenaicorum, Epicureorum consideratio *finiebatur*'. His version may be slightly longer than the original, by the addition of simple explanatory phrases or doublets: Ficino's phrase about the inspired soul, 'superat omnia, et a nulla rerum inferiorum inquinari, vel superari potest', appears as 'ne peult estre souillee, ou vaincue d'aucune chose basse et terrestre: mais au contraire surmonte et surmarche toutes ces viltez'.[2] But he often abridges, and occasionally compresses a borrowing till it becomes incomprehensible: thus he denies that June was named after Junius Brutus, 'nonobstant la fable de la Deesse Carna et ses féves au lard'.[3] This is explained only by the source:

Nonnulli et a Iunio Bruto denominatum putant, qui primus Romae consul factus calendis Iuniis pulso Tarquinio rege sacrum Carnae deae in Coelio monte voti reus fecit. . . . Huic vero deae pulte fabacia et larido sacrificabatur.

But Tyard colours by his own personality, by minute and significant alterations, even his most servile borrowings; and as his mind became more flexible, so did his technique of vulgarization. His *Leon Hebrieu de l'amour*, even if 'una traduzione alquanto libera, specie in certe pagine',[4] was offered as a translation in the true sense. In the *Solitaire premier* of the next year he already rendered Ficino with less fidelity, Giraldi with still less. The *Solitaire second* took earlier textbooks to pieces in order to make them easier and more interesting; Tyard used the wording of their definitions and explanations when it suited him, but otherwise retold their contents in his own words. In 1557 and 1558 he was yet more ready to adapt the order and wording of his borrowings, and to interrupt them with others or with his own comments. Most free of all are his versions of well-known stories, like that of the metamorphosis of the Sirens after the loss of Proserpine, apparently direct from Ovid:

[1] SP, 1552, p. 12; cf. Ficino, *Opera omnia*, Basle, 1576, p. 79 (*Theologia Platonica*, i. 1).

[2] SP, 1552, p. 42; cf. Ficino, op. cit., p. 1282 (*In Platonis Ionem*).

[3] DT, 1556, p. 53; cf. Giraldi, op. cit. ii. 569 (*De Annis*).

[4] Baridon, *Pontus de Tyard*, 1950, p. 23.

elles esmues du juste deuil de la perte de leur chere compagne, entre-
prinrent de n'oublier aucune partie de la terre, en laquelle elles ne la
cherchassent. En fin estant leur travail vain, elles impetrerent des
Dieux les aesles à fin que plus aisément elles peussent suivre toutes les
eaux, et là trouver ce, qui leur avoit esté denié de rencontrer en la terre.
Ainsi elles furent transformees en oiseaux, retenant toutefois la face
feminine, et la douceur de la harmonieuse voix. Mais tel essay n'apporta
aucun fruit, et ne peurent onques rencontrer leur compagne. . . .[1]

It is perhaps in such passages that the quiet charm of Tyard's style
can be best appreciated.

His language, compared with that of many of his contemporaries,
is clear, simple, and fluent. He translates vividly and spiritedly,
breaking the monotony of the original by questions and exclama-
tions, light digressions and colloquial asides: 'ceste derniere et
tant renommee Calliope, ayant d'Achelois engendré les Sirenes, se
fit Apollon tant ami, qu'elle en eut trois filz. . . .'[2] One has the sense
that one is following, not an order of academic discourse laid down
long before, but the turns and twists of a spontaneous conversation.
Tyard has the knack of selecting the most important or interesting
points of a passage, treating them in the right proportion, varying
them at the right moment with interpolations of some other sort,
and at the right moment stopping. Much of his true originality lies
in this artistry of arrangement, and above all in the dovetailing and
interweaving of his borrowings, within the dramatic setting which
he also borrowed and vivified.

I · *Ficino and the Neoplatonists*

The *Discours philosophiques* name Plato more often than any other
writer, disagree with him explicitly on only one subject, the music
of the spheres, and elsewhere cite him as a supreme authority, head
of 'la plus divine secte des Filozofes'[3] and virtually a Christian:
'Platon (dit Hieromnime) à mon avis seroit fait Chrestien facilement, si lon prend garde combien naïvement il touche les plus
secrets et beaus points de notre religion.'[4] The words of Plato must
often have been at the back of Tyard's mind, and their imagery
often tinges his. On the second page of the *Solitaire premier*, in
the middle of a translation from Ficino, references to 'la simple

---

[1] SP, 1552, pp. 84–85; cf. Ovid, *Metamorphoses*, v. 552–63.
[2] SP, 1552, p. 102; cf. Giraldi, op. cit. i. 540.
[3] DT, 1556, p. 68.   [4] U, 1557, pp. 104–5.

consideration des ombres non maniables' and 'la lumiere eternelle
. . . (combien que l'œil de ces terrestres n'en puisse(nt) souffrir
les raiz)' are surely inspired by the myth of the Cave. Later the
Solitaire premier shows a first-hand if rather naïve acquaintance
with the *Ion* and the *Timaeus*, and the *Solitaire second* adds the
Cratylus and the *Phaedo*. Very frequently, however, Tyard
evidently considers it a waste of time to go back to Plato's text;
Giraldi can give him a fuller list of the names of Apollo[1] than the
Cratylus can, and, where the *Republic* fails him, he can find the
name of the Siren of each sphere[2] in Glareanus.

'Les Platoniques' for Tyard may be modern as well as ancient;
and, in particular, the phrase very often disguises Marsilio Ficino.
He is only twice quoted by name, once as a Platonic numerologist[3]
and once as an authority against astrology,[4] a questionable interpretation of his position. But much the greater part of the Neoplatonic material in the *Solitaire premier* comes straight from him, and
is introduced in a dogmatic tone significant of Tyard's reverential
attitude towards him: 'Je veux (poursuiví je) vous effacer ceste
admiration par congnoissance de la cause, qui est telle . . . .'[5] Disagreement, where it does occur, is tacit and to be discerned only
by a comparison of texts; divergences are due mainly to Tyard's
policy of vulgarizing Ficino, occasionally to a failure to grasp
Ficino's thought.

The key in which the *Solitaire premier* was originally conceived
is indicated in its first pages, based roughly but recognizably on the
first chapter of the *Theologia Platonica*. This chapter falls into three
parts: first a picture, which Tyard copies almost literally, of the
misery of man in his earthly state; secondly an assertion of the
soul's immortality, which Tyard indicates in a single phrase, and
its ability to escape from its bodily prison and rejoin God through
contemplation, on which Tyard descants somewhat platitudinously.
Thirdly Ficino gives an account of the five grades of being with
which much of the *Theologia Platonica* is to be concerned, and of
the philosophical schools which appreciated the existence of each
grade; this passage Tyard reduces to a heated denunciation of the
school of Epicurus and a vague list of the others. Ficino's peroration, on the glory of man as the middle link in the chain of being,

---

[1] SP, 1552, pp. 74–77; cf. Giraldi, op. cit. i. 211 ff. (*De Deis*, vii).
[2] SP, 1552, p. 70; cf. Glareanus, *Dodecachordon*, Basle, 1547, p. 99.
[3] DP, 1587, p. 121.   [4] M, 1558, p. 5.   [5] SP, 1552, p. 27.

he replaces by an apology for learning in general and for his *Discours* in particular. In short, Tyard's introduction is a rather disjointed and fumbling attempt to bridge the considerable distance of character between Ficino's work and his own; the borrowing is neither an epitome nor an equivalent of the original chapter, but only suggests an atmosphere and an attitude of mind.

From this point onwards Tyard departs from the *Theologia Platonica*. Instead he proceeds to throw into dialogue form various portions of Ficino's commentaries on Platonic texts. The *Commentarium in Convivium* furnishes descriptions of the outward signs of madness and the physical effects of being in love. The same commentary, rather than that on the *Ion* or the letter *De Divino Furore*, provides the whole narrative of the fall of the soul and its rise by the help of the divine frenzies. The commentary on the *Ion*, however, supplies a theory of poetic inspiration, though Tyard's borrowings here alternate with others from Plato himself. It will be seen that to form the main framework of the *Solitaire premier* Tyard has simply juxtaposed Ficino's views on a few characteristic subjects, all aspects of one study, that of the human mind in a state of 'transport'. He wholly neglects the metaphysical basis of Ficino's philosophy, and postpones until *L'Univers* an account of the cosmological background and even of general human psychology.

The cosmology which Ficino passed on to the sixteenth-century Neoplatonists included, besides the Great Chain of Being, several other sequences. There was the descent of the soul, from perfect union with God, through the states of intuitive contemplation (similar to that of angels), rational argumentation (peculiar to man), and sensuous observation (or 'opinion'), to complete absorption in the body and bodily activity. The reascent takes place when the domination of the body is eliminated by poetic frenzy; sensuous distraction, by mystic frenzy; reasoning, by prophetic frenzy; and the primary separation of the soul from God, by celestial love. All this Tyard adopts. Another method of reascent was that of the lover, passing from love of a single beautiful object to love of all the beauty of the world, thence to a recognition of this beauty as part of his own mind, and so to love of universal intellectual beauty and the beauty of God. It has been seen how far the love of Pasithée inspires the Solitaire in the quest for truth; but otherwise Tyard is much less interested in this, the more genuinely Platonic route taken seriously and even literally in Peletier's *Amour des amours*. It is not love but study which leads Tyard, as dialectic elsewhere leads Plato, up the 'montaigne, qu'est la difficile congnoissance de la divinité'.

Prior to both these series is the quintet of the grades of being, God, Angel, Soul, Quality, Body; and this Tyard hardly mentions. For one thing, he does not appear to be quite sure what Ficino meant by Quality, 'efficacem qualitatem aliquam atque virtutem, ad quam Stoicorum Cynicorumque investigatio sese contulit'. Tyard's parallel passage refers only to 'les vertueux discours des Stoïques'. Also, he is not wholly ready to accept the second and third hypostases of the Trinity of Plotinus, Divine Mind and World-Soul. So when he comes to Ficino's quintet in his rendering of the first chapter of the *Theologia Platonica*, he seems to try to equate it with the stages of the fall of the human soul, of which it is really the cosmic setting. Ficino has been saying that the studies of Democritus, the Cyrenaics, and the Epicureans stopped at the body, those of the Stoics and the Cynics at Quality, those of Heraclitus, Varro, and Manilius at the 'rational Soul', while Anaxagoras and Hermotimus appreciated the existence of the 'Angelic Mind', and Plato proceeded as far as the 'divine Sun itself', 'Solem ipsum . . . divinum, in quem Plato noster purgatam mentis aciem dirigere iussit, docuit, et contendit'. Tyard prefers to cite the more enlightened of these thinkers as witnesses to the insight of the human soul in a state of 'fureur':

la jouissance de la lumiere eternelle, et vraye felicité: laquelle . . . l'Entendement eslevé est capable d'appercevoir, de quoy font foy les vertueux discours des Stoïques, la congnoissance de l'ame raisonnable par Heraclite, Varron, et autres: l'apprehension de l'immuable essence Angelique d'Anaxagore, et Hermotime, et la profonde contemplation, qui conduit l'ame purifiee en reverente admiration de la non jamais comprinse immesurable grandeur de la sourse de bonté, beauté et sapience de l'unique Soleil divin, selon Platon, et Pithagore.[1]

The assertion is in the spirit of Ficino, but scarcely a faithful use of the original text.

Tyard does not exactly reject the Neoplatonic Trinity of the Supreme Unity or First Existent, the Divine Mind or Νοῦς, and the Soul of the All; rather, he carefully avoids mentioning it.

[1] SP, 1552, p. 13; cf. Ficino, op. cit., p. 79 (*Theol. Plat.* i. 1).

Once only does it figure explicitly, among the 1578 additions to the list of ancient conceptions of God in *L'Univers*. The Curieux has just given Plutarch's account of the Zoroastrian Trinity of Ormuzd, Ahriman, and Mithras,[1] and Hieromnime follows it with Francesco Giorgio's interpretation:

par Oromasis ils entendoyent Dieu, par Mitra l'entendement, ou ce que les Latins appellent *Mens* . . . la sapience divine, de laquelle procede la belle disposition de l'ordre et des poids des choses de ce monde. Comme par Araminis qui leur signifioit l'Ame, ils se representoyent les mesures et mouvemens des substances mondaines. Voyez donc si sous les noms de ces trois Dieux ils vouloyent point comprendre la saincte Trinité, commencement, milieu, et fin de toute chose. . . . Aussi faut-il croire que la substance divine espanchant sa puissance par toutes nations, n'a laissé peuple au monde qui n'ait senty quelque odeur de la divinité.[2]

As Frances Yates[3] points out, this comes perilously near equating Ahriman, god of evil, with the Soul (presumably the World-Soul); Mithras, neutral between good and evil, with the Divine Mind; and both these gods with the Second and Third Persons of the Christian Trinity. Tyard's careful orthodoxy in his other mentions of a world-soul shows that he cannot have meant this; only the Augustinian idea that the ancients, with a vague sense that God was triune in nature, constructed erroneous trinities in unsuccessful attempts at grasping the true one.

Tyard refers readily to the 'eternelle sapience', but only as one of the attributes of God, 'ouvrier doüé de tres-grande puissance et sapience tres-excellente, qui n'est ailleurs que dedans ce Monde, lequel il conduit . . .'.[4] He is not prepared to deny that there may also be a world-soul, perhaps even souls of the spheres and elements: but, if so, these are only 'corps animez'[5] and the world a 'grand et parfait Animal'.[6] So when any phrase of Ficino presupposes a Divine Intelligence distinct from the Supreme Being, or a Universal Soul comparable though not equal with Him in rank, Tyard alters or omits the phrase. Ficino speaks of the soul in 'transport' as 'shining with the rays of the divine mind', 'divinae

[1] DD, 1578, p. 97 v°; cf. Plutarch, *De Iside*, 369D–370B.
[2] DD, 1578, p. 98; cf. Giorgio, *De Harmonia Mundi*, Venice, 1525, I. iii. 2. The italics are Tyard's.
[3] Yates, *Academies*, 1947, p. 91.   [4] DD, 1578, p. 104 v°.
[5] DP, 1587, p. 232.   [6] U, 1557, p. 138.

mentis radio claret'; for Tyard 'ceste Ame est esclarcie des raiz de la divine union'.[1] Ficino represents poetic inspiration as descending through a series of beings: 'Jupiter rapit Apollinem, Apollo illuminat Musas, Musae suscitant . . . vatum animas', and he has just explained that the Muses are the 'sphaerarum mundi animas. Jupiter quidem mens Dei est, ab hac Apollo, mens animae mundi.'[2] More cautious even than Ronsard in the *Ode à Michel de l'Hospital*, Tyard omits all this chain and represents 'la fureur divine, laquelle les Muses, et le Musagete (ainsi se nomme leur guide Apollon) inspirent,'[3] as coming only and equally from the Muses and Apollo, who symbolize 'toute puissance de divinité, qui excede le commun cours de la naturelle apprehension'.[4]

It seems that Tyard is attempting to paint the lily, to christianize Ficino. He makes other such attempts. Where Ficino mentions the use of the body as the distinguishing mark of the fallen soul, 'natura velut instrumento utitur', it is only that soul's excessive love of the body which Tyard denounces, 'amie de ces formes particulieres . . . elle se plait à embrasser le corps'.[5] Where Ficino refers to God it is Tyard's habit to interrupt the train of thought with a string of reverential epithets. On the other hand, he may bowdlerize the word 'Deus' itself: 'Deo duce' becomes 'guidez par plus fideles esprits',[6] and the frenzy which for Ficino comes 'a Deo' is for Tyard 'engendree d'une secrette puissance divine'.[7] Obviously he has in mind the less instructed, or more easily startled, of his readers, as he has when he expands difficult terms, omits confusing details like the fall of the soul from eternity through *aevum* and time into space, concurrently with its other descent, or softens apparent exaggerations—according to him the lover devotes 'la plus grande partie de sa puissance',[8] according to Ficino the whole of his vital powers, to thinking of the beloved, whence his digestion suffers. . . . The impression of the *Theologia Platonica* which is to be gained from the *Solitaire premier* is simplified to the point of distortion. Tyard has selected for the 'Dames Françoises', to whom his popularization is dedicated, the romantic,

---

[1] SP, 1552, p. 32; cf. Ficino, op. cit., p. 1361 (*Comm. in Conv.* vii. 13).
[2] Ficino, op. cit., p. 1283 (*In Platonis Ionem*).
[3] SP, 1552, p. 49.   [4] Ibid., p. 43.
[5] Ibid., p. 33; cf. Ficino, op. cit., p. 1361 (*Comm. in Conv.* vii. 13).
[6] SP, 1552, p. 13; cf. Ficino, op. cit., p. 79 (*Theol. Plat.* i. 1).
[7] SP, 1552, p. 25; cf. Ficino, op. cit., p. 1357 (*Comm. in Conv.* vii. 3).
[8] SP, 1552, p. 27; cf. Ficino, op. cit., p. 1346 (*Comm. in Conv.* vi. 9).

personal, pictorial elements of Neoplatonism which might be expected to appeal most to them and be easiest to understand, with the addition of a devotional colouring to satisfy any Oisille among his readers.

The earlier part of the *Solitaire premier* relies on Ficino almost exclusively. When Tyard turns to Giraldi as his main source, he still maintains the Neoplatonic atmosphere, partly by selecting and stressing any particularly relevant details in Giraldi's work, but partly by timely interpolations from Ficino like the notion of the three types of beauty, 'triplex . . . pulchritudo, animorum, corporum atque vocum', which is allowed to interrupt the Solitaire's account of the Graces.[1] This is the beginning, however, of a decrease in borrowing from Ficino which becomes more and more marked. It is true that the Neoplatonic background produces in the *Solitaire second* a theory of music presupposing a 'fureur' in performers and listeners, tints the melancholy opening and close of the *Discours du temps*, and affects Tyard's cosmology in the other three Discourses. But very few verbal borrowings from Ficino are to be observed, and even those which may be traced are buried in passages inspired much more by other sources. Tyard still retains his respect for Ficino, never extends to him the slight flippancy which sometimes develops in his references to 'les Platoniques', and leaves his earlier borrowings intact; but, so far as the evidence of the *Discours philosophiques* goes, within a few years of the first publication of the *Solitaire premier* Ficino's direct influence on Tyard almost ceased.

A Neoplatonic influence which lasted longer, though in a rather different way, was that of Leo Hebraeus. The *Discours* rarely borrow verbally from him and never mention him; after all, Tyard had translated him; but doing so seems to have left Tyard taking many of Leo's ideas for granted and taking a lasting interest in many of Leo's subjects. The *Dialoghi d'amore* and the *Solitaire premier* both speak of the relation between virtue, knowledge, and happiness, of the disciplines, of why the philosopher should speak obscurely, and of why some men were called sons of the gods. The *Solitaire second*'s question whether sight or hearing is superior is argued in Leo's Dialogue II, which also devotes much space to astrology, the subject of *Mantice*; and both Dialogue III and the *Discours du temps* treat of ancient chronological cycles. Dialogue II

[1] SP, 1552, p. 57; cf. Ficino, op. cit., p. 1322 (*Comm. in Conv.* i. 4).

may have supplied what became the *Second Curieux* with a few of its 'correspondences' between man and the universe; Dialogue III almost certainly contributed to the *Discours du temps* some unorthodox arguments that Time had no beginning. And it may be that the sources of many commonplaces in Tyard are to be sought in Leo, if they are worth seeking at all: for example, the fact that laurel is sacred to Apollo is not in Giraldi, who provided the rest of Tyard's passage on laurel, but is in the *Dialoghi*.[1]

But what Tyard appears to owe above all to Leo is the manner of presentation of the two *Solitaires*, the conversation between Pasithée and her lover, and the tone of this conversation. Of the various forms of the Platonic dialogue, the most popular among Renaissance Neoplatonists was the symposium; Ficino used it in his *Commentarium in Convivium*, Castiglione in his *Cortegiano*, Estienne Pasquier in his *Monophile*. Tyard himself was gradually to move towards it; *L'Univers* and *Mantice* are recognizably symposia. But Leo followed rather the model of the medieval textbook such as the *Margarita philosophica* of Gregor Reisch, a duologue between the *discipulus* and the *magister*, whose function is neither to lecture like Timaeus nor to ask questions like Socrates, but to answer at length the questions of the pupil. At times a little humour is allowed to creep in, the simplicity of the pupil giving scope for the wit of the master. The pupil of Reisch has his revenge: when the master, after treating of purgatory, announces his intention of 'descending lower', the student retorts, 'Go first, and I will follow.'

To all this Leo adds only the complication that the pupil is a woman with whom the master is in love; and all this, including both this complication and the occasional humour, is exactly reproduced in the *Solitaires*. The task of both Leo's Filone and Tyard's Solitaire is to answer the questions put by their ladies; the questions are apt and intelligent, and both ladies make their own contributions to the discussions. Both, however, are clearly in the position of learners: 'Più corretto vorrei che parlassi, o Sofia'; 'Il vaut mieus (dit elle) que j'essaye si j'auray compris ce qu'avez dit.'[2] And each lady has to thwart her tutor's attempts to make the conversation a more personal one: 'Non tante cose, o Filone! ch'io veggo bene che negli amanti più abbonda la lingua che le passioni';

---

[1] *Dialoghi d'amore*, ed. Caramella, Bari, 1929, p. 140; cf. SP, 1552, p. 88.
[2] SS, 1555, p. 87; cf. Leo, op. cit., p. 224.

'Ce commencement de harangue melancolique et pleintive (dit elle) tend bien loin du musical entretien, lequel vous m'avez promis.'[1]

One may even compare the opening of Leo's first Dialogue, where Sofia queries Filone's assertion that love and desire coexist in him, with that of the *Solitaire premier*, where Pasithée demands an explanation of the Solitaire's remark that he is agitated by frenzy. One may parallel the close of Leo's first and last Dialogues with the close of the two *Solitaires*: both authors refuse further instruction on the ground that it is too late at night. And it may be Sofia who gave Tyard the idea of representing the fourth *fureur* not in theory but in practice: 'Non vedi tu [che] ciò ch'io voglio da te è la teorica de l'amore, e quel che tu vuoi da me è la pratica di quello?' says she, and the Solitaire replies, 'Je n'ay autre travail en plus songneuse recommendation, que de la vous representer devant les yeux.'[2] Nevertheless, the dialogue form used by Leo is almost as rigid and bare as that of the *Margarita*; it is the personal introductions and interpolations, more reminiscent of the *Cortegiano*, which afford the charm and humanity of the *Discours philosophiques*.

A passage in the *Solitaire premier*, on the role of the number three in the universe, recalls the method of Francesco Giorgio. But there is no reason to believe that Tyard used him in that Discourse; their lists of triads have only one in common, the obvious one of beginning, middle, and end.[3] Nor is there reason to believe that, except in the field of astrology, Tyard took much from Giovanni Pico della Mirandola. On several occasions when a borrowing from him might be expected, as in the proofs that sight excels hearing or that Time had no beginning,[4] no such borrowing is to be found. On several occasions when one seems recognizable, as in Tyard's passages on the garden of archetypes, the microcosm, and the Trinity,[5] the source will be found to be Giorgio. One at least of the Kabbalistic borrowings added in 1587 to the *Premier Curieux* is in the *Heptaplus*,[6] but Pico is certainly not Tyard's only source of that type of learning. The closest parallels

---

[1] SS, 1555, p. 10; cf. Leo, op. cit., p. 55.
[2] SP, 1552, p. 120; cf. Leo, op. cit., p. 200.
[3] SP, 1552, p. 55; cf. *De Harmonia Mundi*, I. iii. 2.
[4] SS, 1555, pp. 118–19; DT, 1556, pp. 5–9.
[5] DD, 1578, p. 75 v°; U, 1557, p. 115 ff.; DD, 1578, p. 98.
[6] DP, 1587, p. 237 v°, last six lines; cf. *Heptaplus*, i. 7.

will be found in their attacks on astrology; but their final conclusions differ.

Tyard turned not to other Neoplatonists, but to the mythological manuals, to supplement Leo and Ficino.

II · *Giraldi and the Mythologists*

As the earlier part of the *Solitaire premier* depends on Ficino, so the latter part depends on Lilio Giraldi of Ferrara, one of Montaigne's 'deux tres-excellens personnages en sçavoir . . . morts en estat de n'avoir pas leur soul à manger'.[1] Tyard does not use his *Historiae Poetarum* . . . *Dialogi decem* nor his *De Poetis Nostrorum Temporum Dialogi duo*; but he undoubtedly had under his hand the *Syntagma de Musis*, published first in 1507 and enlarged in 1539, the *De Annis et Mensis caeterisque temporum partibus* . . . of 1541, and the *Historia Deorum* or *De Deis Gentium varia et multiplex historia, libris* . . . *XVII comprehensa* of 1548, three systematic and pedantic manuals of mythology. One or more of these was quoted in the original version of every one of the *Discours philosophiques*, and all three works were further used in the seventies and in 1587.

Yet for Tyard Giraldi seems to have been in no way a master, perhaps hardly a person; he never refers to him by name or by implication. In prose and verse alike he uses Giraldi's books merely as standard works of reference, containing facts on which anyone has a right to draw; and his borrowings are introduced not with the formality accorded to those from Ficino, but as matters of common knowledge: 'la plus frequente et vulgaire opinion est, que Jupiter engendra en Mnemosine les Muses. . . .'[2] Tyard is no longer drawing attention to a great work; he is paying tribute to nothing in the original except its usefulness:

et ne vous ennuirois de ce discours, si je ne savois, que le souvenir de telles choses vous servira de quelque lumiere à la lecture des œuvres de tant de doctes Poëtes de ce tems, qui decorent si richement leurs vers des ornements de l'antiquité, que mal aisément y pourront les ignorans et grossiers rien comprendre.[3]

One is therefore surprised, and the innate weakness of Tyard's creative powers is confirmed, by the evidence that Giraldi fur-

[1] *Essais*, i. 35.
[2] SP, 1552, pp. 67–68; cf. Giraldi, op. cit. i. 533 (*De Musis*).
[3] SP, 1552, p. 106.

nished him not only with facts but with basic plans for half one Discourse, the whole of another, and a considerable section of a third. Midway in the *Solitaire premier*, making a somewhat awkward transition from Plato's and Ficino's remarks on the Muses' role in inspiring poets, Tyard promises to

> declairer une grande partie de ce, que les fables Poëtiques ont touché des Muses, souz l'escorce de quoy le suc et la moelle se treuve de plusieurs bonnes doctrines. . . .[1]

He proceeds to reproduce almost the whole of Giraldi's compendium of the legends about these goddesses, only slightly altering the order to make it more pleasing. Like Giraldi, he begins by considering the number of the Muses; their relation to the spheres, to Jupiter, and to Apollo; and the meaning of the name 'Muses' and of some of their attributes. He omits for the moment Giraldi's next section, on the surnames given to the Muses collectively, and splits into three sequences the section following, which treats of each of them in turn. Giraldi's last two pages, on the worship offered to the Muses, are discarded in favour of the passage on their surnames, reduced to a bare list, and further remarks on their attributes. From time to time Tyard pauses to insert material from other sources, literary theory or amorous badinage; but he always returns after a few pages to the framework provided by the *De Musis*. The result, while almost completely irrelevant to Ficino's conception of the Muses, yields a charming promenade through late classical mythology, accompanied with much good advice, moral and educational, for Pasithée:

> les Muses (à fin qu'encor je vous declare quelques unes de leurs façons de faire) entrelacees l'une avec l'autre dansent en chantant des hymnes appropriez aux louenges des Dieux: et signifie tel entrelacement, que la vertu ne peult estre separee, ou desjointe des studieux, et sinceres amateurs de sapience et doctrine.[2]

Tyard, at least, was sufficiently satisfied with the effect to adopt the *De Annis* in 1556 as a similar basis for his *Discours du temps, de l'an, et de ses parties*. He ruthlessly abridges the ponderous treatise, but it is clear that he relies on its rigidly systematic construction. Giraldi opens with definitions of eternity and time, which Tyard

---

[1] SP, 1552, p. 50.
[2] Ibid., pp. 80–81; cf. Giraldi, op. cit. i. 535.

takes for granted when he drifts into his unorthodox suggestion that the world had no beginning; Giraldi's next topic, the age of the world, is replaced by a closely related one, the chronology of the Bible. The main part of Giraldi's book, on the divisions of time, Tyard almost exactly reverses. Giraldi begins, where Tyard ends, with a list of the cycles of antiquity, and passes on to the years; the seasons, which Tyard studies together with the hours, the Greek word being the same; the months, followed by the history of their names in Latin and then in Greek, which Tyard throws into a single sequence; the problem of adjusting the calendar to the real movements of the celestial bodies; the day and its variations, to which Tyard adds a disquisition on lucky and unlucky days. Giraldi ends, where Tyard begins, with the hours, and adds a paragraph on methods of telling the time; Tyard concludes in a moral strain.

By the time of *L'Univers* and *Mantice* Tyard appears to be emerging from Giraldi's influence. However, not only does sporadic borrowing persist, but it seems demonstrable that the ten pages of *L'Univers* which treat of God and the gods[1] were primarily modelled on the first book of the *De Deis*, though Tyard seems either to have lost interest at about the sixteenth of Giraldi's seventy-two closely printed folio pages, or to have decided that his reader would do so. Both works begin with orthodox descriptions of God. The Curieux enters on a more secular discussion by quoting the threefold classification of deities, fabulous, civil, and natural, which could of course be found in the *De Civitate Dei*, but which Giraldi's page 12 conveniently supplies. Emphasizing that God is unknowable, the Curieux is enabled to return to Giraldi's observation on page 2 that His Hebrew name was deliberately chosen as unpronounceable. Tyard's digressions on Hebrew words in Christian worship and on Zoroastrianism, and the twenty-page argument about the existence of God, date only from 1578; in 1557 the Curieux continued with Giraldi through the other names of God to the theological opinions of various philosophers and of various nations of antiquity. Several examples of ancestor-worship, deification of abstract qualities, and totemism are then taken from Giraldi's last two pages 'de stulto . . . cultu, et falsa opinatione . . . '. The Curieux concludes, 'Je vous ennuyrois des Theologies Pheniciennes, Atlantides, Africaines, Phrigiennes,

[1] U, 1557, pp. 125–35 (DD, 1578, pp. 95–114 v°; DP, 1587, pp. 298–317 v°).

Persiennes',[1] which are, in order, the subjects of five successive paragraphs of pages 6–7 of the *De Deis*.

Giraldi may have shaped Tyard's views and works in more subtle ways. To delight in allegorizing classical mythology is, of course, both medieval and Neoplatonic, but Giraldi and Tyard agree in the extent to which they indulge in it, and in many examples. They agree too in believing, or in accepting for literary purposes the belief, that the first inventors of various arts can be traced. On the other hand, they are critical enough to account euhemeristically for certain antique deifications; according to Giraldi, 'Jupiter . . . ambitiosus sibi divinos honores comparavit', and he mentions many 'praestantissimos virtute, prudentia, viribus, appellatos Jovis filios'.[2] Tyard extends the principle to a long list of

ceux, qui, impatiens de se contenir sous la peau de l'humanité, se sont eslevés au souhait desnaturé d'estre Dieux: ou, defaillant la puissance d'atteindre à celle impossible majesté, s'en acquerir du moins, les honneurs et la reputation.[3]

As for the Muses,

pensez, que ceux, qui les ont feint si fecondes, entendoient ceux estre leurs enfans, qui se sont trouvez excellens professeurs des arts ou disciplines, qui leur sont particulierement dediees.[4]

It may even be that Giraldi influenced the development of Tyard's views on astrology. Giraldi is frankly a sceptic about it; quoting Firmicus and Manilius on the government of the parts of the body by the signs of the Zodiac, he comments, 'Sed et hunc et illum mecum rideas licebit.'[5] Usually Tyard takes Giraldi's facts and neglects his opinions; but the marked dependence of the *Discours du temps* on Giraldi may have something to do with the number of flippant references to astrology there.

Above all, Giraldi must share with the Brigade the responsibility for turning Tyard away from his early manner of composition, inspired by Ficino and Scève, towards the ornate, pictorial, allusive work that Ronsard loved and Giraldi facilitated. The change of style half-way through the *Solitaire premier* echoes exactly the change of style in the *Erreurs amoureuses* between 1549 and 1551. Perhaps it was even Giraldi, rather than Ronsard or Du Bellay,

---

[1] U, 1557, p. 130. [2] Giraldi, op. cit. i. 7–8 (*De Deis*, i).
[3] M, 1558, p. 1. [4] SP, 1552, p. 102.
[5] Giraldi, op. cit. i. 15 (*De Deis*, i).

who prompted Tyard's first infidelity to Neoplatonism. It was not impossible to combine a belief in the *fureurs* with the writing of *docte poésie*; the contradiction pervades the work of the Pléiade. But it was next to impossible to combine an antiquarian's detached interest in all mythology with the almost religious attitude required in a Neoplatonist; and Giraldi and his fellow mythologists, for the most part, were not Neoplatonists. Giraldi, for example, dissociates himself from belief in the Platonic conception of Cupid:

> Plato in Symposio scribit, Cupidinem natum ex Poro . . . et Penia . . . quod plerique omnes magno mysterio a Platone confictum prodidere. Quae si minus placeant, quae a philosophis Platonicis traduntur, vel prolixiora sunt, accipe quae paucis Eusebius pie et religiose scribit . . .;[1]

and Giraldi, Conti, and Cartari refer only cursorily, if at all, to such traditions as those of the twofold Venus and Cupid and of the Androgyne. Sending Neoplatonic inquirers away empty, and supplying instead a rich panorama of paganism in general, they may have joined in bringing about the gradual discarding of Neoplatonic themes from sixteenth-century literature; they certainly contributed to the first interruption in the course and change in the character of the *Discours philosophiques*.

Deliberate alterations in borrowings from Giraldi are rarer than in borrowings from Ficino; but this is not because Tyard accepts all Giraldi tells him. Where he is dissatisfied with what he finds, he simply neglects it and passes to another source or subject. By the time of the *Discours du temps* he comes flatly to contradict Giraldi: the latter describes a representation of the Horae and identifies the god accompanying them as Apollo; Tyard repeats this but adds: 'Mais je le jugeay Jupiter foudroyant. . . .'[2] The adaptation of Giraldi's material to the Neoplatonic atmosphere of the *Solitaire premier* results at least once in a distinct tampering with the thought: Giraldi's explanation of the Muses as 'mentis conceptus . . . aeternarum rerum contemplatores' is translated as 'les Entendemens *eslevez* aux conceptions, et contemplations des choses eternelles',[3] reverting to the idea of the soul's mystical ascent.

And, again, Tyard tends to christianize his source. Giraldi himself is no pagan nor syncretist; he uses the old myths to draw

---

[1] Giraldi, op. cit. i. 389 (*De Deis*, xiii).
[2] DT, 1556, p. 14; cf. Giraldi, op. cit. i. 402 (*De Deis*, xiii).
[3] SP, 1552, p. 68; cf. Giraldi, op. cit. i. 533 (*De Musis*).

general moral conclusions, or compares them with Christianity to
their disadvantage; but often he leaves the facts to speak for themselves. Tyard brings out the Christian view much more explicitly:
Giraldi's 'Jupiter . . . rerum omnium parens' becomes 'le Createur
souverain de tout (que les anciens couvroient du nom de Jupiter)'.[1]
The sub-title of the *De Annis*, 'difficili hactenus et impedita
materia, dissertatio facilis et expedita', simply offers knowledge
for knowledge's sake. Tyard's reason for pursuing the same study
is that 'si jamais les ames *genereuses* se sont *elevees* en contemplation de quelque *excellence*, le Ciel me semble en avoir esté le plus
louable sujet . . .'.[2]

It seems that any mythological manual might have supplied
Tyard's wants equally well; he may have adopted Giraldi's merely
because it came first into his hands. He must already have had
a sound general education in mythology, and it is pointless to try
to trace his more hackneyed references, unless anything indicates
some particular source. However, Natale Conti's *Mythologiae* of
1551 is so indicated. Tyard's passage on the Sirens contains some
details which are to be found in Conti and not in Giraldi, others
which are in Giraldi but where Tyard's wording is closer to Conti's
and, especially, Conti's explanations, moral or scientific:

. . . loca quaedam marina in angustias quasdam praeruptis montibus
contracta fuisse, in quas . . . fluctus sonum cum suavitate et harmonia
emittentes navigantes allicerent ad visendum, quo cum appulissent
undarum impetu delati absorbebantur.

. . . la vraye histoire des Sirenes est, qu'en quelques destroits de la
Mer se treuvent des rochers, qui dedens leurs concavitez reçoivent les
flots ordinaires des eaux contraintes, et faites impetueuses entre ces rocs,
d'ou s'engendre (comme il est evident, et aisé à croire) une voix aigue
et sifflante.[3]

The passage is something of a digression from the main thread of
the *Solitaire premier*, and could have been added at the last
minute.

Conti also offers a neat differentiation, not brought out clearly
by Giraldi, between Tethys and Thetis: 'Tethys putanda est ipsa
aquae moles, quae ad generationem coaluerit. Thetis vero aquae

---

[1] SP, 1552, p. 68; cf. Giraldi, op. cit. i. 533 (*De Musis*).
[2] DT, 1578, dedication (DP, 1587, p. 334).
[3] SP, 1552, p. 87; cf. N. Conti, *Mythologiae sive explicationum fabularum
libri decem*, Venice, 1551, VII. xiii.

elementum. . . .'[1] This may account for the 1575 substitution of 'Thetis' for 'Tethis' in the Ode with which the *Solitaire premier* concludes, describing sunset over the sea. There are a few other fragments which Conti may or may not have supplied to this Discourse and the scientific ones. The suggestion is that Tyard met with the *Mythologiae* towards the end of the composition of the *Solitaire premier*, but that his work was already too near completion, and his interests soon diverged too far from Conti's, for the latter to be of great use to him. Cartari's *Immagini* of 1556 also came out too late for him; there seem to be no borrowings from it in any of the Discourses.

But it is certain that after completing the *Solitaire premier* Tyard used Alessandri, the Neapolitan antiquarian who won himself some ridicule by his pseudo-classical *nom de plume*, Alexander ab Alexandro, but who inspired widespread respect for his erudition. The six books of his *Dies Geniales* each start vaguely from a conversation with a certain friend on a certain day, and go on to wander at will through Roman history, law, philology, and archaeology. From the chapter 'Quando dies tam apud Rhomanos quam exteros gentes incipiat: et qui dies atri, quive fausti sint' are taken almost bodily four pages of the *Discours du temps* of 1556, perhaps six pages,[2] though the first two might equally come from Giraldi. At least one more passage in the three pages before, and at least one of the 1578 additions to those pages, can be traced to the same chapter of Alessandri. A passage in the *Second Curieux* of 1578:

> Quel poisson n'eust receu pour compagnon au nager . . . un Scyllis Sicyonien, et le matelot Neapolitain, qui en un jour est allé et revenu nageant, d'Ischia à Porezzo, à l'entree du golphe de Naples? ou bien Colan, surnommé Poisson, natif de Catania en Sicile, qui comme en un bain par esbat ordinaire alloit nageant par la mer depuis Gaiette jusques en Sicile?[3]

refers unmistakably to the chapter 'Miraculum de homine, qui plus in mari quam in terris degebat, maximaque aequora velocissime tranabat'.

These certainties suggest a further possibility, that Alessandri's account of the tarantula and the effects of its bite inspired the

---

[1] *Mythologiae*, VIII. ii.
[2] DT, 1556, pp. 21–26; cf. *Dies geniales*, Rome, 1522, IV. xx, and Giraldi, op. cit. ii. 587–98.   [3] DD, 1578, p. 91; cf. *Dies geniales*, II. xxi.

passage in the *Solitaire second* where the Curieux provides the only evidence of an Italian tour by either Tyard or Des Autelz:

J'ay souvenance d'avoir vù en meints lieus d'Italie des Phalanges (petite espece d'araignes) nommees entre eus Tarantola, si dangereuses, que mal pour celui qui en est piqué, principalement en la Pouille, ou je me suis rencontré quelquefois, à voir la diverse misere qu'engendre la pointure de si petit animal: Les uns rient incessamment, les autres pleurent, les autres chantent, les autres dorment, les autres sont afligez d'un veiller perpetuel, d'une Phrenesie, d'une manie Lymphatique, aumoins de semblables aigues passions, toutes diverses (cróy je) pour la diference du venin de l'un à l'autre Tarantole, ou pour la diversité de la complexion des piquez. De remede, il n'en est nouvelle que d'un souverein, duquel la preuve vuë, mal aisément vous permetroit de contenir le rire: car, aupres du malade lon fait venir un joueur de Lut, de Lyre, ou autre harmonieus instrument, à l'ouïe duquel, soudein, le languissant perd sa grande douleur, et commence ou à se réveiller, s'il est endormi: ou s'il veille, à dancer: et de peu à peu reprenant le sens, est remis en son premier naturel.[1]

Ficino, who has been suggested as a source,[2] could have furnished Tyard with only two or three phrases:

Esse vero Phoebeam medicamque in sono, et eo quidem certo, potentiam, ex eo patet, quod quae in Apulia tacti Phalangio sunt, stupent omnes, semianimesque iacent, donec certum quisque suumque sonum audiat. Tunc enim saltat ad sonum apte, sudat inde, atque convalescit.

Alessandri devotes nearly the whole of a chapter to the phenomenon, with a fuller introduction than Ficino's:

... *tarantula, id est, phalangio* percussos, quos vulgo tarantatos dicunt, haud aliter ex ancipiti morbo convalescere vidimus, quam si *tibicen vel citharista* iuxta eos diversos modulos incinat ...;

a fuller description of the insect:

... Tarantula enim *aranei genus* est, *dirum animal, tactu pestilens*: eam si casu spectes, *futilem* et sine noxa putabis ...

and of its habitat, 'Apuliae campos, ubi *peculiare* hoc malum existit'. His description of the victims is fuller than Ficino's, though still not so full as Tyard's:

... *abalienati mente* et semivivi, continuo *stupore* et hebeti sensu oculorum auriumque affecti, vitam *miserabilem* aegerrime ducant ....

---

[1] SS, 1555, p. 117; cf. Ficino, op. cit. i. 564 (*De Vita Coelitus Comparanda*, III. xxi); *Dies geniales*, II. xvii.

[2] Young, in *Bibl. d'Hum. et Ren.*, 1960, 364.

He recounts a patient's recovery in detail:

... velut e gravi *somno excitus*, oculos attollit parumper, mox se in pedes erigit, ac *sese recipiens, paulatim* ... in *saltus* gestusque ... erumpit ...

and claims to have watched such a recovery himself, 'res ... *risu* prorsus digna'.

Even in an age of plagiarism, to pass off as personal experience a thirty-year-old scientific report is something of a serious matter. But such a treatment of Alessandri's text goes little farther than Tyard's other borrowings from him, where the mere essentials are taken and reworded in pithy and racy language, while it is not unknown for Tyard to introduce borrowings from other sources as if they were original. It may still be, of course, that as well as reading Alessandri Tyard went to Apulia and observed the tarantula for himself. . . .

III · *Growing Mastery*

At first glance the *Solitaire second* appears to be a mere pendant or sequel to the *Solitaire premier*; but as one studies it more closely one senses a different atmosphere, of harder work in the light of more expert knowledge. The hybrid character of the *Solitaire premier* is almost confessed in the sub-title itself, not 'Discours de la Poésie' but 'Prose des Muses, et de la fureur poëtique'. In contrast, the *Solitaire second* is precisely subtitled 'Prose de la Musique', and soon reveals itself to be a serious technical treatise, thrice the length of the *Solitaire premier* and, as Nan Cooke Carpenter suggests,[1] probably a source of Ronsard's 'Préface au Roy François II'. Tyard is obviously master of his subject to a degree unparalleled in the Discourses before *Mantice*; though, except for a few remarks on notation, he omits what was styled in his time the *musica practica*, ostensibly because Pasithée knows it 'trop familierement'[2], really perhaps to conform to the 'philosophical' nature of the Discourses, to their early theory of artistic intuition, and to the principle of *odi profanum vulgus*. For Boethius, though Tyard does not go so far as to quote this passage, it is 'nobler' to understand musical theory than to be able to perform:

Multo enim est maius atque altius scire quod quisque faciat, quam

[1] Carpenter, in *M.L.N.*, 1960, 126.   [2] SS, 1555, p. 14.

ipsum illud efficere. . . . Quanto igitur praeclarior est scientia Musicae in cognitione rationis, quam in opere efficiendi atque actu cantum, scilicet, quantum corpus mente superatur.[1]

In the *Solitaire second* Tyard is much more ready to acknowledge his sources; there are some dozen references to Boethius, and a passage in praise of Glareanus and Gafori, 'Franchin, (auquel je doy, apres Boëce, le plus en cete discipline)'.[2] Franchino Gafori, the cleric and musician of Milan, had died in 1522. His *Theorica Musicae* of 1492 clearly derives from Boethius, and is complemented by his *Practica Musicae* of 1496; his *De Harmonia musicorum instrumentorum* of 1518 is at once more broadly based and more detailed, and Tyard uses it for preference, supplementing it sometimes by the *Theorica* but never by the *Practica*. In 1508 Gafori extracted and translated from his own Latin works an *Angelicum ac Divinum Opus musicae* in simple Italian, and a copy was in the library of Tyard's great-nephew in 1638. It may be merely natural that Tyard, making a similar extract and translation, should several times parallel the movement and phrases of the *Opus*; but one question, why the Greater Complete System is divided into tetrachords and not pentachords,[3] is mentioned by Gafori in the *Opus* alone, and is not raised at all by Boethius or Glareanus. If this is really a borrowing from the *Opus*, it provides one of the few instances of Tyard's using a source written in a modern language.

'Henri Glarean, amateur et congnoissant de toutes disciplines',[4] not only music but arithmetic and chronology, philology and geography, was an elder contemporary of Tyard's, by birth Heinrich Lorit of Glarus in Switzerland. There seems no evidence of Tyard's using his *Isagoge in Musicen* of 1516; but he certainly used the *Dodecachordon* of 1547. It summarizes Boethian music very briefly, sweeps away most of its irrelevancies and proceeds to present an interpretation of the Greek modes in direct opposition to that of Gafori—a revolutionary paradox likely to arouse the lively interest of the Pléiade, with their concern for taking music as well as poetry back to its classical sources, and to fascinate Tyard, with his passion for embracing new ideas and attempting to reconcile them with the old.

---

[1] *De Musica*, I. xxxiv.
[2] SS, 1555, p. 119.
[3] Ibid., p. 59; cf. *Angelicum . . . opus*, I. xiii.
[4] SS, 1555, p. 119.

In respect of some ancient systems of notation, Tyard also acknowledges a debt to 'un vieil livre escrit en main' and to 'un fort vieil exemplaire, venu en mes mains par la grace de . . . Maurice Sceve'.[1] The borrowings that can be traced to Boethius, Gafori, or Glareanus leave little else that may be from these two works, and they are not recognizable in Baridon's *Inventaire de la bibliothèque de Pontus de Tyard*. For the introduction of the *Solitaire second*, extolling temperance as 'le vrey moyen de s'alonger une vie, vreyement vie' and music as 'le vrey pourtrait de la Temperance',[2] no likely model has yet been found either in Ficino or in Tyard's known musical sources. It might well represent the opening of one of the two unnamed sources, and provide a means of identification.

After the introduction, Pasithée and the Solitaire reappear, regretting, in company with many musicians of the age,

que la Musique . . . soit en basse et vulgaire estime pour ce tems . . . demeuree par je ne say quel desastre sans plus louable nom, que celui qu'un chantre vagabond et sans savoir, ou un mercenaire menestrier lui en aura aquiz. . . .[3]

Tyard then proceeds to follow faithfully but discriminatingly the first book of Boethius's *De Musica*, that of Gafori's *De Harmonia* (with occasional excursions into the *Theorica*), and that of Glareanus's *Dodecachordon*, taking what is more interesting, passing over what is less so, using the volume best suited to his purpose of the moment, and expanding its contribution by fragments of the others. A brief survey of the history of music comes from the first chapter of the *De Musica*, with the help of the *Theorica*; half a page on the three meanings of music, mundane, human, and instrumental, is related to Boethius's second chapter; and some elementary definitions from the first chapter of the *Dodecachordon* are followed by a 'plus sufisante descripcion' from the first two chapters of the *De Harmonia*.

So Tyard comes, with his three sources, to the longest, though hardly the most important, section of his Discourse: a process of building up or plotting out the diatonic, chromatic, and enharmonic scales by calculating the positions of their notes from the ratios of their intervals. The raw material is taken almost in entirety from the latter part of Book I and the earlier part of Book II

---

[1] SS, 1555, pp. 25 and 28.   [2] Ibid., pp. 5 and 8.   [3] Ibid., p. 10.

of the *De Harmonia*, though simpler diagrams are substituted and the approach is less impersonal, a very pleasant collaboration between the Solitaire and his pupil. In the course of it Tyard finds himself confronted with the fact that the musical tone cannot be divided into two equal semitones; this leads him to push his Gafori aside, to recapitulate Boethius's references to the paradox, and to try to refute them out of Boethius himself. The section finally founders among assorted borrowings from Gafori, such as a passage on the ease with which the senses are deceived, connected originally with the argument about the semitone, but fitted by Tyard into his description of the enharmonic scale with its still smaller intervals. One has the impression that Tyard has skimmed through the remainder of Book II and Book III of the *De Harmonia*, preserved the few points he thinks interesting enough, and decided that it is time to make some sort of break before passing to Book IV, on the classical modes and the music of nature.

The break is provided by the entrance of the Curieux, who transforms the duologue, where Leo Hebraeus's inspiration was becoming exhausted, into a spirited triangular conversation. But there is little change in the way in which Tyard chooses or uses his borrowings. Though it is the Curieux who raises the subject of the Greek modes, it is the Solitaire who pursues it in the same style as before; and though this subject is the speciality of Glareanus, whose view Tyard ends by adopting, he first gives the views of Boethius and Gafori, and digresses as they do to the 'effects of music'. Tales of its 'guerison des perturbacions d'esprit, et des corporelles maladies . . .'[1] formed a common stock served up in a conventional style by any Renaissance writer who wished; but there seems no doubt that most of Tyard's examples are translated directly though freely from Boethius, supplemented by Gafori.

Moindre eficace n'avoit la Phrygienne, par laquelle un jeune Taurominitein fut irrité, et mis en tant extreme colere, que, plus que transporté, à feu et à armes il vouloit forcer une maison voisine, en laquelle la jeune fille, qui lui poingnoit le cœur en quelque endroit, faisoit part de soy à un sien favorit. . . .[2]

'. . . cum scortum in rivalis domo esset clausum, atque ille furens domum vellet amburere. . . .' The Neoplatonic close of the digression, where the psychological effects of what is heard are compared with those of what is seen, is not in Tyard's musical sources.

[1] SS, 1555, p. 113.   [2] Ibid., p. 113; cf. *De Musica*, I. i.

Tyard now returns to the *Dodecachordon* to treat again of the modes in themselves, and then of modulation and whether it is more 'estimable' to be able to compose harmony or melody. To conclude the Discourse, he lets the Curieux turn to the 'musiques mondeine et humeine', the 'proporcion de parfette Symmetrie'[1] between the intervals which compose the scale, the positions of the planets, the parts and elements which make up the human body, and anything else it may seem relevant to mention. Even Glareanus devotes a chapter to the Muses, and it would have been a sign of very advanced thought had Tyard omitted the subject. The *De Musica*, *Theorica*, and *De Harmonia* contribute about equally to his anthology of fancies, but so do other sources. The practical appendix on how to construct a monochord is, as Tyard admits, based on Boethius and Glareanus, but is for the most part an excellent illustration of his knack of putting simply and clearly what earlier writers tended to assume one knew already.

Apart from such simplification, Tyard makes few alterations in his borrowings; his method of treating an opinion with which he disagrees is now to reproduce it fairly before indicating disagreement. He is not a competent original thinker on the subject of music, though he struggles gallantly to find French equivalents for Latin technical terms, 'mépartemens (car je ne say comme dire autrement ce qu'ils nommoient proporcionalité ou medieté)' and 'treize nonanteneuviemes, que je ne puis exprimer en plus gracieus mot'.[2] Confuting Aristoxenus, Boethius proved that the musical tone cannot be exactly bisected. The Solitaire repeats as best he can the mathematical proof, from the absence of a geometric mean between two numbers in the ratio of 8 to 9:

... 17, raporté à 16, contient 16, et la seizieme partie de 16: et ce mesme 17, raporté à 18, est contenu par ledit 18, avec une sienne dix et settieme partie: tellement que la moindre partie est la dixsettieme, et la plus grande est la seizieme, qui doivent representer deus parties du ton divisé en deus le plus egalement qu'on peut. . . .[3]

He supports this proof, as Boethius does, with arguments from the imperfection of the senses and from experiment; his last argument, that the tone could not be exactly bisected without throwing out the proportions of the whole scale, comes nearer than Boethius ever

---

[1] SS, 1555, pp. 134–5.   [2] Ibid., pp. 29 and 90–91.
[3] Ibid., pp. 40–41; cf. *De Musica*, I. xvi.

does to the way in which a modern musician would express the problem of temperament:

qui voudroit hausser la Diese d'un Schisme, en tous lieus ou elle se rencontre, l'ordre seroit entierement troublé et confondu: demeurant tout le Systeme sans proporcion ni consonance.[1]

But Tyard does not seem to see any special value in that phrase, puts none of the arguments really clearly, and obviously sympathizes with Pasithée as much as with the Solitaire. She insists with feminine logic on the very names of 'demi ton' and 'diesis', and on the possibility of halving any given length of string on the monochord; and the two conclude only that neither Aristoxenus's view nor Boethius's can ever be demonstrated in practice, 'pource que la voix ne peut estre si aisement coulee, ni articulee tant intelligiblement, que lon puisse en juger le milieu . . .'.[2]

The Solitaire later queries the whole notion that the spheres make music; but again he is fair-minded enough to let the Curieux first state his case fully: 'Peut il estre, que des corps si grans et si violens en leurs cours que les Cieus, fissent un continuel mouvement sans aucun son?'[3] and a page[4] is added to the Curieux's arguments in 1587, nothing to the Solitaire's. He finds no real counter-arguments till he reopens the question in the various editions of L'Univers; in 1555 he can only reiterate that 'toute l'Academie ne pourroit, sans plus vives raisons, me faire croire, que les Cieus rendent aucun son'.[5]

Except for this point, Tyard still tries to maintain a Neoplatonic atmosphere in his work, though Gafori and Glareanus give him no more help than Giraldi did. As much as possible of the thought of the Solitaire second is still conformed to the theory of the perfection of the soul by learning, ecstasy, and temperance. To hold music in high esteem was, of course, not peculiarly Neoplatonic; but even where Tyard models his defence of music on Gafori he gives a twist to the argument. He cites Plato at the earliest suitable moment, representing his attitude to music as unequivocally favourable: 'Superfluz seroit le discours emprunté de Platon et d'Aristote, qui la louent, et l'apellent, l'un en sa civilité, et l'autre

[1] SS, 1555, p. 64.
[2] Ibid., p. 44.
[3] Ibid., p. 135; cf. De Musica, I. ii.
[4] DP, 1587, p. 116.
[5] SS, 1555, p. 146; cf. U, 1557, p. 56; DP, 1587, pp. 230 v°–231 v°.

en sa Republique.'[1] And soon he reverts to Plato's conception of the musical frenzy:

> . . . en sa Republique . . . la Musique servoit d'excercice pour reduire l'ame en une parfette temperie de bonnes, louables, et vertueuses meurs, emouvant et apaisant par une naïve puissance et secrette energie, les passions et afeccions, ainsi que par l'oreille les sons estoient transportez aus parties spirituelles: qui fut ocasion prestee aus premiers Poëtes et Theologiens de l'acompagner de Poësie, au nom de fureur souz la charge des Muses, comme je vous diz hier. . . .[2]

To concord with this lofty conception of music, Tyard takes care to soften any suggestion by Gafori or Glareanus that the effects of some musical modes might be bad. The Subdorian mode leads, for Gafori, 'ad segniciem atque desidiam'; for Tyard, 'à la contricion et penitence'.[3] Of the notoriously relaxing Lydian mode Tyard says only that it was 'propre aus paroles . . . tristes et lentes', 'pleintes et lamentacions'.[4] And, while he admits that the Ionian mode was 'mise en usage pour les danses et vers lascifs', he does not feel it necessary, as Glareanus does, to extend the same accusation to the Subionian, 'propre anciennement aus réveils amoureus et aubades de nuit'.[5]

Tyard attributes the effects not merely to the associations of the music, but to mysterious inherent properties of the modes, 'chacune douëe d'une secrette puissance'.[6] This is clearly shown in his anecdotes of the power of music. A peculiarly interesting development is undergone by the tale, which Nan Cooke Carpenter calls rare in musical treatises, of the minstrel left with Clytemnestra by Agamemnon, and killed by Aegisthus. To Homer, this minstrel seems to have been a mere chaperon or private detective, 'to whom Agamemnon when he left for Troy had given strict orders to watch over his queen'. Gafori represents him as under orders to sing especially edifying songs, 'qui uxorem Clytemnestram per muliebrium virtutum laudes ad pudiciciam probitatemque conjugalem cantu hortaretur'. He is almost a magician for Tyard:

> Quelle force avoit la Dorienne, par laquelle Clitemnestre estoit conservee pudique sous le chant d'un Musicien, laissé aupres d'elle, à cet

[1] SS, 1555, p. 11; cf. *Theorica*, I. i.   [2] SS, 1555, p. 11.
[3] Ibid., p. 126; cf. *De Harmonia*, IV. vi.
[4] SS, 1555, pp. 126 and 106.
[5] Ibid., p. 128; cf. *Dodecachordon*, II. xx and xxvii.
[6] SS, 1555, p. 113.

efet, par Agamemnon allant au siege de Troye? demeura elle pas constante contre les lascives importunitez d'Egiste, qui n'emporta d'elle lavantage amoureus, jusques à ce que le malicieus l'ust privee de ce parfet Musicien?[1]

In the same way Tyard puts into Neoplatonic terms the whole of his argument, based on Glareanus, that a good melody is as hard as harmony to compose, and therefore equally 'estimable'.[2] For Glareanus, the composer of either must be gifted with 'naturali quadam ac ingenita virtute, magis quam arte'; for Tyard,

la Musique requiert une naturelle veine, poussee par mesme *Enthusiasme*, plus necessairement (possible) en *l'invencion* d'une seule mutacion de voix à exprimer une parole, qu'on apelle l'air ou le suget d'une chanson, qu'en *l'industrie* de savoir contre un suget raporter deus, trois, ou plusieurs voix harmonieusement. . . .

Glareanus desires a tune which will 'stick in the mind', 'qui hominis animo insideat'; Tyard's ideal tune 'vous *ravit* la part qu'elle veut'. And, obedient to the law *odi profanum vulgus*, Tyard suppresses entirely Glareanus's point that pure melody will appeal to the unlearned as well as to the learned.

Finally, for Tyard the universe conforms, as the human soul should, to a philosophy of 'temperance':

merci de laquelle, les humeines accions, autant intellectuelles que corporelles, toutes assemblees en un compartiment bien proporcionné, forment l'Idee de l'homme heureus. . . . De cete Temperance se treuvent infiniz simulacres en notre vie, tant aus Ars mecaniques, conduiz tous par nombres ou par mesures, qu'aus disciplines honnestes et liberales. . . .[3]

So, when he takes from Gafori a parallel between the intervals of the scale and the 'mouvemens de l'Ame',[4] Tyard stresses the moral implications by defining several of the virtues enumerated by Gafori; interpolates the comment that the health of the soul depends on that of its three Platonic parts, Desire, Ire, and Reason; and concludes in praise of Justice, 'qui raporte et acorde les afeccions, passions, et puissances, corporelles et intellectuelles, l'une à l'autre', a Platonic rather than a scholastic definition.

It seems to have been Tyard's intention to keep apart by itself

---

[1] SS, 1555, p. 113; cf. *Odyssey*, iii. 267–8, tr. E. V. Rieu; *De Harmonia*, IV. iv.
[2] SS, 1555, pp. 132–3; cf. *Dodecachordon*, II. xxxviii.
[3] SS, 1555, p. 8.
[4] Ibid., pp. 150–1; cf. *De Harmonia*, IV. xvi–xvii.

the knowledge he gained from Boethius, Gafori, and Glareanus. They probably supplied the *Solitaire premier* with some points not to be found in Giraldi, such as the passages on the instruments and notes which the Muses sometimes symbolized,[1] and the responsibility of each Muse for a celestial sphere.[2] But they contribute little or nothing to the last four Discourses, and the *Solitaire second* borrows little from any writer except these three. Contributions from elsewhere, Plato or Ficino, Giraldi or Alessandri, are confined almost entirely to the last section of the Discourse, on the 'effects of music' and the 'harmony of the universe', and do not divert the train of thought. It is in that section that one first finds a long borrowing from Francesco Giorgio's *De Harmonia Mundi*, on the mathematical relationships between the elements and the geometrical figures which symbolize them.[3] One more unexpected source, acknowledged by Tyard and available to him in Camerarius's Latin translation, is 'Albert Durer . . . en ce qu'il ha escrit de la Symmetrie du corps humein'.[4]

The *De Symmetria* is a textbook of figure-drawing, and Tyard may well have been attracted to it as such; he was always interested in practical applications of his learning. But in the *Solitaire* he does not speak of Dürer from that point of view, and does not translate any particular passage; he merely selects from Book I certain details, such as the proportion of the nose to the face, which illustrate the role of number and order in the human body. Dürer serves Tyard as Giraldi and his fellows do, as a storehouse of useful or curious facts. However fascinating such storehouses may be, Tyard has not allowed them to distract his attention and alter his purpose as in the *Solitaire premier*; the *Solitaire second* welds a single group of sources into a strong artistic unity.

iv · *Tyard's Mature Manner*

In the scientific Discourses, *L'Univers* and *Mantice*, Tyard is no longer vulgarizing individual authors, and one can only comment generally on his preferences and methods. To assess the truth of astrology, he simply accumulates in the first speech of the Discourse all the arguments he can gather against it, in the second

[1] SP, 1552, pp. 52–54 and 61–62.
[2] Ibid., p. 70; cf. *Dodecachordon*, II. xiv.
[3] SS, 1555, pp. 136–8; cf. *De Harmonia Mundi*, I. iii. 13 and 17.
[4] SS, 1555, p. 148.

speech all the counterblasts, and in a third speech his own conclusions. In his survey 'des parties, et de la nature du monde' he follows the Chain of Being, descending through the spheres and the
elements to the earth, reascending through plants, animals, and man
to God. Into the appropriate places in this framework he inserts
any relevant and interesting information that he may obtain from
any source; and in just the same way, after 1558, he will insert into
appropriate places in what he has already published anything which
might be relevant and interesting in a new edition.

One encyclopædia which has been suggested[1] as a source of
L'Univers, and also of the *Solitaire second*, is Gregor Reisch's
Margarita philosophica of 1503. This manual for undergraduates
covers in turn the Trivium, the Quadrivium, and Natural and
Moral Philosophy, in twelve books, each giving the bare bones
of one subject. The definitions are often word for word those of
earlier experts, and it is always possible that a writer who appears
to have used the *Margarita* may really have gone behind it to its
own sources. This clearly happened in the composition of the
Solitaire second: Reisch's renderings of Boethius and Gafori are
even simpler than Tyard's, and the material taken by Reisch from
other sources is not used by Tyard. The order of Reisch's books
on natural science is so conventional that its correspondence with
Tyard's order proves nothing, unless more detailed correspondences can be traced. In *L'Univers* Tyard's studies of the three
divisions of the air, 'comme vous diriez estages, ou regions du lieu
qu'il occupe',[2] and of how the soul can suffer 'tourment d'un feu
corporel'[3] after death, echo those of Reisch, but not exactly. A
closer parallel, which may be a true borrowing, concerns the three
movements ascribed to the eighth celestial sphere;[4] this is represented as an 'interruption' by the Curieux, which may be a symbol
of Tyard's unaccustomed recourse to Reisch. He may also have inspired a few lines of Tyard's comparison of the earth and the
human body:

Pro visceribus et intestinis habet concavitates et cavernas multas,
in quibus ex vaporibus ibidem inclusis diversa generantur metalla,
mineralia, et flumina quae sunt ut sanguis in animali. . . .

---

[1] Saulnier, *Maurice Scève*, 1948, i. 389.
[2] U, 1557, p. 74; cf. *Margarita*, ix. 7.
[3] U, 1557, p. 70; cf. *Margarita*, xi. 47.
[4] U, 1557, pp. 17–18; cf. *Margarita*, vii. 6.

Encores pourroís je estendre, que les Eaus interieures de la Terre,
les cavernes spiriteuses et venteuses, les matieres et liqueurs d'ou les
pierres s'endurcissent, les viscositez bitumineuses, sont en l'homme les
veines, qui reçoivent le sang. . . .[1]

But most of these pages come from elsewhere. It is not till 1578
that an unmistakable borrowing from Reisch will be found.

Three main sources for *Mantice* have been proposed in various
quarters: Cicero's *De Divinatione*, Pico's *Disputationes adversus
Astrologos*, and a collection edited by Gervasius Marstallerus in
1549, *Artis Divinatricis, quam astrologiam seu judiciariam vocant,
encomia et patrocinia*. In this field, especially, parallels of method
and occasional aphorisms prove little; some must necessarily and
many may accidentally be common to all discussions of astrology.
Closer investigation of parallels of wording shows that Pico's work
is the chief but by no means the only source.

The introduction of the *De Divinatione* is reflected in some
phrases of Tyard's introduction:

Gentem quidem nullam video . . . quae non significari futura et a qui-
busdam intellegi praedicique posse censeat . . . magnifica quaedam res
et salutaris, si modo est ulla, quaque proxime ad deorum vim natura
mortalis possit accedere. . . . Etenim nobismet ipsis quaerentibus, quid
sit de divinatione iudicandum . . . saepe et paulo accuratius nuper . . .
disputatum est. . . .

. . . en toutes nations ha tousjours esté creu parmi les hommes estre
une capacité de predire l'avenir. . . . Science vrayment, qui (si elle est
vraye) doit sans empesche passer devant toute autre, comme salutaire,
et utile aux humeins: et par laquelle le but desiré de ceux, qui aspirent
à estre estimés Dieux, se pourroit atteindre de plus pres. Mais autour de
l'ouy et du non de sa verité, est un neud fort difficile à deslacer. . . . Ce
qui nous empeschoit bien embesongnément, n'a pas long temps. . . .[2]

Later Cicero and Tyard, like all the other controversialists, discuss such points as whether the errors of practitioners invalidate
an art, or the difference between causes and signs; but there is no
correspondence in order, and little in matter and wording. If
Tyard does seem to echo a principle of Cicero's, it is almost always
in another context and using other examples; it would be simpler
to believe in another source.

The speech of the Curieux attacking astrology does adopt much

---

[1] U, 1557, p. 119; cf. *Margarita*, vii. 1.
[2] M, 1558, pp. 4–5; cf. *De Divinatione*, I. i. 2, I. i. 1, I. iv. 7, and I. v. 8.

of the basic order of the *Disputationes adversus Astrologos*, and at times much of their wording. Both cite historical condemnations of the art, the failures of astrologers, especially Firmicus Maternus and Ptolemy, and the honour given in antiquity to all achievement except the astrological. Both give the same interpretation of the myth of Icarus:

Qui enim Homerum allegorice exponunt, per illam Icari fabulam, qui facticiis pennis caelo tenuiore se committens in mare praecipitatus est, astrologos aiunt designari, qui pennis temerariae professionis in caelum se substollentes, cum de caelestibus suis dogmatis, quibus sublimari videntur, quid sint praedicturi, in pelagus ruunt mendaciorum.

Car Icare, j'enten le Divinateur temerairement eslevé sus unes ailes mal jointes, se haulsant jusques au Ciel, d'ou il pense extraire les causes secrettes, et là orguilleusement s'accompagner trop familiere-ment des Astres, tombe par un precipice ruïneux en la Mer profonde de mensonges.[1]

Both go on to a theory of natural causes, including Pico's important notion that celestial heat is a universal cause of terrestrial pheno-mena, but that no influences from particular planets can account for all the differences manifested in the objects affected:

... calor quidam non igneus, non aereus, sed caelestis ... quare, si caelesti calore destituantur, nec frigiditatem agere frigus poterit, nec calor caliditatem; non enim calor ille sidereus frigori contrarius, sicuti calor igneus vel aereus, sed omnes continet elementares qualitates eminentia simplici, sicuti caeli natura continet omne corpus, sicuti motus circularis omnes motus, sicuti lux omnes colores.... Idem igitur ille calor, filius lucis, suscitans e terrenis corporibus vaporosos halatus, extenuans crassa, faeculenta dissolvens, parit ea quae fiunt in sublimi. ... Operatur ... omnia igitur calor et universaliter omnia....

La chaleur entén je non ignee, ou aërienne: mais premiere qualité pure, simple et non contraire aux qualités Elementaires: mais au con-traire, sans laquelle le froid ne pourroit refroidir, ou la chaleur eschaufer: brief contenant d'une singuliere simplicité les qualités de tous les Elemens, comme sa lumiere toutes les lumieres, et son mouvement circulaire tous autres mouvemens. ... Ceste chaleur donq est celle, qui attirant en l'air des vapeurs et exhalations, sert de cause à toutes les impressions et apparences aëriennes, par ce moyen rapportables aux Cieux. Au reste je nie toutes ses [*sc.* ces] influences, desquelles on les feint gracieux, ou mal faisans aux corps inferieurs. ...[2]

[1] M, 1558, p. 21; cf. *Disputationes*, ii. 9.
[2] M, 1558, pp. 21–22; cf. *Disputationes*, iii. 4.

Both end with detailed criticisms of astrological methods, for example the choice of the moment of birth rather than of conception as determining character and fate.[1]

But Tyard treats his source freely throughout. He omits many of its explanations, developments, and illustrations, and substitutes his own simpler or more topical ones; he goes back from it to its own sources such as Plotinus;[2] and, as usual, he takes progressively less from its later chapters, which become steadily more technical. It cannot, of course, furnish much of Mantice's reply, though the latter[3] uses its chapter 'Quinque rationes quibus astrologia roborari posse videtur'. The Solitaire, closing the debate, returns to Pico for the three or four arguments which strike him as most powerful; but his final conclusion diverges from those of both Pico and the Curieux.

One of the sources of Mantice's reply has been discovered by Baridon[4] in the *Artis Divinatricis*, a copy of which was in Tyard's library as catalogued in his great-nephew's time, and bears scribbles which appear to be in Tyard's hand. Baridon shows incontrovertibly that a page by one of Marstallerus's contributors, on the signifying of Christ's birth by a star, is the source of fourteen consecutive lines of *Mantice*:

Nous n'entendons pas, donc, rendre la nativité de Jesus-Christ, sujette aux astres: de l'influxion desquels elle ait tiré son estre necessaire. Car nous le recognoissons bien pour Createur du Ciel et des estoilles: mais sera-ce diminution de sa grandeur, de croire qu'alors qu'il estendit le Ciel comme une peau (dit le Prophete) de laquelle il forma le livre contenant tout le discours de l'Univers, il ne voulut oublier d'y escrire, en ces beaux et lumineux caracteres, parmy les autres esmerveillables effects futurs de la providence, sa remarquable nativité d'une Vierge? non que la disposition du Ciel à telle heure soit cause de ceste miraculeuse naissance. Car elle n'est seulement que signification, et non cause que la chose soit ainsi advenuë.[5]

But these lines appear in the edition of 1587 only. The similarity between three of the eleven lines which date from 1558,

. . . la passion, voire toute la vie de Jesus Christ, ha esté predite par les

---

[1] M, 1558, p. 29; cf. *Disputationes*, iv. 5, iv. 11, and vii. 2.
[2] M, 1558, pp. 25–26; cf. *Disputationes*, i; *Enneades*, III. i. 5.
[3] M, 1558, pp. 69–71; cf. *Disputationes*, iii. 2.
[4] Baridon, *Pontus de Tyard*, 1950, pp. 207 and 220–31.
[5] DP, 1587, pp. 185 v°–186.

Prophetes, qui toutefois ne sont reputés coulpables des effectz avenus selon leurs propheties . . .[1]

and one clause of the *Artis*, 'Non quod . . . oracula prophetarum causa fuere, quod Jesus pateretur', is less impressive without the rest, and so are Baridon's parallels on other topics.

Tyard's definition of astrology coincides with Melanchthon's in respect of two phrases, with Milich's in respect of three:

. . . l'Astrologie, qui se promet par consideration des mouvemens celestes de discourir sur les temperamens des Elemens simples, et des corps meslés et composés: et de prevoir les effectz qui par le moyen de ces temperamens aviennent en tous les corps du Monde inferieur.[2]

. . . inquirit causas efficientes universales *in motibus* ac viribus *syderum*, quae movent materiam *in inferioribus corporibus*.

. . . docet *quos effectus* astrorum lumen *in elementis et mixtis corporibus* habeat, *qualia temperamenta*, quas alterationes, quas inclinationes pariat.

But he must surely have learnt some definition before the *Artis* came out in 1549, and it would have been hard to construct one without foreshadowing any of the five phrases. One of the passages underlined in the *Artis* by Tyard, and two others quoted by Baridon, stress the usefulness of astrology; but it is astronomy whose usefulness Tyard stresses, for example in composing the calendar:

Grandement me delecte (repríns je) la consideration des mouvemens celestes utile et necessaire, pour diverses raisons, à l'entretien des Republiques, par l'observation des saisons, guide des constitutions religieuses, et autres causes, desquelles l'usage est familier aux hommes plus vulgaires. Mais je ne puis embrasser de bon cueur la Judiciaire. . . .[3]

The proof of stellar influence from solar and lunar influence is naturally to be found in all astrological works, and Mantice's version may equally well be drawn from Pico's.[4] Any treatise on astrology must also include a study of the influence of the nativity on the life; but Mantice's speech on how 'le bon Astrologue . . . voit comme en un livre, là haut, les mœurs complexions et autres conditions futures de l'enfant',[5] cited by Baridon as inspired by the *Artis*, is again an addition, of 1573.

Otherwise, what Baridon observes in Tyard is his knowledge,

---

[1] M, 1558, p. 81. [2] Ibid., p. 5. [3] Ibid., pp. 96–97.
[4] Ibid., p. 69; cf. *Disputationes*, iii. 2.
[5] M, 1573, pp. 95–96 (DP, 1587, p. 185).

like Cicero's, that μαντική is Greek for 'divination'; 'analogies' between his Ciceronian dialogue with its three speakers and Pontano's 'dialogus', really a fourteen-page tirade by Pardus to a single auditor, Franciscus Pudericus, who has only a dozen introductory lines; and a 'contatto . . . con Melantone, piuttosto diffuso e di consenso generico', 'un lavoro di adattamento più sottile, una sorta di alimentazione controllatissima' unlike Tyard's usual technique of borrowing. Certainly the *Artis Divinatricis* influenced his ideas generally, and made a particular contribution to the text of 1587; but this collection of miscellaneous essays and extracts can hardly have been a 'canovaccio sul quale potè poi comporre con facilità il suo ricamo'.

It is clear, however, that Tyard still felt the need to have a master's work before his eyes as he wrote. Just as *Mantice* is sustained first by Cicero's train of thought and next by Pico's, now by a passage from Plotinus and then by one from the *Artis Divinatricis*, so, even more clearly, section after section of *L'Univers*, two or five or ten pages long, reveals itself as based largely on one source. Giraldi's *De Deis* inspired the penultimate section, on God and the gods. Reisch and Alessandri contributed to the preceding section, on man as the microcosm:

> Qui niera que l'homme ne soit seul animal celeste et divin . . . ?
> . . . notre Microcosme, l'homme, le plus beau et accompli animal que Nature cree, nourri de la plus belle Ame. . . .[1]

But the main source of this section is certainly Francesco Giorgio.

The *De Harmonia Mundi* which this Italian Franciscan published in 1525 is a monumental work divided into three 'canticles' each of eight 'tones' with a varying number of chapters, making up the hymn of praise which all nature utters to its Maker through its numerical proportions and correspondences. The elaborate cosmology is Neoplatonic: three groups of nine orders of angels, spheres, and elemental creatures, emanate from God and provide for man a means of ascent to Him. The *Solitaire premier* showed a resemblance between the mentalities of Giorgio and Tyard, the *Solitaire second* one long borrowing; in *L'Univers* five consecutive pages,[2] almost all the section except for its last few pages of afterthoughts and the interpolations of the later editions, are made up

---

[1] U, 1557, pp. 115–24.
[2] Ibid., pp. 116–20; cf. *De Harmonia Mundi*, I. vi. 5–12.

of closely translated extracts from the *De Harmonia Mundi*. It must be confessed that parts are barely readable; much of what Giorgio says is of little or no importance, and his style, which Tyard reflects, can be very colourless:

> Est quoque in carne vegetativa virtus praebens alimentum, et augmentum manifestum. . . . Incisa nanque planta iterum pullulat, etiam duriusculus cortex. . . .
>
> La chair est comparable aus plantes en sa vertu vegetative, prenant nourriture et accroissement: car tout ainsi qu'une plante coupee recroit, se rejoint, ou reprend, aussi fait la chair.[1]

Yet there is a certain impressiveness in the magnitude of the whole conception, and Tyard will return twenty years later to borrow other passages of real beauty.

It would seem indeed that for Tyard Giorgio was the Neoplatonic master who came to replace Ficino and Leo. Tyard's borrowings seem to have had a greater importance for him than their wording alone reveals. They are placed at a central point of *L'Univers* and, in the first edition, in the mouth of the Solitaire who gives Tyard's personal views. They are governed by a principle which Giorgio has drawn from the Wisdom of Solomon: 'Tribus etiam (ut sapiens ait) Deus mundum disposuit, numero, pondere, et mensura.'[2] This principle holds a place of honour in the first pages of *L'Univers*: 'par nombres, par poix, par mesures, par saisons, par tems, et observacions celestes toutes choses sont conduites, recueillies, et distribuees.'[3] Tyard will later add to the text of the *Second Curieux* and the *Solitaire second* so as to give the principle yet more prominence:

> la secrette doctrine et salutaire cognoissance du nombre ternaire, tant reveré, que l'essence du Monde est entierement attribuee en sa disposition de nombre, de poids et de mesure.[4]
>
> De ceste Temperance se treuvent infinis simulacres en nostre vie . . . aux Arts mecaniques, conduis tous par nombres, *par poids*, ou par mesures. . . .[5]

As for Giorgio, so for Tyard, this principle must have been one

---

[1] U, 1557, p. 119; cf. *De Harmonia Mundi*, I. vi. 11.
[2] Ibid., I. iii. 2; cf. Wisd. of Sol. xi. 21.
[3] U, 1557, p. 9.   [4] DD, 1578, p. 98.
[5] DP, 1587, p. 40; the italicized words are added in the author's final corrections.

of the 'traiz grossiers, et (comme on diroit) monogrammes' which explain the universe.

A more up-to-date encyclopædia, Gasparo Contarini's posthumous *De Elementis* of 1548, Tyard treats more boldly. *L'Univers* refers to it once, on the topic of the 'divorce' between 'la seicheresse et l'humidité . . . comme d'une diserte abondance ha escrit l'honneur du pourpre Rommein de son tems, le docte Cardinal Contaren . . .',[1] but this hardly reveals the extent of Tyard's debt to Contarini. Their general sections on the elements cover the same ground as one antique encyclopædia after another; but Tyard's three pages on the 'quatre premieres qualitez'[2] translate or abridge the main part of Contarini's Book III, though disarranging its order with what seems almost a perverse pleasure. The next two pages continue with its account of fire; but then Tyard's attention is diverted to the problem of the 'feu logé au milieu du Monde . . . eternelle prison des malheureux dannez'.[3] On this the *De Elementis* cannot help him, and thereafter it is recalled by barely half a dozen phrases on air and a couple on water and on earth. Evidently Tyard has now opened another main source, though his Contarini is still within reach to furnish an explanation of the Milky Way,[4] a description of ocean currents,[5] and, in 1578, an explanation of tides:

La cause en est vulgairement rejettee (comme vous avez dit) sur le corps et mouvement de la Lune, à laquelle aucuns donnent pour ayde la force du mouvement solaire. Mais de quelle faculté procede cest effet, personne ne l'a (que je sçache) encor bien descouvert: si le docte Contaren n'a fait la subtile rencontre, disant que le Flux n'est autre chose, qu'une enfleure et elevation de la Mer, procedante de la rarefaction de la substance aquee, attiree à ceste elevation par la chaleur des rayons de la Lune. . . .[6]

Some of Tyard's shorter borrowings are still more topical. The subject of the air and its 'meteors' is enlivened by a quotation from the *Georgics* put into a French quatrain by Peletier.[7] Elsewhere Tyard quotes a few lines of Lucretius[8] translated into three couplets by Des Autelz, and even two of Ronsard's latest compositions,

---

[1] U, 1557, p. 66.   [2] Ibid., pp. 64–66.   [3] Ibid., p. 69.
[4] Ibid., p. 79; cf. *De Elementis*, Paris, 1548, p. 26 v°.
[5] U, 1557, p. 89; cf. *De Elementis*, p. 32.
[6] DD, 1578, p. 63; cf. *De Elementis*, p. 32 v°.
[7] U, 1557, p. 75; cf. *Georgics*, i. 365–7.
[8] U, 1557, p. 129; cf. *De Rerum Natura*, 646–51.

the 'Hymne de l'Eternité' in *L'Univers* and the 'Hymne des Astres' in *Mantice*.[1] On the subject of the earth he makes his famous reference to the heliocentric system of Copernicus—though the first edition gives only a half-page account of it, not borrowed directly from the *De Revolutionibus Orbium Coelestium*, and chiefly concerned with tracing classical antecedents for it:

> Nicolas Copernic (prĭns je la parole) d'une dextre et admirable sutilité ha renouvellé un Paradoxe presque semblable à celui d'Aristarque Samien, duquel Archimede en son denombrement d'Areine fait mencion, donnant au centre du Monde, le Soleil immuable. . . .
>
> Aussi semble entendre Martian Capella en son Astronomie (entrerompit le Curieus). . . .
>
> Copernic ne l'a oublié (reprĭns je) bien que ce soit sans servir à ces Hypotheses: car selon Martian, par eschange Venus, et Mercure, sont ores l'un ores l'autre plus voisins du Soleil: mais Copernic fait continuellement Mercure plus voisin.
>
> A la verité (dit le Curieus) ses demonstracions sont ingenieuses, et ses observacions exactes, et dignes d'estre suivies. Toutefois vraye ou non que soit sa disposicion, la connoissance de l'estre de la Terre telle que nous la pouvons avoir, n'en est aucunement troublee: et ne nous empesche de croire que ce soit un Element pesant, froit, et sec: lequel par reçue, vulgaire, et comme religieuse opinion, nous croyons immobile. . . .[2]

Here Tyard appears to be reverting to Contarini's 'terra infimo mundi loco, in centro . . . sita, gravissima . . . sicca . . . frigida . . . semper immobilis . . .'.

But the scientific Discourses show a widening in the range of Tyard's borrowings not only from the moderns but from the classics. The earlier Discourses hardly go farther than to insert short passages from Plato among long passages from Ficino, or to interweave Boethius, a classic for Tyard, with Gafori. In *L'Univers* Giorgio and Contarini still represent the early Renaissance; but Tyard seems at last to be ready to make direct use of ancient writers on equal terms with those of his father's generation, and of pagans on equal terms, almost, with Christians.

He takes less delight than Giorgio in adorning his work with Biblical texts. In the *Solitaires* there are only the vaguest echoes of the Bible, such as a veiled reference to the pronunciation of the word *shibboleth*: 'entre les Hebrieux combien ont engendré de

[1] U, 1557, p. 12; M, 1558, p. 59.
[2] U, 1557, p. 99; cf. *De Elementis*, p. 36 v°.

differens les lettres, qu'ilz nomment Schin, et Samec, et quelques autres . . .?'[1] In the *Discours du temps* and *Mantice* all the characters prefer Biblical allusion rather than quotation. In *L'Univers*, as well as such allusion, there are real quotations, added to slightly in the second edition and rather more in the third. Naturally, considering his subject, Tyard makes most use of Genesis, and then of Job and the Psalms; but he can throw his net wide, and draws on the Septuagint as well as the Vulgate. His translations are both close and vivid: 'les Cieus . . . passeront bruyans comme tempeste: les Elemens eschaufez se dissoudront, mesmes la Terre, et toutes ses euvres se bruleront.'[2] But he is often content with a free paraphrase, or the remark that 'De cetui . . . les saintes lettres font ordinaire conte'.[3] Tyard does not wish to appear a pedant or a bigot; he uses the Bible just as much as is permissible in polite society.

His use of Plato extends to the *Critias*, 'Platon en son Atlantique',[4] and to doubtful works, the *Epinomis* and *Epistles*; his personal tendency is to accept congenial works like the monotheist letter to Dionysius, 'si l'epistre est sienne, comme il n'est sans apparence',[5] and to reject uncongenial ones like the 'livres imposteurs'[6] on astrology. For the ideas of such Platonists as Plotinus and Iamblichus he seems to rely almost entirely on later commentators; though he may have gone back to the *Enneades* for a page of *Mantice* which reflects not only Plotinus's thought but some of his order and wording.[7] He must surely have read with interest St. Augustine's chapters on classical mythology; but often what can be traced from them in the *Discours* is to be found word for word in Giraldi. Where Tyard appears to fuse two widely separated passages of the *De Civitate Dei* on the 'Trois sortes de Dieus entre les anciens',[8] one finds that those passages have already been abridged and juxtaposed in the *De Deis*, and that Tyard's expansion of the abridgement bears no relation to the remainder of Augustine's text.

Tyard treats one old Platonist very differently. As he himself states, it is to Philo Judaeus's *De Opificio Mundi* that he owes Philolaus's description of God;[9] but, as Du Verdier points out, a much

---

[1] SP, 1552, p. 112; cf. Judges xii. 6.

[2] U, 1557, p. 155; cf. 2 Peter iii. 10.

[3] U, 1557, pp. 142–3.   [4] Ibid., p. 135.

[5] Ibid., p. 133.   [6] M, 1558, p. 14.

[7] Ibid., pp. 25–26; cf. *Enneades*, III. i. 5.

[8] U, 1557, p. 126; cf. *De Civitate Dei*, iv. 27 and vi. 5; Giraldi, op. cit. i. 13 (*De Deis*, i).   [9] U, 1557, p. 132; cf. *De Opificio Mundi*, xxxiii. 100.

longer direct borrowing follows soon after. The fifteen-page argument that the world is indestructible[1] is almost all supplied by the *De Aeternitate Mundi*, whose authorship was unquestioned in Tyard's time. He follows its order almost exactly, though with many omissions and a few interpolations. Often he translates it literally, unabridged, unexpanded. Where it breaks off, in spite of the promise of a sequel with counter-arguments, the Curieux, 'qui sembloit vouloir dire d'avantage', is interrupted by Hieromnime, who takes over the defence of the orthodox position. The material does not lend itself readily to lively dramatic treatment; but Tyard has made an interesting attempt to apply to a classical author the technique by which he popularized Ficino.

The Aristotelians come to join the Platonists. The *Solitaire premier* neither uses nor mentions Aristotle; either Tyard considered poetic frenzy to be outside Aristotle's jurisdiction, or his interest in him was still undeveloped. In the *Solitaire second* the references to him are rare and vague; the judgements on music in the *Politics* are cited accurately,[2] but otherwise only two passages raise Aristotelian questions, that of the supremacy of hearing over sight and that of the music of the spheres, and neither shows direct borrowing. In 1557–8 Tyard's mentions of Aristotle come to exceed even his mentions of Plato, and to rank the two nearly equally. Where Plato is 'Divin', Aristotle is 'Tout-sachant', and Mantice, to prove that wine intoxicates, even proceeds, 'A l'autorité d'Aristote peult estre ajoutee la familiere experience'.[3] The *Meteorologica* seems to have been one main source of at least two sections of *L'Univers*, those on comets and thunder. Tyard also refers to the *De Caelo*, the suspect *Marvels* and *Physiognomy*, and some of the treatises on animals.

But one cannot always be certain that apparent borrowings from Aristotle are true ones; Tyard often gives them in the form to which they have been reduced by centuries of compilation. A passage on Aristotle's theology follows the original wording closely though hesitantly:

il appelle Dieu, ζῷον ἀΐδιον ἄριστον que nous pourrions dire eternellement vivant, et tresbon: pour ne l'appeler animal, nom difficilement recevable en telle dignité . . .[4]

[1] U, 1557, pp. 135–50; cf. *De Aeternitate Mundi*, especially iii–viii, xvii, xx–xxvii.   [2] SS, 1555, pp. 11 and 113.
[3] M, 1558, pp. 8 and 79.   [4] U, 1557, p. 134; cf. *Metaphysica*, 1072ᵇ.

and the phrase is not in Giraldi, Tyard's main source for the section. But when Tyard cites Democritus, Epicurus, and finally Aristotle on the eternity of the world, it is from Philo that he takes not only these names but an account of Aristotle's opinion which it seems impossible to substantiate from Aristotle's own works:

Aristote en fin, croyant le Monde eternel, diffamoit du titre d'impieté ceus qui avoient contraire opinion, comme outrageus contre Dieu: duquel ils sembloient estimer l'ouvrage de mesme, ou pareille condicion, que les euvres et manufactures des fragiles humeins. . . .[1]

Especially, Tyard quotes many of the opinions of Aristotle from the catalogues wrongly attributed to Plutarch, the De Placitis Philosophorum.

For, even in his maturity, Tyard seems to see no special merit in using a great classical work at first hand; it may sometimes have taken his fancy, it was certainly not his habit. The occurrence of a name in the Discours philosophiques is no proof that Tyard knew anything of its bearer except what his favourite compilations had told him, and, even where he could have recalled or looked up considerably more, he often did not trouble to do so. What is to be seen in the scientific Discourses is less a shift from encyclopædias to original texts, than a shift from medieval or Renaissance encyclopædias to ancient ones.

The poets themselves are treated as sources of information. No special place is given even to Orpheus or Homer, except by right of their early date: '. . . Orphee, et . . . Homere . . . croyoient la Terre estre une Isle environnee de l'Ocean. . . .'[2] The highest compliment is paid to Hesiod, in passing and not without prejudice:

O que Hesiode (dit HIEROMNIME) avoit bien fueilleté les livres de Moyse, envelopant si cautement les secrets de la creacion, et le repos de Dieu souz le repli de ses fables.
Je croy bien (respondí je) qu'il n'estoit sans Theologie. . . .[3]

Euripides and Ovid, whom alone Tyard considers for a moment as artists, are soon amusingly subjected to his usual approach; he, like Montaigne, 'ne se laisse plus chatouiller . . . au bon Ovide'.[4] Prettily translated in the Solitaire premier, Ovid is criticized in L'Univers as scientifically unreliable, 'trop leger en choses serieuses

[1] U, 1557, p. 136; cf. De Aeternitate Mundi, iii. 10.
[2] U, 1557, p. 101.   [3] DT, 1556, p. 27.   [4] Essais, ii. 10.

Filozofiques, et Naturelles',[1] when he describes the sun as growing
weary. In the *Discours du temps* the Solitaire sighs: 'Hoo . . . combien me plait ce mot d'Euripide: . . . la vie n'est point vie mais
calamité';[2] but the quotation is so misused as to suggest that
Tyard lacked either a knowledge of its context or a sense of its
humour. In the *Alcestis* Heracles offers a drink to one whom he
declares to look as if he held that opinion.

Cicero and Plutarch would surely have appealed to Tyard as
perhaps the greatest vulgarizers of the ancient world. Cicero's
influence on the form of the *Discours philosophiques* is certain; but
in the sixteenth century his works needed no popularizing, and
most of Tyard's Discourses seem even to avoid overlapping. The
Solitaire premier uses Cicero's assessment of the roles of 'nature'
and 'art' in poetry,[3] and perhaps his definitions of madness,[4] but
not those of rhetoric. The *Solitaire second*, like the *Somnium
Scipionis*, compares the planets with the notes of the scale, and,
like the *Tusculanae*, the bodily with the mental virtues, but there
are several points of difference. The *Discours du temps* barely mentions Cicero's cycle of 15,000 years, as reported by Macrobius; and
it has been seen that *Mantice* uses little more than the introductory
remarks of the *De Divinatione*.

One must therefore also view with caution the alleged pro-
venance of *L'Univers* from the *De Natura Deorum*. This is indicated
by Busson[5] as furnishing Tyard's lists of atheists, opinions on the
nature of God, and proofs for and against His existence; Lapp adds
that 'he borrows liberally from Cicero's *De natura deorum* in the
second edition of the *Premier Curieux*',[6] and offers in support three
lists, already given by the Curieux in *L'Univers*, of 'philosophers
and scientists who discussed the sun', the primary element and the
shape of the earth.[7] But though Cicero, or Giraldi who copies him
almost exactly, could have contributed about half the phrases
which make up Tyard's page on Thales', Anaximander's, Anaximenes' and Anaxagoras' conceptions of the 'principe de tout',[8] the

[1] U, 1557, p. 40; cf. *Metamorphoses*, ii. 63–66.
[2] DT, 1556, p. 80; cf. *Alcestis*, 799–802.
[3] SP, 1552, p. 49; cf. *Pro Archia*, vii. 15 and viii. 18.
[4] SP, 1552, p. 24; cf. *Tusculanae*, III. v. 11.
[5] Busson, *Rationalisme*, 1922, p. 410; 1957, p. 401.
[6] Lapp, *Universe*, 1950, p. liv.   [7] Ibid., pp. 194–6.
[8] U, 1557, pp. 60–61; cf. *De Natura Deorum*, I. x. 25–xi. 26; Giraldi, op. cit.
i. 8–9 (*De Deis*, i); *De Placitis*, i. 3.

page could have come almost as a whole from the *De Placitis Philosophorum*. So could the pages on the sun[1] and on the earth:

... Thales et les Stoïques ont esté d'accort de sa forme ronde: contre l'opinion d'Anaximandre, qui la figuroit en colomne: et d'Anaximene, qui la disoit estre plate comme une table: aussi pertinemment que Leucipe la descrivant en Tympane, et Democrite assurant qu'elle estoit creuse au milieu, et tendue en largeur à la forme d'un plat.[2]

In 1572 Amyot was to translate the *De Placitis* thus:

Thales, et les Stoiques, et ceulx de leur eschole, tiennent qu'elle est ronde comme une boule. Anaximander, qu'elle est semblable à une pierre en forme de coulonne. Anaximenes, qu'elle est platte comme une table. Lucippus, qu'elle a la forme d'un tabourin. Democritus, qu'elle est platte comme un bassin, mais creuse au milieu....

Cicero gives nothing more than some of the proper names, in very different contexts:

ista enim flagitia Democriti sive etiam ante Leucippi, esse corpuscula quaedam levia, alia aspera, rotunda alia, partim autem angulata, curvata quaedam et quasi adunca, ex his effectum esse caelum atque terram....

In the part of *L'Univers* which became the *Second Curieux*, Tyard is certainly working on the same subject and with the same material as Cicero; but minor differences of presentation suggest another immediate source and another attitude. The page and a half[3] which is all that *L'Univers* gives to the atheists and natureworshippers, and which would have had to be compiled from widely separated parts of the *De Natura Deorum*, could have been made up much more easily out of the first dozen pages of Giraldi's *De Deis*, seemingly the main source of the surrounding ten pages. Giraldi gives Tyard some personages not in Cicero—Callimachus and Lucretius, Cecrops and Melisseus of Crete, Melissus of Samos and Varro—and a summary of Epicurean theology closer to Tyard's wording than Cicero's 'hominis esse specie deos confitendum est. Nec tamen ea species corpus est, sed quasi corpus ... '. For Giraldi:

Epicurus Atheniensis, ex atomis deos suos constituit, et eos quidem corporeos putavit, ab hominibus tamen discretos, hominum tamen figura.

[1] U, 1557, p. 41; cf. *De Placitis*, ii. 20.
[2] U, 1557, p. 95; cf. *De Placitis*, iii. 10; *De Natura Deorum*, i. xxiv. 66.
[3] U, 1557, pp. 128–9.

For Tyard, 'Epicure constitue ses Dieus Atomiques en humeine figure bien que separee des hommes'.[1] The argument for and against theism is lacking in L'Univers, as in Giraldi; and Giraldi offers Hieromnime the story of Simonides[2] in the same words as Cicero. There is no doubt that Tyard read Cicero; but in the fifties, at least, it would seem that he took his borrowings, like those from Plotinus and Aristotle, by way of media which neutralized or even christianized any dangerous effects of paganism or rationalism.

Plutarch's Lives, like Cicero's works, needed no popularizing in that decade. The Life of Alcibiades is used in the Solitaire premier, those of Demetrius and Theseus in the Discours du temps, and perhaps that of Romulus there and that of Antony in Mantice; but it is like Tyard to be more interested in the less familiar Moralia. However, in the fifties not all had been translated into Latin, and it is possible that he found the Greek difficult. Busson[3] has pointed out the parallel between the ideas of the De Amore and the Solitaire premier, but there seem to be no verbal borrowings. The 1552 dedication of the volume, Lapp[4] has shown, uses the De Mulierum Virtutibus, but Sauvage's translation was available, and Tyard alludes rather than translates: after opening his feminist polemic with Plutarch's well-known citation of Thucydides, and before closing it with that of Gorgias, he confines himself to listing the names of Plutarch's and other heroines.

But Tyard seems to have had no doubt of the authenticity and value of the De Placitis Philosophorum, and of another work wrongly ascribed to Plutarch, the De Fluviorum Montiumque Nominibus, on both of which, even in the fifties, he drew heavily. The latter work, besides forming the chief inspiration of the Douze fables de fleuves et fontaines, started him on a quest for 'eaux miraculeux' which furnished several decorative if futile pages to the Erreurs amoureuses, L'Univers, and Mantice.[5] His pages of 'opinions which pleased the philosophers' on many scientific subjects come directly from the Greek or, more likely, from a Latin translation of the De Placitis; he only added a little general

[1] U, 1557, p. 129; cf. De Natura Deorum, I. xviii. 48–49; Giraldi, op. cit. i. 11.

[2] U, 1557, p. 134; cf. De Natura Deorum, I. xxii. 60; Giraldi, op. cit. i. 12.

[3] Busson, Rationalisme, 1922, p. 398; 1957, p. 389.

[4] Lapp, in M.L.N., 1949.

[5] TLE, 1555, pp. 17 and 18; U, 1557, pp. 91–94; M, 1558, p. 79.

knowledge, retouched the order, and varied the mechanical and monotonous constructions. Seneca's *Natural Questions* and Pliny's *Natural History* also seem to have contributed directly to *L'Univers*, and so do such works as Aelian's *Variae Historiae*, from which comes one long and close translation,[1] and Pausanias' *Itinerary*, used at first hand, it appears, even in the *Solitaire premier*.[2]

It is these collections of interesting natural or antiquarian facts which are most representative of Tyard's favourite type of classical source in the scientific Discourses. For explanations of the universe he is up to date enough to go to a scientist like Contarini or a theologian like Giorgio. But before the universe can be explained it must be 'contemplated', and in as much detail as possible; and to provide this detail, Tyard finds the old encyclopædias as good as any and better than most:

l'homme est nay pour contempler le Monde. . . . Opinion, que vous savez avoir esveillez de tous tems les plus beaus, et meilleurs entendemens, à se despendre et employer aus contemplatives consideracions des choses: Dont il nous reste encores, malgré les injures de l'outrageus, et oublieus envieillissement des aages, tant de belles et non perissables restes, que mal aisément pouvons nous rien discourir, que par redites. . . .[3]

---

[1] U, 1557, pp. 103–4; cf. *Var. Hist.* iii. 18.
[2] SP, 1552, p. 104; cf. *Itin.* iv. 33.   [3] U, 1557, p. 6.

IV · VARIANTS

WHERE a modern re-edition is described as 'revised', the favourite description in Tyard's century was 'augmented', and the word was significant: the works of Reisch and Giraldi, for example, swelled quietly and steadily year by year and even posthumously. Montaigne took up and transfigured this procedure; Tyard's use of it was more conservative but equally unsystematic. All the Discourses but one went through the same three stages: an original publication in Lyons between 1552 and 1558, a new edition in Paris some twenty years later, and a definitive edition in 1587. It was in 1578 that *L'Univers* was split into *Deux discours . . . le premier Curieux, traittant des choses materielles: et le second Curieux, des intellectuelles*; the second part was almost doubled in length, and the *Discours du temps* was increased by half in the same year. The longest Discourses, *Mantice* and the first part of *L'Univers*, had been increased by rather less, and the *Solitaire premier* by little more than a page in all; the *Solitaire second* was not reprinted in the seventies. The 1587 volume was the only one to print all six dialogues together, under the title of *Discours philosophiques*; the three Discourses reissued in 1578 were there lengthened by about one-tenth, and the others by much less. The insertions far outnumber the deletions; there are many small stylistic changes, but rarely any extensive redrafting, and surprisingly rarely any serious modification of the train of thought.

1 · *To Occasion Another Edition*

Montaigne's variants usually represent second thoughts; but Tyard's additions often seem to represent merely further reading, on his old principle of seeking and passing on knowledge for its own sake. In the *Solitaire second* of 1555 he argues that long life depends on the health of the soul: 'Dequoy, si ce lieu le requeroit, j'alleguerois autres exemples que de Platon et d'Aristote . . .'[1] who lived to eighty-one and sixty-three respectively. He is quite conscious that the 'place' does not require it, that the two examples

[1] SS, 1555, p. 6; DP, 1587, p. 38 v⁰.

suffice; yet in 1587 appears a third, that of 'Xenophile musicien qui arriva jusques au cent cinquiesme an de son aage sans avoir souffert aucune maladie'. He met with the new fact in Pliny, it struck him as worth repeating, and he dovetailed it into his work in an appropriate spot, even at the expense of the immediate context. It seems that even from 1557 he had in mind to 'augment' his works in this way; he makes the remarkable assertion that that was one reason for publishing his first editions:

je n'ay voulu refuser à mes François, en ce Discours que je vous donne, partie du fruit que j'y avois fait, pour en ouvrir le chemin à quelque autre studieus et diligent, ou pour m'ocasionner par ci apres une seconde edicion, en telle polissure que je la pourray redresser, avec l'aage. . . .¹

The only general principle which seems to govern his additions is a certain care that his statements shall attain an encyclopædic precision and completeness. To prove 'que les Planettes gettent raiz assez clairs pour faire ombre',² *L'Univers* records Tyard's and Peletier's excitement at seeing shadows cast by the light of Jupiter. The next edition extends the affirmation to cover Mars and Sirius, and in 1587 a similar passage in *Mantice*³ is corrected to match. Philosophers, according to the early *Solitaire second*, have even lived to eighty-four, 'si la fortune . . . ou la tyrannie des Princes et Magistrats, ou la lacheté de quelques particuliers haineus n'ont coupé le chemin'.⁴ The 1587 edition takes care to add, 'ou quelques autres causes estrangeres'.

But the content and distribution of the additions indicate very clearly a shift in Tyard's interests, prolonging his development in the fifties, and also reflecting the interests of the circles in which he moved. The most frequent additions occur in the scientific Discourses, the most lengthy in the speculative ones, the fewest in the Neoplatonic ones.

After 1573 Tyard seems to have cooled towards the subjects of poetry and music, as Frances Yates shows Baïf's Academy to have done during its evolution into the Palace Academy. Tyard wrote next to no poetry after the *Recueil de nouvelles œuvres poëtiques*, never published his promised treatise on Greek music, and inserted only one new verse quotation into his Discourses,⁵ from his own unpublished *Vers astronomiques* which *L'Univers* shows

---

¹ U, 1557, p. 7.   ² Ibid., p. 35; DD, 1578, p. 20.
³ DP, 1587, p. 142 vº.   ⁴ SS, 1555, p. 6; DP, 1587, p. 38 vº.
⁵ DP, 1587, p. 281; cf. U, 1557, p. 15.

to have been composed by 1557. The waning of his Neoplatonism also continued; the brief revival of it in the 1573 *Recueil*, like that in Parisian circles generally and even in the *Sonnets pour Hélène*, is singularly unconvincing. In the additions to the four later Discourses still less Neoplatonic colour can be seen than in their first editions, and one or two passages even suggest something of Ronsard's derisive attitude. About the music of the spheres Tyard declares in 1578: 'Je n'en puis croire le bon Pamphylien, introduit par Platon au X. de sa Repub.'[1] An astrologer described in 1558 as a 'Planetaire contemplatif' becomes in 1587 a 'Planetaire contemplatif à la Platonique'[2].

Almost the only exception in Tyard's treatment of the Neoplatonists is still in favour of Francesco Giorgio. In 1578 the *De Harmonia Mundi* is the source of more esoteric learning: a Kabbalistic correspondence between the letters of the alphabet and the 'Principes et Elemens du Monde',[3] the Magian interpretation of the Zoroastrian Trinity,[4] and, very probably, an identification of the rivers of Eden.[5] Above all, it supplies the beautiful description of Paradise:

paradisus voluptatis . . . non terrestris (ut vulgo dicitur) sed coelestis, divinusque . . . hortus ille plantatus a coelesti agricola, et opifice summo in terra quidem non hac feculenta, sed in terra viventium figurata per terram illam promissam. . . . Ecce quam clare innuit vineam illam meliorem, et consequenter omnes arbores sacri horti plantatas esse in filio, et in verbo divino. . . . Est itaque paradisus voluptatis locus et mansio in Archetypo omnibus delitiis consita ubi sunt gradus omnium creaturarum et in medio omnium Christus tanquam arbor et fons vitae ac omnium bonorum plenissimus. . . .

ce Paradis, ou jardin de delices, et sejour de felicité . . . non un jardin terrestre: mais bien un celeste et divin vergier, planté par un celeste et divin Jardinier: non point en ceste terre corruptible et fangeuse, mais en celle eternelle terre des vivans, figuree aussi par la mesme histoire sous le nom de Terre de promission, vray heritage des enfans du Seigneur et createur du Monde. Nostre escole s'exerce souvent aux saintes contemplations de la vigne, plantee de la dextre de Dieu en son Fils et saint Verbe divin, figure du jardin ou vergier de vrayes delices et pures voluptez. Recerchons-nous le lieu? il est en l'archetype, primitif exemplaire, et principale idee de l'Univers: où se treuvent toutes les creatures

---

[1] DD, 1578, p. 34. [2] M, 1558, p. 35; DP, 1587, p. 154 v°.
[3] DD, 1578, p. 40; cf. *De Harm. Mundi*, I. v. 17.
[4] DD, 1578, p. 97 v°; cf. *De Harm. Mundi*, I. iii. 2.
[5] DD, 1578, p. 76; cf. *De Harm. Mundi*, I. vii. 22.

chacune en son degré, au milieu desquelles est Christ, vray arbre et fonteine de vie coulante tous biens en abondance.[1]

All the new borrowings are allotted to Hieromnime, the spokesman of the Church. Giorgio still presides over Tyard's much attenuated and christianized Neoplatonism.

More typical of the additions of the seventies are antiquarian interests, the same that irrupted into the *Solitaire premier* in 1552 and largely inspired the *Discours du temps* and the latter part of *L'Univers*. The 1575 additions to the *Solitaire premier* consist of four passages on Greek mythology and archaeology;[2] the 1587 additions to the *Solitaire second*, except for two brief scientific observations,[3] are of the same type and may well date from the same period; and general information, unnecessary to the argument, is particularly frequent in the 1573 additions to *Mantice*. Tyard makes use again of Giraldi, Conti, and Alessandri, and still more of the classics at first hand. Especially, there is a sharp increase in his borrowing from Plutarch and Cicero.

His choice among the *Moralia* is characteristic: the *De Defectu Oraculorum* and *De Iside et Osiride*. Giraldi had directed his readers to both, but the first editions of the Discourses probably use neither; the only parallel with the *De Iside*, the description of Harpocrates,[4] was a commonplace, and the only echo of the *De Defectu* may well be an indirect one, the haunting introduction of *Mantice*:

. . . la diabolique Goëtie est destruite avec l'antiquité Egyptienne: les evocations Phitoniques, et Euriclites, sont abolies: et n'est plus vraye nouvelle, comme au vieil temps, de Demon ny d'Esprit. Des Pyromanties, Hydromanties, et autres de semblable denomination, ne restent que les noms. . . .[5]

But in 1578 appear half a dozen unmistakable and lengthy borrowings. It may be that Tyard had to wait for the help of Latin versions; these two texts seem to have remained in Greek till 1564. It may even have been Amyot in 1572–3 who first fully revealed Plutarch to Tyard, as to many of his contemporaries; the incontestable borrowing from the *De Iside* in the 1573 *Mantice*[6] is slipped into the ninth page from the end, while an earlier bor-

[1] DD, 1578, p. 75 v°; cf. *De Harm. Mundi*, I. vii. 21.
[2] SP, 1575, pp. 21, 36, 39, 64; cf. SP, 1552, pp. 46, 71, 75, 117.
[3] DP, 1587, pp. 105 and 116; cf. SS, 1555, pp. 117 and 135.
[4] DT, 1556, p. 57; cf. *De Iside*, 377C and 378C.
[5] M, 1558, p. 4.   [6] M, 1573, p. 105; cf. *De Iside*, 354E.

rowing,[1] which seems to be from Diodorus Siculus but to which the *De Defectu* could have supplied a proper name, had to wait till 1587 for the name to be inserted. Tyard's passion for Plutarch in the seventies may have been like his passion for Ficino and Giraldi in the fifties, a prompt reaction to a recent stimulus.

Lapp is surely right to suggest[2] that the new dedication of the *Second Curieux*, on the Romans who enriched their language as Tyard was enriching his, was modelled on the *Academica*; and certainly much of the new argument about the existence of God runs closely or roughly parallel to the *De Natura Deorum*. But the presentation and tone are much altered. Cicero could put the views of all his three speakers with spirit and gusto; if Tyard can do this in the case of the theistical views, he handles the opposing ones with a perfunctoriness that suggests distaste:

Qualem autem deum intellegere nos possumus nulla virtute praeditum? Quid enim? prudentiamne deo tribuemus . . . ? cui mali nihil est nec esse potest, quid huic opus est dilectu bonorum et malorum?

Ils adjoustent: que s'il est prudent, il est capable de consulter, et de prendre conseil: et s'il consulte, c'est de quelque chose qui luy est incertaine. . . .[3]

Cicero's arguments are completely rearranged, and often two or three are woven together; for instance, the argument from the 'sympathy' running through the universe, 'rerum consentiens conspirans continuata cognatio', proves for Balbus that the universe is maintained by 'uno divino et continuato spiritu'; for Tyard it proves only that 'le Monde est un corps uny en soy',[4] which must still be proved to be maintained by a reasonable and perfect 'nature',[5] described much later by Balbus. To complicate a borrowed argument is not the habit of Tyard, the born simplifier.

Some passages clearly come from outside, like two pages[6] translated very faithfully indeed from Xenophon's *Memorabilia*, from which Cicero used two lines only, and the argument from the *Timaeus*, that the Creator could not be so 'envious' as to deny existence to the universe.[7] The atheists' list of virtues which cannot

[1] M, 1558, p. 79; cf. DP, 1587, p. 184; *De Defectu*, 433D.
[2] Lapp, *Universe*, 1950, p. 197.
[3] DD, 1578, p. 109; cf. *De Natura Deorum*, III. xv. 38.
[4] DD, 1578, p. 101 v°; cf. *De Natura Deorum*, II. vii. 19.
[5] DD, 1578, p. 101 v°; cf. *De Natura Deorum*, II. xi ff.
[6] DD, 1578, pp. 103–4; cf. *Memorabilia*, I. iv. 2–8.
[7] DD, 1578, p. 104 v°; cf. *Timaeus*, 29E ff.

be predicated of God is extended by the Curieux to include what seems to be the Thomist conception of 'art', which 'attouche les choses incertaines', while 'rien n'est incertain à Dieu'.[1] There is still the possibility that Tyard's immediate source was some Renaissance Latin compilation, which recast the order and form of Cicero's and others' arguments while retaining much of their wording. However, this time it may be Tyard who performed the delicate synthesis for himself; the possibility of a development in his technique of composition over twenty years cannot be denied. But if the reworking is Tyard's, so is the devotion of extra care and space to all the arguments in harmony with Christianity.

Comparative religion and natural science, the chief subjects of the new borrowings from Cicero and Plutarch, seem to have become Tyard's dominating interests from 1557 onwards. Once again, he seems to have been partly responding to his environment; they were the subjects which, rather than pure literature, were absorbing intellectual Paris and particularly the Palace Academy. With them he continued to ponder the questions of the truth of astrology and the music of the spheres; with ecclesiastical circles, he was agitated by the problem of calendar-reform, and the *Discours du temps* shows that he was not completely satisfied even by Gregory XIII's resolution of it in 1582. The rationalists' growing doubt of the existence of God elicited the pages of argument which Tyard had evidently felt no need to write in 1557; and the accounts of returning explorers supplemented Giraldi's study of totemism and Contarini's explanation of tides. Lapp has even identified two Spanish sources of the *Discours philosophiques*, Lopez de Gómara's account of West Indian worship[2] and Fernández de Oviedo's account of West Indian tides;[3] though by the time the borrowings appeared, the former in 1578 and the latter in 1587, Tyard could have read both accounts in Poleur's, Cravaliz's, or Fumée's French or Italian translation.

The *Premier Curieux* of 1578 includes five and a half new pages on another very topical subject, the significance of comets. Again, it is possible that Tyard's mind was set in motion by a particular event, the transit of the comet of 1577, though he does not mention it. But ever since the comet of 1556, which he does mention, the

[1] DD, 1578, p. 109 v°; cf. *De Natura Deorum*, III. xv. 38.
[2] DD, 1578, pp. 111 v°–112; cf. Lapp, *Universe*, pp. xlii and 198.
[3] DP, 1587, p. 262; cf. Lapp, *Universe*, pp. 195–6.

attention of scientists had been increasingly attracted to comets, in the hope of checking the theories of Copernicus. Tyard's approach, however, is characteristic. He makes no new reference to Copernicus, ignores the new evidence that comets pass above the moon rather than below, and models not only his phrasing but his attitude, usually cited as a notable example of his 'rationalism', on a source seventy-five years old, the *Margarita philosophica*.[1]

The remarks of Reisch 'De Cometa et bellis . . .' open with the definition, 'Cometes est exalatio terrestris, calida et sicca, pinguis et viscosa: virtute astrorum ad supremam aeris partem elevata: et ibidem incensa.' His theory is Aristotelian with medieval elaborations, but surprisingly free from astrological superstition. It is the heat of the stars, including that of the sun, which draws up the exhalations; their various types may be named after the planets, but their differences are due to the material forming them. 'Significationes cometarum sunt variae, generaliores autem sterilitates, pestilentiae et seditiones', but this is for physical reasons independent of astral influences. By the loss of the very exhalations which compose a comet, 'privatur . . . terra . . . omni foecundo humore'; drought ensues, except in marshlands, where the result may be fertility. Meanwhile the atmosphere becomes poisoned:

nam . . . aliae exalationes . . . impuriores et venenosae elevantur. . . . Ex his itaque aer infectus et continuo inspiratus, vitalem spiritum debilitat, et tandem extinguit. . . .

One observes especially deaths of princes:

quod Principes ut magis delicati vel intemperati ab aere corrupto citius inficiuntur. Aut quod mors Principis unius plus quam multorum popu-larium divulgatur. . . .

Through the body the mind becomes affected, 'fantasia perturbatur: appetitus irascibilis et concupiscibilis excitatur: ad cuius impetum nonnunquam ratio condescendit', and such emotional disturbances may issue in sedition or revolution. Clearly for Reisch a comet is a sign only in the sense of a symptom; and he comes to the sensible Ptolemaic conclusion that 'the sage is master of the stars', 'sapiens . . . dominabitur astris'.

Tyard translates almost literally Reisch's definition:

ce n'est autre chose qu'exhalation chaude, seiche, visqueuse et capable d'estre enflammee: elevee et attiree en la plus haute region de l'Air, par la vertu du Soleil et des autres Astres. Là ceste matiere s'enflamme. . . .

[1] ix. 23; cf. DD, 1578, pp. 49–52.

The theories he is willing to accept come from Reisch:

J'advoueray seulement, que la Comete signifie de grandes et abon-
dantes exhalations passees: que les Elemens (mais l'Air principalement)
sont fort intemperez: et que de telles elementaires intemperies se peuvent engendrer des maladies et vens impetueux. . . . Mais de la mort des
Princes, je ne sçay pourquoy lon en peut prendre prognostic ou signification: si ce n'est que les Rois et Princes (comme dient les devins pour
preuve fort subtile) sont d'une complexion plus delicate, plus fragile,
et capable de souffrir la malice des contagions elementaires, que les
autres hommes. . . .

As for wars,

j'ose asseurer que si tous les ans il apparoissoit trois Cometes, il se
rencontreroit assez d'accidens en la terre pour leur en appliquer la
cause et signification. . . .

Tyard is here no more of a rationalist than Reisch or Jean de
Meung; theirs is not Renaissance free-thinking, but medieval
realism.

Indeed, as Tyard's life became more public and varied, even
his philosophical works became perceptibly less academic and
more realistic; the additions are less concerned with words and
ideas, more with people and things. His experimentalism went
farther: it is in the *Deux discours* that he first reports his observations of Sirius and his experiment on the salamander, 'toute rostie
assez soudainement'.[1] His arguments were completed by concrete illustrations: rain, he suggests in 1587, originates 'en gros
floz' which break into drops while falling, 'comme si l'on verse
du haut d'une Tour un seau d'eau',[2] and stone hardens in extreme
heat and cold, 'comme tressensiblement nous voyons aux *tuilleries
et* grands hyvers gelez'.[3] He became more interested in popular
speech: he who refused in 1552 'de se baisser, et accommoder
à la vilté du vulgaire'[4] records in 1557 the Mâconnais term *Avis*[5]
for the will-o'-the-wisp, in 1578 the shift of meaning of *temps* in
'Quel temps fait-il?'[6] and in 1587 the phrase 'vous me portez
bissexte'[7] for 'vous me portez malheur'. And it is in the 1578
dedication of the *Second Curieux* that his defence of the vulgar
tongue is most explicit.

[1] DD, 1578, p. 44. [2] DP, 1587, p. 253 v⁰.
[3] Ibid., p. 279; U, 1557, p. 108, lacks the italicized words.
[4] SP, 1552, p. 109. [5] U, 1557, p. 48.
[6] DT, 1578, p. 3 v⁰. [7] DP, 1587, p. 363 v⁰.

The additions of 1587 show to some extent the same trends as the additions of the seventies; but they give especially strongly the impression of being gleaned on the impulse of the moment from any book Tyard happened to be reading, and they show two new characteristics. Many concern not so much natural philosophy as theology—understandably, since that would form Tyard's professional reading after 1578. New quotations from the Bible almost outnumber those in his first editions; the Fathers of the Church are consulted as hardly ever before; and, still perhaps reacting to rationalist discussions, Tyard goes much farther than before into purely Christian problems such as the situation of Eden and the nature of angels. He counterbalances these by lighter interpolations, but they are professional too: amusing heresies like the 'folie de Basilide, disciple juré de Simon le premier heretique qui amonceloit 365 cieux faits par les Anges',[1] or Kabbalistic gems like the suggestion that the 'Hebrieux ont nommé la Terre *Arets*, du verbe *Ruts* qui signifie courir'.[2]

It would seem indeed that it was not until he became a bishop that Tyard made a serious study of the Hebrew language. The remarks on 'les Hebrieus' in the first editions of the Discourses could all have been made without a knowledge of Hebrew; for instance, the comment that the name of Adam symbolized 'de grans secretz: par Aleph, la partie divine: par Daleth, la nature celeste: par Men, le corporel et corruptible',[3] was drawn wholly from Giorgio. The additions of 1578 were less superficial, but seldom before 1587 did Tyard attempt to put forward any opinions of his own. The point is well illustrated where he had said in 1557 that 'Paradis, fait avant le Ciel et la Terre, à l'interpretacion de saint Hierome, fut situé en Orient'.[4] In 1578 the proposition was reconsidered:

la situation de ce Paradis est estimee en Orient. N'oubliant toutesfois que S. Hierosme rapporte le Milkedem Hebrieu, non pour ORIENT, mais interpreté pour AU COMMENCEMENT, signifiant que ce Jardin fust fait avant le Ciel et la Terre.

The 1587 edition devotes half a page to the subject:

à mon advis . . . Moyse escrit fort clairement, que le Seigneur Dieu

---

[1] Ibid., p. 204.   [2] Ibid. p. 269 v°. The italics are Tyard's.
[3] U, 1557, p. 116; cf. *De Harmonia Mundi*, I. vi. 5.
[4] U, 1557, p. 105; cf. DD, 1578, p. 76, where the author's corrections substitute 'Mikedem'; DP, 1587, p. 276.

planta le Jardin en Hgeden (car il s'escrit par Hgain et non par Hé) qui signifie une place, une region, ou bien un lieu delectable, ainsi nommé: duquel Moyse donne un confin Mikedem, c'est à dire, qu'il estoit tourné du costé de Kedem, qui signifie, costé Oriental. Combien que sainct Hierosme a interpreté quelquefois ce mot, pour, au commancement. . . .

The 1587 insertion goes on to argue for another page that in any case longitude is a purely arbitrary concept, 'figuré par la volontaire imagination de celuy qui traite la Geographie', and only latitude can cause climatic differences. Here is shown the other characteristic of the 1587 additions. Both the theological ones and the equally numerous scientific ones, whether original or borrowed, are often highly technical. A second and much more detailed page[1] on Copernicus appears, balanced elsewhere by three lines praising one of his opponents, 'le docte Fracastor'.[2] Tyard studies echoes[3] and 'vapeurs odorantes',[4] the precession of the equinoxes[5] and the number of possible arrangements of the stars,[6] eight different opinions on the origin of the soul.[7]

Had he forgotten the readers represented in his first Discourses by his little Pasithée, 'en si jeune aage, en si delicate personne moins propre pour endurer le labeur de l'estude', on which she could spend only 'le tems desrobé'?[8] His stylistic alterations show that even in 1587 he was still very conscious of his vocation as a popularizer. It must be that by then he was able to count on a more educated public, less afraid of minute detail, obscure authorities, and special terminology, more prepared to work hard even when reading his comparatively simple encyclopædia.

II · Better Polished than Before

Tyard shows himself in his poetry, and in the introductory pages of both the *Curieux*, to have been highly conscious of style. He even seems to stress improvements of manner rather than matter in the dedication of the 1575 *Solitaire premier*, 'ce discours des Muses et des Graces . . . mieux limé que celuy qui sortit . . . il ya ja long temps, en lumiere'. The peculiarity of his method of revision is that, while adding to the Discourses in so many ways, he felt it necessary to alter so very little.

[1] DP, 1587, p. 270.   [2] Ibid., p. 205.   [3] Ibid., p. 245.
[4] Ibid., p. 293.   [5] Ibid., p. 365.   [6] Ibid., p. 196.
[7] Ibid., pp. 289 v⁰–290 v⁰.   [8] SP, 1552, pp. 92–93.

Real corrections, where he has caught himself out on points of fact, amount to barely a score, and even so some of the mistakes may have been made by the printers: the second *Mantice* has to substitute the name of Pliny for that of Theophrastus,[1] and meanwhile translates *scarabaeus* as 'escargot',[2] which the third edition has in turn to correct to 'escarbot'. Major reworkings concern two astronomical matters only, the reform of the calendar, in the *Discours du temps*, and the mode of movement of the planets: *L'Univers* presents unfairly the theory attributed to the Curieux, that, for example, 'Saturne, je di l'Estoile mesmes, court par la rondeur de son Epicicle . . .'[3] and the *Deux discours* correct all the statements, 'Saturne (je dy le poinct de l'Epicycle auquel il est cloué) court . . .'. Material deletions are so few that it is difficult to find any general principle governing them: a naïve apology for the ugliness of Hebrew consonants,[4] a weak argument concerning the solidity of the sky,[5] the suggestion of a quarrel in the *Discours du temps*,[6] and some out-dated dedications and compliments.

In contrast, Tyard's works even show an odd method of correction by addition. In 1557 he states that igneous exhalations from the earth can rise 'jusques à la plus haute aëree region';[7] in 1578 he continues contradictorily 'voire jusques dedans la place plus haute ordonnee pour le feu'. In 1578 a Hebrew word is translated 'rouge',[8] in 1587 'rouge, ou roux'. Until 1587 Tyard abstains from expounding the religious position of Plato and Aristotle, 'bien difficile à connoitre';[9] the apology is allowed to stand when the omission is repaired. Montaigne often uses this method, but is ready to delete too; Tyard seems unwilling to sacrifice his old text, even where he has changed his attitude or discovered his facts to have been wrong.

One group of corrections, combined with the longer additions of the seventies, might suggest a real evolution of the Discourses in the direction of rationalism. In the realm of pure scientific inquiry there is certainly an increase in the scepticism expressed by Tyard.

[1] M, 1558, p. 78; M, 1573, p. 93.
[2] M, 1573, p. 80; DP, 1587, p. 176 v°.
[3] U, 1557, p. 32; DD, 1578, p. 17 v°.
[4] SP, 1552, p. 112; cf. DP, 1587, p. 33 v°.
[5] DD, 1578, p. 32 v°; cf. DP, 1587, p. 229 v°.
[6] DT, 1556, p. 10; cf. DT, 1578, p. 3 v°.
[7] U, 1557, p. 74; DD, 1578, p. 47 v°.
[8] DD, 1578, p. 77; DP, 1587, p. 278.
[9] U, 1557, p. 129; cf. DP, 1587, p. 302 v°.

To the story of the bear-cub's birth[1] as 'une masse de chair qui ne monstre aucune vitale figure' he adds the phrase 's'il est vrai ce qu'on en dit'; to the story of the burning of the salamander[2] he adds 'quoy qu'en ait escrit Aelian, curieux, et, croy-je, trop credule rechercheur'. The sudden formation of 'une montagne de sablon'[3] 'est avenu de notre siecle au Royaume de Naples' according to *L'Univers*, 'se raconte estre advenu' according to the *Premier Curieux*; and a reference to the 'tems de Romule'[4] becomes in 1578 'à l'heure que Romule se trouva perdu, laissant opinion de sa deïfication'. In the same year Tyard's dissatisfaction with the calendar goes so far as to denounce its 'bien chastiable desordre'.[5]

However, the *Discours du temps* brings all its characters to a final 'sceptique chrétienne'. Scève is made to declare in 1587 that we must content ourselves with an approximately correct calendar, 'puis qu'il est impossible ou tant difficile de rencontrer une parfaicte et exacte reformation', and Hieromnime concludes 'que Dieu s'est particulierement et uniquement reservé la cognoissance de l'entiere science de la verité des mouvemens celestes'.[6] Hieromnime's role is extended and improved, in all the Discourses where he appears, so as to stress their orthodoxy; two of the *Deux discours*' additions[7] are violent attacks on those who disbelieve the Christian creed:

Que puissent ceux qui ne le croyent entrer en meilleur chemin, et se mettre devant les yeux ce que recite Theophraste des Acrothoites, peuple sans religion, qui fut soudainement englouti de la terre par une miraculeuse et divine punition.

Quant aux Sceptiques qui nient tout, j'en souhaitte la memoire estouffee.

It is worth noting too that the further polish given in 1587 to the Curieux's arguments for the existence of God is entirely refused to the arguments against it.

Yet more significant is what seems, for once, to be a methodical process of correcting passages which might savour of free-thinking. *L'Univers* speaks of the daemons, inferior to angels, that inhabit

---

[1] DD, 1578, p. 79; DP, 1587, p. 280.
[2] DD, 1578, p. 44; DP, 1587, p. 242.
[3] U, 1557, p. 109; DD, 1578, p. 79 v⁰.
[4] DT, 1556, p. 69; DT, 1578, p. 23 v⁰.
[5] DT, 1578, p. 28.
[6] DP, 1587, pp. 366 v⁰ and 367.
[7] DD, 1578, pp. 114 v⁰ and 112 v⁰.

the different 'regions Elementaires',[1] 'toutefois moins croyable-
ment'; in 1578 these three words are deleted. The *Deux discours*
describe Eden as 'non un jardin terrestre';[2] in 1587 'simplement'
is added. *L'Univers* mentions the Solitaire's 'profession de ne
croire de leger';[3] in 1587 'parlant de choses naturelles' is added.
And the peroration of the section on God, Hieromnime's profession of faith,[4] undergoes a change of construction; in 1557 it is
presented hypothetically:

> Je ne suis (respondit Hieromnime) si presomptueus, que de m'usurper
> la suffisance d'exprimer l'ineffable divinité, de laquelle assez me suffiroit
> de retenir la seule et continuelle souvenance en l'esprit: si je ne voulois
> que la langue portast publique témoignage de ma foy, appuyee en l'espe-
> rance de sa sainte bonté. . . .

In 1578, as if in the presence of a more urgent peril, it is affirmed
positively: '. . . assez me suffit. . . . Mais je veux bien que tousjours
ma langue porte . . . .' This whole movement towards expressing
greater orthodoxy runs parallel with that towards expressing greater
scepticism, and, in the end, counterbalances it.

Tyard's indulgence in general towards what he has once written
is not unsuited to the nature of the Discourses; a survey of learning
may continue to list old beliefs even when it adds new ones, and
the dialogue form allows and calls for the display of conflicting
viewpoints. Tyard's variants, however, betray both how weak is
the unity of the Discourses, philosophic and artistic, and also how
few changes in his views after 1558 were marked enough to catch
his own attention and make him reject his former opinions. He
might have pleaded Montaigne's theory of 'bransle et inconstance',
that one's inconsistencies and errors are to be accepted and recorded as the only means of obtaining a complete picture of one-
self; but his aims and methods are very different from Montaigne's,
and the fact that he makes no such defence suggests that he did not
feel he needed it. His mind was open to receive new ideas, but
seldom to reconsider his old ones in the light of the new. Despite
his growing love of exact information and his occasional rationa-
listic doubts, truth remained multiple for him; addition without
deletion was an essential part of his way of thinking.

[1] U, 1557, p. 114; DD, 1578, p. 82 v⁰.
[2] DD, 1578, p. 75 v⁰; DP, 1587, p. 275 v⁰.
[3] U, 1557, p. 22; DP, 1587, p. 207 v⁰.
[4] U, 1557, p. 131; DD, 1578, p. 112.

He was much more ready to alter form than content; but even in matters of style he tended to complacency, to leave intact a page once written, except where it might take a higher polish. The extent to which he rehandled his work fluctuated with his interest in its content, and often variants group themselves so as to suggest that, after making a major addition, he dallied over the passage making minor changes until his attention flagged and he turned away, 'las et remiz . . . ainsi que le Dieu l'a laissé'.[1] The 1575 *Solitaire premier* offers an example of this grouping of variants, where nearly a page is added to the 1552 description of Apollo.[2] On the same page occur three other minor alterations, such as the substitution of 'aussi' for 'et'; on the next page four more, on the next two, on the next none. His revisions, however, show a continual attempt to present knowledge more and more precisely and attractively.

He developed a nice sense of words, availing himself more often of technical terms like 'ichnographie' and of grammatical resources such as the use of *lequel* or the distinction between *de* and the partitive. By 1578 he felt that the sudden formation of the sand-mountain could not really be classed as a 'monstre', as in 1557, but only as a 'nouveauté'; at the same time the sky's 'blancheur d'ordinaire lumiere' became the charming 'serenité d'ordinaire lumiere'.[3] But Tyard's efforts to achieve euphony and balance usually resolve themselves into seeing that one construction reigns throughout a sentence; in the description of the madmen[4] 'frappant, rompant, dessirant tout' the last word is deleted in 1587.

He seems ruled less by the artistry of the young Pléiade than by a sort of logic which foreshadows Malherbe's. Pasithée's native tongue being French, he ends by seeing no sense in her remark[5] that 'la langue Grecque ne m'est la plus familiere et usitee', and deletes 'la plus'. He tends especially to reduce plurals to singulars when used in a general sense: according to the earliest editions[6] astrology is alleged by Mantice to rest on 'vrayes experiences', man dies 'de maladies procedantes de sa propre nature', and in hell souls suffer 'une peine de feus non esteingnables . . . pource qu'elles sont tachees et soillees des pechez'; by 1587 all the nouns are singular.

[1] SP, 1552, p. 49.   [2] Ibid., p. 75; SP, 1575, p. 39.
[3] U, 1557, p. 55; DD, 1578, p. 33 v°.
[4] SP, 1552, p. 23; DP, 1587, p. 4 v°.
[5] SP, 1552, p. 73; DP, 1587, p. 21.
[6] M, 1558, p. 55; U, 1557, pp. 137 and 71.

An illogical order of words, particularly in lists, is frequently altered; and the precision element in Tyard seems to find satisfaction in the most minute changes, like the repeated interchange of *et, mais, aussi,* and *voire.*

Seldom, however, does pedantry spoil the stylistic effects of the Discourses. One may regret the loss of some of the *naïveté* of the earlier editions, where the realistic sigh 'Hoo' is later replaced by 'Las!'[1] The 1587 page of alternative opinions on the fate of the sky at the end of the world forms a sad anticlimax to Hieromnime's impressive peroration[2] in *L'Univers.* More often the animation and force of Tyard's style increase in later editions. Unnecessary words are eliminated, like 'bien' in 'il vous bien plaira entendre',[3] and strong phrases substituted for weak: 'Qui est-ce qui donnera aux autres quelque foy? Qui croira Guide Bonat . . .' replaces a flat 'tous les autres, comme Guide Bonal . . .' in a denunciation of unreliable astrologers.[4] Tyard is also to be congratulated on his decision that the final page of the *Discours philosophiques* should be not that of *Mantice,* expressing an attitude to a single problem, but that of the *Discours du temps,* expressing an attitude to the whole of life; and yet more on his earlier decision to split the increasingly unwieldy *Univers* into two parts, the first to be closed and the second opened by delightful pictures of a typical evening and afternoon at Bissy.

Throughout the Discourses the presentation of the setting and characters grows richer and more dramatic. Scève's gesture, 'monstrant de la main un petit et clair ruisseau, qui couloit contre le canal, environnant l'isle de mon jardin',[5] is new in 1578, and so in 1587 is the Curieux's reference to the Solitaire's orrery: 'Nous contemplons avec grand esbahissement *vostre globe mouvant (s'adressant à moy) imitant* la Sphere d'Archimede....'[6] A reference to the 'Empereur aujourdhuy vivant' and a demonstration of how to find the date of the new moon for the years 1555-9[7] are retouched in 1578 when they risk giving the *Discours du temps* an old-fashioned air—though Tyard does not trouble in 1587 to make further changes. Laughter breaks in oftener: 'respondit elle'[8]

[1] DT, 1556, p. 80; DT, 1578, p. 32.
[2] U, 1557, p. 156; DP, 1587, p. 331.
[3] SP, 1575, p. 9; DP, 1587, p. 5 v°.
[4] M, 1558, p. 13; DP, 1587, p. 140 v°.   [5] DT, 1578, p. 2.
[6] DP, 1587, p. 309; DD, 1578, p. 105 v°, lacks the italicized words.
[7] DT, 1556, pp. 24 and 73-74.   [8] SS, 1555, p. 9; DP, 1587, p. 40 v°.

becomes 'respondit-elle souriant', and Hieromnime, also 'sous-riant', tells a Manichaean legend with great success, 'Ceste sub-tilité nous ayant à tous trois presté occasion de rire'.[1] On the other hand, there appears to be some wish to idealize Scève in the later editions of the *Discours du temps*: the less elevated passage[2] where a quarrel nearly arises,

Cette dispute s'eschaufoit entre nous, quand pour quelques raisons qu'il me dist à l'oreille, et pour le respet lequel la presence des personnes qui escoutoient, nous commanda d'avoir, nous entrames en propos de la diversité des Ans . . .,

is abridged to 'Ceste dispute s'eschaufant entre nous, nous en-trasmes en propos de la diversité des Ans'; and speeches are allo-cated to Scève showing wider and deeper research on Tyard's own part. The re-editions of *L'Univers*, too, transfer speeches to other speakers where appropriate. Surprisingly, it was only after pub-lishing two editions of the *Solitaire premier* that Tyard noticed that to conform to the poetic theories of the couple the Solitaire should discover Pasithée singing an 'Ode Françoise' and not an 'Ode Italienne'.[3]

Though Pasithée takes no part in the scientific Discourses, Tyard bears in mind her special needs. He adds translations of technical terms, '*les Tables des mouvemens, ou* les Ephemerides'[4] and 'une Ichnographie *ou plant*'.[5] He strives to make his language more com-prehensible: 'expresse' becomes 'faite expressement à cest effect',[6] 'simmetriez' becomes 'composez et rapportez l'un à l'autre',[7] and words or phrases are readily repeated or rearranged. In the case of the 'observacions Egipciennes, qui assuroient desja par deus fois, le Soleil avoir changé d'Orient et d'Occident',[8] the 1578 reading '. . . qui asseuroyent le Soleil desja par deux fois avoir changé . . . ' makes it clear that the error was supposed to have been repeated by the sun and not by the Egyptians. Above all, the long and loose sentences of the first editions are broken up, in the *Soli-taires* mainly by repunctuation, but in the scientific Discourses by repetition of subject or verb, substitution of personal for relative

---

[1] DP, 1587, p. 281. [2] DT, 1556, p. 10; DT, 1578, p. 3 v°.
[3] SP, 1552, p. 17; DP, 1587, p. 3.
[4] M, 1573, p. 107: the italicized words are new.
[5] DP, 1587, p. 198: the italicized words appear in the author's corrections.
[6] M, 1573, p. 3; DP, 1587, p. 133 v°.
[7] SS, 1555, p. 135; DP, 1587, p. 115 v°.
[8] U, 1557, p. 135; DD, 1578, p. 115.

pronouns, or yet more drastic rephrasing; though some care is also taken to avoid abruptness, by inserting adverbs like 'donc' and 'toutesfois'.

This process may form part of another interesting development. Tyard seems to have made a real attempt to adapt his language to changing fashion. At the time of the Pléiade's experiments with vocabulary and syntax he took a modest and tasteful part, with a few neologisms of his own, though fewer than Marty-Laveaux claimed. In the seventies he retreated to safety among more generally accepted forms: 'pie'[1] is replaced by 'orné de pieté' or 'pieux', and 'prouvable'[2] and 'taisement'[3] give ground to 'probable' and 'tacitement'. By 1587 the movement is away from Latin, to 'adroitement', 'entrerompre', and 'blasme' instead of 'adextrement',[4] 'interrompre',[5] and 'vitupere',[6] and even 'haute montaigne' instead of the bolder 'ardue montaigne'.[7]

Archaisms, 'chacunes'[8] and 'ores'[9], fade out. The absolute construction 'le croyant Aristote' is replaced by 'quand Aristote le croira'.[10] The accusative and infinitive construction is used less, especially in the marginal headings: 'Le Monde estre fini' becomes 'Le Monde est finy'.[11] Even one subjunctive construction is eliminated, 'je n'ay (que je me souvienne) jamais' becoming 'je n'ay (s'il me souvient) jamais'.[12] *Ne* is inserted in phrases such as 'rien se peult trouver'[13] and 'plus . . . que je m'en saurois forger'.[14] Genders change, *hymne*[15] and *œuvre*[16] becoming feminine, *doute*,[17] *foudre*,[18] and *mensonge*[19] masculine. Prepositions are repeated more scrupulously, articles and subject pronouns are expressed more often, and in 1578 a distinct preference is shown for forms such as 'vingt cinq', usually with no hyphen, rather than the 'vingt & cinq' of

---

[1] U, 1557, pp. 9 and 132; DD, 1578, pp. 3 v⁰ and 113.
[2] M, 1558, p. 42; M, 1573, p. 48.
[3] U, 1557, p. 16; DD, 1578, p. 7 v⁰.
[4] M, 1558, p. 21; DP, 1587, p. 146.
[5] SP, 1552, p. 42; DP, 1587, p. 10 v⁰.
[6] SP, 1552, p. 65; DP, 1587, p. 18 and author's corrections.
[7] SP, 1552, p. 13; DP, 1587, p. 2.
[8] U, 1557, p. 11; cf. DD, 1578, p. 4 v⁰.
[9] DT, 1556, p. 3; cf. DT, 1578, p. 1 v⁰.
[10] SS, 1555, p. 146; DP, 1587, p. 123.
[11] U, 1557, p. 10; DD, 1578, p. 4.   [12] SP, 1552, p. 84; SP, 1575, p. 44.
[13] SP, 1552, p. 14; cf. DP, 1587, p. 2.
[14] SP, 1575, p. 4; cf. DP, 1587, p. 3.   [15] Masc. in SP, 1552, p. 81.
[16] Masc. in U, 1557, p. 47.   [17] Fem. in M, 1558, pp. 10, 16, 92.
[18] Fem. in U, 1557, p. 85.   [19] Fem. in M, 1558, pp. 9 and 46.

the fifties. By this time, however, one begins to ask oneself whether these are really Tyard's preferences or only those of his printers.

The question recurs insistently as regards the orthography of the Discourses, and as regards their marginal headings and notes. The marginalia of the 1552 *Solitaire premier* are in a class by themselves, and certainly Tyard's work; they are all Greek derivations of terms and names used in the text, and come from its own sources. The other Lyons editions are equipped with subject headings, not unhelpful, though sometimes obvious, ill chosen, or misprinted. Many are drawn from the text; many simply draw attention to persons such as 'Jan, Comte de la Mirande'[1] mentioned there; a few, mostly in the *Solitaire second*, add further information.

The editions of the seventies add many more subject headings, to old as well as new passages. None reflects independent knowledge, except that one Greek root is noted against an interpolation[2] in the *Solitaire premier*, and a few slips are corrected. Meanwhile fresh slips occur, and it is very hard to see how Tyard himself could have made them. Beside such *naïvetés* as 'Allusion' and 'Consideration necessaire'[3] one finds a misquotation of Tyard's most loved master in 'Delie, object de plus *grande* vertu',[4] the description 'Exclamation de Demetrie aux Muses' applied to a speech beginning 'O bien-heureuses et vrayement sages Cigales,'[5] and the heading 'Proprietez d'aucuns poissons'[6] introducing the assertion that man can rival any fish in swimming.

The 1587 edition substitutes 'Nageurs admirables' and makes some other corrections, but adds barely half a dozen marginalia and even deletes a few. The suggestion is that Tyard accompanied his original manuscripts with a few learned notes, supporting especially the mythological *Solitaire premier*. In the fifties and again in the seventies he submitted to his publishers in letting them supplement and clarify his work by subject headings. In 1587 he revised these printers' headings, but, like his own matter and style, not very thoroughly or carefully.

Even more, the orthography of the Discourses seems attributable to their printers. At their publication by Jean de Tournes they all appeared in a simplified semi-phonetic spelling. The editions of the seventies vary, but often tend towards the archaizing ortho-

---

[1] M, 1558, p. 67. [2] SP, 1575, p. 21.
[3] M, 1573, pp. 47 and 27. [4] SP, 1575, p. 59.
[5] Ibid., p. 63. [6] DD, 1578, p. 91; cf. DP, 1587, p. 294.

graphy of Robert Estienne, a tendency carried much farther in the complete edition of 1587. According to Baridon,

il semble fort probable que les différences orthographiques entre les trois éditions soient dues à Pontus lui-même. . . . Pontus de Tyard . . . se rattache décidément à l'école conservatrice . . . et . . . devient en réalité, parfois, esprit novateur, puisqu'il ne conserve point des formes préexistentes, mais en introduit au contraire de purement chimériques. . . .[1]

Most sixteenth-century authors left questions of spelling to be decided by the habits of the publisher or even the needs or whims of the compositor. Sauvage let his printers 'orthographier à leur mode . . . pourveu qu'ils ne s'esloingnassent des raisons, que l'Antiquité peut avoir pour soy'.[2] Montaigne confessed, 'Je ne me mesle ny d'ortografe, et ordonne seulement qu'ils suivent l'ancienne, ny de la punctuation . . . '.[3] Ronsard let his programme of reform be obscured by traditionalism—'tu escriras écrire';[4] and Beaulieu discovered reforming tendencies in a single gathering of the Bignon 1538–9 edition of Marot.[5] Without positive evidence, it cannot be assumed that an author of this period took any personal interest in the presentation of his printed works; and Tyard showed a complete lack of method even in his attention to mistakes or misprints in the Discourses, some, like 'avec toute les graces de bien dire',[6] persisting through all the editions.

It is hard to imagine any of the orthographical systems of the Discourses to have been constructed by an author with strong views of his own, whether reforming or conservative. The simplifying editions of the fifties prefer *i* to *y*, single consonants (except *f*) to double, and suppress preconsonantal *d* (*avis*) and *s* (*vingtieme*), the *ç* of *sçavoir* and unsounded consonants in forms such as *ars*, *grans*, *tems*. However, there are *praticien* tendencies in such forms as *il ha*, *il peult*, and final *-z*, and latinizing tendencies in forms like *fantasie*, *volunté*, and *il void*. Illogical and incompletely sustained in itself, the system is only partly in accord with what little is known of Tyard's personal orthography. No manuscripts of his

[1] Baridon, *Le Solitaire premier* . . . *édition critique*, 1950, preface.
[2] *L'Histoire et chronique de messire Jehan Froissart, reveu par Denis Sauvage*, Jean de Tournes, Lyons, 1559, preface.
[3] *Essais*, iii. 9, ed. Strowski, iii. 230.
[4] *Œuvres*, ed. Laumonier, xiv, Paris, 1949, p. 30 ('Art Poëtique').
[5] *Histoire de l'orthographe française*, Paris, 1927, ii. 36.
[6] SP, 1552, p. 92.

survive except some letters, and these are not all holograph; but half a dozen, mostly dated after 1587, are so. They show, among other characteristic traits, a marked preference for single consonants (except *f*) over double, but also for *y* over *i*; suppression of preconsonantal *d* and of *p* in *tems*, but also of *l* between *u* and *t*, and yet retention of preconsonantal *s* (*vostre*) and *c* (without cedilla) in *scavoir* or its forms; a distaste for *h*, a taste for final -*s* (*assés*, *vous verres*), and a neglect of accents and punctuation, except for the apostrophe neglected in the first editions.

It might be that in the fifties Tyard had been under a reforming influence which later, with others among his interests, lost its attraction; but it is difficult to find a suitable influence of sufficiently early date. Neither Ronsard's nor Peletier's is reflected exactly, the school of Scève was hardly interested in orthography, and Guillaume des Autelz was opposed to simplification. Many of the characteristic graphies of the fifties, however, are paralleled by those which appeared in the poetical works of Heroët as re-edited by Jean de Tournes in 1547. Double consonants are reduced (*tranquile*); derivatives are latinized (*voluntaire*); preconsonantal *l* is retained, and *il a* once becomes *il ha*; and, where Jean de Tournes's sources and Tyard's letters use forms of *esloigner*, the editions of 1547 and of the fifties alike use forms of *eslongner*. It seems possible that if these graphies entered Heroët's text in the publishing house of Tournes, their appearance in Tyard's text may be traced to the same source, and at least some of them to the regular practice of the house.

The late Renaissance orthography of the final *Discours philosophiques*, more traditional in its use of *y* and of superfluous letters though more modern in its use of accents and punctuation, diverges equally from the early editions and the late letters of Tyard. Here too a house style may be in question: some of the differences between the orthography of Tyard's letters and that of the 1587 edition are very similar to the differences between Montaigne's orthography and that of the 1588 edition of the *Essais* by the same printer, Abel L'Angelier. Voizard[1] shows that L'Angelier doubled the single consonants preferred by Montaigne, as by Tyard; added the accents neglected by Montaigne, as by Tyard; and substituted -*ez* as a verbal flexion where Montaigne, like Tyard, persisted in using -*es* (*que vous ayes, vous receves*). Montaigne's

---

[1] *Étude sur la langue de Montaigne*, Paris, 1885, pp. 15, 18–19, and 29.

instructions to his printer further reveal that L'Angelier had tam-
pered with Montaigne's word-division ('Qu'il serre les mots
autremant qu'icy les uns aus autres'), and had added to his use of
capitals ('Ne mettez en grande lettre que les noms propres'); on
these points all the editions of the Discourses differ. Even when
L'Angelier follows Tyard's practice, as in inserting *s* before *t*, it
may be merely by coincidence; for Montaigne had to rebuke him
on this point, 'montrer . . . cet home . . . escrives le sans /s/'.

Between the editions of Tournes and L'Angelier appeared those
of the seventies, Mamert Patisson's *Deux discours* and *Discours
du temps*, which largely anticipate the spelling of the *Discours
philosophiques*, and Galiot du Pré's *Mantice* and *Solitaire premier*,
which tend the same way but vacillate much more in both principles and practice. The mere fact of the existence among the
Discourses of a third orthographical system, if system it can be
called, raises problems; and that Tyard cannot have supervised it
entirely is shown by a series of slight but impressive differences
between the first four pages and the rest of the *Solitaire premier* of
1575, relating the spelling of those four pages rather to that of the
1552 edition than to that of either the 1587 edition or Tyard's
letters. Surely we are to picture compositors bewildered among the
simultaneous influences of the work they were copying, the house
styles of their employers, their own habits, and such needs as that
of roughly equalizing the number of letters in each line of type;
and perhaps, beginning the *Solitaire* of 1575, a novice unused to
Galiot du Pré's house style, imposed rather more firmly soon after.

Certainly one cannot imagine Tyard making line-by-line alterations in the Discourses from the point of view of spelling only, or
giving his printer more detailed instructions than Montaigne's. It
would seem that there was nothing 'decided' in his views on orthography. His personal practice, around 1587 at least, was a rather
pleasant blend of tradition and moderate simplification. For the
rest, he gave a free hand to his publisher: his nearest approximation to a pronouncement on the subject promotes not system but
freedom. The Muses may be surnamed 'Aonides, ou Aoniennes
(car je ne veux donner loy à la deduction des vocables, autant ami
de la liberté d'autrui, comme de la mienne) . . . '.[1]

---

[1] SP, 1552, p. 113. For a more detailed demonstration see my thesis, *An Introduction to the* Discours philosophiques *of Pontus de Tyard*, in the Bodleian
Library, Oxford.

V · IDEAS

CONSIDERING so many influences under which Tyard passed, so many sources on which he drew, one would like to be able to determine how much he accepted deliberately and sincerely, how much he merely echoed with what Bremond called 'une adhésion psittaciste'.[1] His sudden abandonment of the Neoplatonism of Ficino, a philosophy of a highly artificial character and chiefly of literary interest, leads one to ask whether he ever really believed in it; and certain provocative remarks in the scientific Discourses led Busson and Lapp to consider him as secretly 'épris de rationalisme' and mirroring, if not expressly fostering, the drift away from belief in Christianity itself. Clements and Frances Yates have not pursued these suggestions, but they too suspect that Tyard is not always to be taken as meaning what he appears to say: 'the poet "hides" his inspired meanings in a system of images'.[2] Even Baridon finds 'la difficoltà di pronunciare un giudizio definitivo sulla vera essenza del pensiero di Pontus'.[3]

Certainly the *Discours philosophiques* introduce plagiarisms as if they were matters of personal knowledge or experience. 'Si le souvenir ne me deçoit',[4] begins Pasithée, and proceeds to translate literally from Ficino; 'je tascheray, non par tel ordre que vous pourriez desirer, mais comme je pourray l'arracher de ma memoire, de vous entretenir de ce, dont il me souviendra',[5] returns the Solitaire, and does the same with Giraldi. The Curieux makes Alessandri's experience of tarantulas his own; and it seems very probable that Tyard borrowed three of Giraldi's descriptions of antique objects with as little scruple. Of the Graces he says, 'je vous en pourrois faire voir un pourtrait de main (quelle qu'elle soit) tres-experte . . .';[6] of the Hours, 'Il me souvient . . . d'avoir vù une medaille antique . . .';[7] and of Janus, 'Je ne puis oublier une forme

[1] H. Bremond, *Autour de l'humanisme d'Érasme à Pascal*, Paris, 1936, p. 55.
[2] Yates, *Academies*, 1947, p. 84.
[3] Baridon, *Pontus de Tyard*, 1950, p. 181.
[4] SP, 1552, p. 22; cf. Ficino, op. cit., p. 1357 (*Comm. in Conv.* vii. 3).
[5] SP, 1552, p. 67; cf. Giraldi, op. cit. i. 533 (*De Musis*).
[6] SP, 1552, p. 58; cf. Giraldi, op. cit. i. 403 (*De Deis*, xiii).
[7] DT, 1556, p. 13; cf. Giraldi, op. cit. i. 402 (*De Deis*, xiii).

de statue . . .'[1]—and he describes each of them in wording suspi-
ciously similar to Giraldi's.

But such literary devices are not necessarily signs of insincerity;
they may be signs that Tyard relies on his sources so greatly as to
identify himself with them. A secret vein of scepticism, indeed,
would nullify the very principles on which the *Discours philosophiques* have been found to be constructed. The act of composing
an encyclopædia attests some belief in the certainty of knowledge;
the act of borrowing attests some belief in authority. But to hold
beliefs and to hold that they should be 'hidden' would in its turn
be incompatible with Tyard's aim of popularization.

The Pléiade shared something of the Renaissance tendency to
concealment and cryptography, erected into a law for the poet by
Tyard himself: 'il n'ose selon les preceptes de son art representer
une verité, si elle n'est revestue de robe de mensonge.'[2] But the
Pléiade are usually, and Tyard is always, referring to verse composition. In the realm of prose we have found him arguing the
opposite, insisting on the right to use French and the duty to
publish, to make the results of study available to all who are capable
of appreciating them. He will defend the obscurity of Scève and
Ronsard, but he casts himself for the role of a Muret, 'pour servir
de fueille aux escrits de tant de bons esprits',[3] 'de quelque lumiere
à la lecture des œuvres de tant de doctes Poetes'.[4]

It must surely be taken that Tyard accepts, and offers for the
acceptance of his readers, the major part of the pronouncements of
the *Discours philosophiques*, rather than a minor and mysterious
'substantificque mouëlle'. The frequent agreement of all his characters, the alterations which his borrowings and earlier versions
undergo, and the personal comments which he adds, all point
in one direction more than is sometimes realized, and, in the present writer's opinion, not in the direction of either mysticism or
free-thinking. A unity pervades Tyard's work which is surely due
to sincerity, since he simply did not possess the genius to simulate
it, and since it squares with what is known of his life. Only a be-
liever in the theory of the *Solitaires* would and could have written
them; a great break occurred before the writing of *L'Univers*, but
there remain enough traces of the earlier attitude to render it
impossible that a secret free-thinker should have written it. In

[1] DT, 1556, p. 43; cf. Giraldi, op. cit. i. 148 (*De Deis*, iv).
[2] DD, 1578, p. 51.   [3] SP, 1552, p. 16.   [4] Ibid., p. 106.

between these works, the *Discours du temps* is not perhaps so insignificant as it seems.

1 · *The Neoplatonism of the* Solitaires

Tyard's contribution to the Petrarchist revival of the seventies certainly seems artificial. The flimsiest stage properties, supplied by Ronsard rather than Ficino, adorn his *Recueil de nouvelles œuvres poëtiques*:

> Quelle douce Python dictera la harangue
> De ma conception si hautement pensée?
> De quelle tienne ardeur (Phebus) sera poussée
> L'Ame pour deslier suffisamment ma langue?
> De quel Laurier faut il que la feuille je mange?
> Et de quel son faut il que ma voix soit haussée,
> Pour d'un parler disert descouvrir ma pensée,
> Chantant de voz vertus une digne louange?
> Mais quelle autre Python faut il que je reclame?
> Mais quel autre Appollon peut eslever mon Ame?
> Quel Laurier pour ronger faut il que je souhaitte?
> Vous seule me seres Python, Phebus, Parnasse:
> Et rendrez (s'il vous plaist me prester vostre grace)
> Pour vous persuader, ma voix assez parfaicte.[1]

All the collection does not ring equally false—for instance, the 'Epistre à Mademoiselle de Saillant' and the 'Epitaphe de la Contesse de Beine' achieve real beauty—but there the Retz *salon* is far away. The dedication even comes near to discrediting Tyard's Neoplatonism of a quarter of a century before: describing himself as 'fort jeune . . . eschauffé de l'ardeur d'Apollon', he continues almost at once, 'je ne fuz aidé que de la force de la beauté qui me commandoit, pour complaire à laquelle je mis peine d'embellir et hausser le stile de mes vers'. One is tempted to translate, 'I only wrote as a Neoplatonist because my lady liked it.'

However, by 1573 Tyard may well have been deceiving Madame de Retz or himself. His earlier life and work give a very different impression. Guillaume des Autelz, the best possible witness, did not suspect his cousin's studies of being other than sincere:

> Mon Dieu quelle soif de gloire
> Luy fait dessous Platon boyre
> Ce vin puissant-gracieux!

[1] RNOP, 1573, Sonnet 2.

Quelle sienne faim devore
Du renaissant Pythagore
Les nombres religieux!
Cette douce nourriture
Se tourne en substance pure,
Par justes concoctions. . . .[1]

All Tyard's publications from 1549 to 1555, and all that is known
of his way of living at that time, reflect Neoplatonism, almost the
whole of Neoplatonism, and very little but Neoplatonism.

We have seen in the *Solitaire premier* his profound belief in the
value of knowledge, surpassed only by faith; but not only religious
faith. Neoplatonism is perhaps the philosophy which rests more
than any other on arbitrary human authority. It was built up from
the work of Plato, from Alexandrian commentaries on it, from
Florentine commentaries on them; to support itself it had fabri-
cated its own type of dialectic and its own body of so-called experience. On Plato's authority one can 'asseurer' that poetry is
the gift of a divine frenzy; this can be proved from Plato's own
'impugnable' incontestable argument that any phenomenon too
regular to be the work of chance and too irregular to be the work of
art must be the work of God; and it can be illustrated by the
'exemple' of Ion, 'nommé honnorablement par Platon . . .'.[2] The
train of thought is Ficino's, the words are the Solitaire's, and they
naïvely reveal the fideistic character of his allegiance. Throughout
the *Solitaire premier* his attitude is exactly that required from the
Neoplatonic novice: opinion and reason must alike yield to faith—
and, pending direct mystical experience, faith in those who have
enjoyed it or say they have: 'je ne me suis dit possedé de telle
fureur . . . .'[3] 'Toutefois je vous diray, pour resolution, ce que j'en
ay peu comprendre . . . .'[4]

In the opening of the first Discourse, before the Solitaire appears
on the scene, Tyard has already placed himself in an anti-rationalist
position. All knowledge found on the way to God, 'diverses rencontres de choses, neaumoins rares, et precieuses, comme rien se
peult trouver autre en lieu tant rare et precieux',[5] may and must
be accepted as containing a certain aspect of truth; and especially

---

[1] G. des Autelz, 'A Pontus de Tyard, troysieme façon par dizains', *Amoureux
Repos*, Lyon, 1553.   [2] SP, 1552, pp. 44–47.
[3] Ibid., p. 26.   [4] Ibid., p. 32.
[5] Ibid., p. 14.

Neoplatonism, which, Tyard takes Ficino's word for it, has come nearest to 'la sourse de bonté, beauté et sapience de l'unique Soleil divin'.[1] The whole Discourse is constructed on the basis of a wholesale acceptance, first of the 'secrets' of Ficino, then even of the 'fables' of Giraldi, for the sake of 'le suc et la moelle . . . de plusieurs bonnes doctrines'[2] which they contain. None of this meets with criticism, either direct like the dispute in *Mantice* or oblique like the ambiguous remarks in *L'Univers*. Pasithée's questions are designed to elicit further authoritative utterances rather than to bring reason to bear, and her occasional levity is answered with a crushing seriousness whose absurd side Tyard never appears to see. Even when he admits that it is unprofitable to spend too long on interpreting 'fables', what checks him is only the fear of boring his audience: 'vous m'estimeriez plus ocieux, que discret à la despense du tems, et des paroles'.[3]

It is hard to see at what point Tyard the writer may be separated from the Solitaire his hero. One may surely take it that when writing the *Solitaire premier*, so far as he understood Ficino, he really believed in Neoplatonic dialectic, cosmology, and psychology. More fundamentally, in 1552 his position was one of almost complete reliance on the authority of his teachers. It is typical that the method of study which he most praises, 'la maniere, et lordre parfait',[4] he owed ultimately to Fulgentius:

> Ergo hic erit ordo. Primum est velle doctrinam. Secundum est delectari quod velis. Tertium est instare ad id quod delectatus es. Quartum est capere id quod instas. Quintum est memorari quod capis. Sextum est invenire de tuo simile ad id quod memineris. Septimum est iudicare quod invenias. Octavum est eligere de quo iudicas. Nonum bene proferre quod elegeris.

The first five steps trust wholly to authority; not till the sixth does the imagination awake, the reason not till the seventh.

The *Solitaire second* emphatically reaffirms Tyard's Neoplatonism, and by implication his intellectual fideism, in spite of his more mature approach to his sources. The Solitaire encourages Pasithée's objection that one type of chromatic scale was misnamed by Aristoxenus; he dares to deny that the soul is a harmony and that the spheres emit sounds; and he conducts an anti-Aristotelian

---

[1] SP, 1552, p. 13.   [2] Ibid., p. 50.   [3] Ibid., p. 86.
[4] Ibid., p. 89; cf. Gafori, *De Harmonia*, iv. 12; Fulgentius, *Mythologia*, i, Fabula de novem musis.

argument 'que la vue fait soufrir aus meurs autant de mutacion
que l'ouïe'. Timid is the rebel, however, who argues about names
and primacies; and the fact is that throughout the Discourse
Tyard's boldness is inspired and sheltered by the highest authorities he can find. The opinion of Aristoxenus was not 'autorisee de
ceus qui lui ont succedé'.[1] It was Socrates who pronounced 'que
l'ame n'est harmonie'.[2] The praise of sight was a Neoplatonic
commonplace and capable of support from Aristotle himself,
'mesmes ce que je vien de dire est à peu pres tout emprunté de lui';[3]
and on him the Solitaire relies for a decision about the music of the
spheres: 'Aussi je le croiray, le croyant Aristote.'[4] Though Tyard
represents the Solitaire as protesting, he still thinks it worth while
for the Curieux to recite his long medley of borrowings on the
'Estranges efets de puissance de Musique'[5] and the 'Musiques
mondeine et humeine'.[6]

Where authorities trusting to reason and to the senses differ,
he would like to have it both ways:

ceus là me plaisent en leurs sutiles speculacions, et ceus ci m'atirent par
leurs preuves familieres et evidentes: Mais plus me satisfont ceus qui
ont suivi une moyenne voye avec Ptolemee, donnant à la raison place
tres-honorable, et toutefois ne refusant en rien le merite dù au senti-
ment corporel.[7]

Pasithée upholds authority as much as reason when judging a
quarrel between the Curieux and the Solitaire, Tyard's old credulity and his dawning critical spirit:

considerez la raison sans autorité, elle est beaucoup hardie, et non sans
danger d'estre cavillee: l'autorité sans la raison, supersticieusement
creintive, et facile à decevoir: mais, ou les deus se peuvent acoupler, lors
la reverence due à l'autorité, et la vive force de la raison, forment une
vreye resolucion de la chose disputee en nos espriz.[8]

And in matters that trouble Tyard, such as the lack of quantity
in French, his cry is always for an absolute legislator:

l'usage, et les hommes doctes, pourroient donner quelque loy en ceci
qui nous releveroit de doute . . . avec peu de labeur de quelqu'un, qui
par venerable autorité et acomplissement des parties requises par
Platon en l'inventeur ou correcteur des langages, tireroit les François

---

[1] SS, 1555, p. 102.   [2] Ibid., p. 153.   [3] Ibid., p. 118.
[4] Ibid., p. 146.   [5] Ibid., p. 112.   [6] Ibid., p. 133.
[7] Ibid., p. 43.   [8] Ibid., p. 147.

à son opinion, nous pourrions estre enrichiz de ce qui nous defaut en cet
endroit . . . .[1]

Bien voudráy je que quelqu'un plus hardi, et plus que moy sufisant,
entreprint, et vint à chef d'un art Poëtique aproprié aus façons Françoises: je requerrois qu'il prescrit des loix . . . .[2]

The same docile Neoplatonism permeates Tyard's poetry from
1549 to 1555. So conventional that it seems vain to talk about
their sincerity, the *Erreurs amoureuses* yet afford valuable glimpses
of Tyard composing originally instead of on another's framework.
Sonnet 4 of 1549 explains the title of the collection by a train of
thought already anticipating the intellectual route described in the
Solitaire premier. Imprisoned in the body, Tyard had yet been free
to use his reason to pursue, as he thought, the good which God had
ordained for him. Love forced him to desert the straight road of
Reason, for a better if more erratic road:

> Aux longs discours de ma libre pensee
> Raison vivoit, et Amour, son contraire,
> Taschant tousjours de son costé m'attraire
> Feit, que par moy elle fut delaissee.
> Lors tout soudain mon ame au vif blessee
> Dit à Amour, ô cruel adversaire
> De mon grand bien, mon grand bien necessaire
> Pour me conduire, ou Dieu m'ha adressee,
> Laisse passer le court fil de ces ans,
> Sans me charger de tes soucis pesans,
> En ceste chair ma prison destinee.
> Amour respond: Tu te dois contenter,
> Car je te veux pour tel bien tourmenter,
> Que tu seras heureusement damnee.

The *Vers liriques* of 1555, which include five Odes first printed
with the *Solitaire premier*, cover a wider field. Two of the Odes,
'Du Socratique' and 'De ses affeccions', provide a fair epitome of
Tyard's Neoplatonism. The title of the former explains it; Busson
is certainly right in his later reading of it as opening with an
attack not on Aristotle but on Epicurus.[3] The speaker, 'un disciple de Socrate', formally dissociates himself from all the opponents of his master, Epicureans, atheists, Cynics, hypocrites,
libertines, and determinists, and personal enemies like Aristo-

---

[1] SS, 1555, p. 27.   [2] Ibid., p. 155.
[3] Busson, *Rationalisme*, 1957, p. 295; cf. 1922, p. 314.

phanes, Anytus, and Meletus. He prays that the world may be
governed by love, truth, justice, pure conduct, and pure worship;
certain that his prayers are inspired ('hauts secretz, qu'il apprend')
and that goodness is at the heart of the universe, he asks only for
it to be more truly reflected throughout the universe:

> O centre, ou sied la bonté
> En non mobile asseurance,
> Fais qu'en ta circonference
> La vagabonde beauté
> Des saints raiz de la clarté
> De ta lumiere feconde
> Incorpore sa couleur. . . .

Meanwhile 'De ses affeccions' analyses, again in Neoplatonic
terms but with less satisfaction, Tyard's own mental state. The
chariot of his soul, falling from heaven because of the vice of its
horse, Instinct, and the unskilfulness of its charioteer, Reason, duly
passed through the spheres of Mars and Venus and acquired

> Deus brandons pernicieux
> . . . d'ireus souci,
> De concupiscible aussi. . . .

> L'espoir d'un fruit vicieux
> Ha longuement combattu
> L'autre espoir ambicieus
> D'atteindre au mont de vertu. . . .

He finds difficulty in purifying his ambition and love, perhaps
because his 'foy outrecuidee' is aiming too high, perhaps because
Pasithée 'en sa cruauté' is uncooperative; and the poem disinte-
grates in a Petrarchist lament. If this jars on the mind practised in
distinguishing between Platonism and Petrarchism, it shows only
that Tyard made no such distinction, that he did not consider
Platonic love as necessitating an equal relationship between the
lovers. The beloved has the privileges merited by beauty, virtue,
and intuitive wisdom; the lover has the one privilege of educating
her, if she will let him perform that service.

During the period of the *Erreurs amoureuses*, so far as it is
possible to put the Neoplatonic way of life into practice, Tyard
seems to have done so. He was temperate, studious, a man of wide
interests but chiefly cultivating the arts, a churchman but otherwise somewhat withdrawn from public activities. He propagated

his beliefs not only through his original compositions but through his translation of Leo Hebraeus, which brought him little glory— Sauvage's was more popular—and must have cost him considerable time and effort. Des Autelz and Peletier witness that he was beginning to form a *salon*, equipped with a library, where he and his friends discoursed and disputed. Des Autelz and Pasquier witness that a woman really existed whom he called Pasithée, and with whom he kept up an intellectual relationship if nothing more.

It may not even be too fanciful to suggest that he attempted to investigate and induce Neoplatonic psychic phenomena. Franchet, Festugière, and Raymond showed how many references to the divine frenzies are mere literary imitations; Clements goes so far as to say that 'the excessive physical disturbances which Ronsard pictures in his poem on the lyre no poet of his time actually experienced'.[1] But what he calls the 'wishful thinking' of the *élite* of the Pléiade may have been sincere belief on its outer fringes. Nan Cooke Carpenter finds that 'to the Pléiade and Baïf's Academy the power of music to sway men's emotions was not an empty theory but a very real phenomenon capable of revival in modern times'.[2] Le Caron represents Jodelle if not Ronsard as genuinely convinced: 'Si les anciens n'eussent esté agitez de cete inspiration, le nom de fureur n'eust jamais eu quelque autorité.'[3]

Le Caron may be responding more credulously than most to the poetic tradition; but there was also a well-established prose tradition, not only among the occultists—Cornelius Agrippa devotes to the *furores* five chapters of the *De Occulta Philosophia*— but among the Platonic party of the natural scientists. Ficino was able to consider the frenzies not only as contacts with the celestial intelligences, but also in medical terms: they exemplified the soul's domination of the body 'ab affectibus rationis',[4] and his incantations, as Walker has shown,[5] were intended as real rites to preserve the health of his spirit. It became the fashion for those Neoplatonic writers who were capable of it to give as much medical support as possible to their psychological theories. Fools, dreamers, the sick or the dying were enabled to prophesy when the disorder of their bodies stirred up their innate knowledge; erotic frenzy was

---

[1] Clements, *Critical Theory*, 1942, p. 247.
[2] Carpenter, in *M.L.N.*, 1960, p. 126.
[3] *Dialogues*, Paris, 1556, p. 135 v°.
[4] Ficino, op. cit., p. 286 (*Theologia Platonica*, xiii. 2).
[5] Walker, *Spiritual and Demonic Magic*, 1958, p. 30.

induced by the entry of alien animal spirits through the eyes, or by spontaneous combustion of the humours.

Tyard was versed, if only at second hand, in such Neoplatonic medicine; from Ficino he borrows the explanation of why lovers grow thin and pale,[1] from elsewhere the explanation of 'Pourquoy au chant les petis enfans cessent les pleurs':

> Le petit enfant pleurant au berceau, s'apaise au chant de sa nourrice, ou à quelque autre son: commençant d'employer la naturelle consideracion à admirer si grande perfeccion, et (s'esmouvant à recueillir tout en un, les puissances de son ame, logee encores en un corps imparfet) deseiche, par la chaleur causee du mouvement, une partie de l'humidité superflue et coulante par les yeus, et repousse l'autre jusques au cerveau, l'induisant à dormir.[2]

He was not unacquainted with occultism; one remembers his 'queste des Daimons et Esprits avec les armes requises en telle entreprinse'.[3] He was always ready to translate his studies as far as possible into practical terms; in 1555 he is found instructing his readers in 'La composicion et l'usage du Monocorde',[4] in 1557 'r'assemblant un Meteoroscope'.[5] How literally is one to take the Solitaire's description of the effect on himself of his own singing?

> ... une nouvelle melancholie, qui, malgré toute mienne dissimulation, s'estoit desjà emparee, et de mon cœur, et de mon visage. ... Car je suis moins disposé à tout entretien, quavant que j'eusse par ce musical exercice esmu mon ame à se passionner. ...[6]

Certainly, as late as November 1555, Tyard seems to believe the much stronger description, which Pasithée claims to have from Jacques de Vintimille, of the power of the lute-player Francesco of Milan:

> il transporte tous ceus qui l'escoutoient, en une si gracieuse melancolie, que l'un, apuiant sa teste en la main soutenue du coude: l'autre, estendu lachement en une incurieuse contenance de ses membres: qui, d'une bouche entr'ouverte et des yeus plus qu'à demi desclos, se clouant (ust on jugé) aus cordes, et qui d'un menton tombé sur la poitrine, desguisant son visage de la plus triste taciturnité qu'on vìt onques, demeuroient privez de tout sentiment, ormis de l'ouïe. ...
>
> Telle puissance (ajoutáy je) est trescerteine, et pourrois moymesme porter témoignage de pareil accident.[7]

---

[1] SP, 1552, pp. 27–28. [2] SS, 1555, pp. 116–17.
[3] M, 1558, p. 89. [4] SS, 1555, pp. 157–60. [5] U, 1557, p. 8.
[6] SP, 1552, pp. 123–4. [7] SS, 1555, pp. 114–15.

II · *Crisis in 1556?*

Hard upon the *Solitaire second* of 1555 followed the *Discours du temps*. At first glance it seems only to continue Tyard's exploitation of the antiquarians. This impression is largely due, however, to the long central borrowing from Giraldi, the dedication of 1578, and the other long additions of 1578 and 1587; the much shorter version of 1556 is startling. Tyard does not deny Neoplatonism; he simply ignores it. Pasithée has gone; so has the Neoplatonic aesthetic and educational theory of the *Solitaires*; so, most fundamentally, has their placid confidence in authority.

The melancholy of the *Erreurs amoureuses* and *Vers liriques*, and of the opening page of the *Solitaire premier*, is conventional and quickly shaken off. The disillusionment of the first three pages of the *Discours du temps* is complete and, one feels, personal; parts of the passage fall into lines of bad verse, often a sign that emotion has overmastered a writer's critical sense. There is no model in the works on which the Discourse is mainly based; if Tyard went to another source, his choice of it was still personal. We cannot rely, says he, on our friends, on our teachers, on ourselves, on life:

l'estat de notre vivre, tant inconstant et incertein, que fable (tant soit elle fabuleuse) ne me semble moins avoir de verité ou vray semblance, qu'il s'en rencontre en nous: soit que nous la cherchions en autrui, ou qu'en nousmesmes essayons de l'assurer. . . . Car le cours de noz ans, ores en heur, ores en malheur, ores en joye, ores en dueil, ores d'une humeur, ores d'une autre . . . nous laisse si peu en un estre durable, que ce qui aujourdhui nous semble vray ou bon, demain nous sera en reputacion de mensonger et meschant: et piz, que ce qu'en nous pensons estre estimable, semble aus plus importans voisins et compagnons, tant peu dine de bonne vuë, que derrier nous ilz en rident le front, et froncent le sourcil.[1]

We can achieve no lasting certainty at all in this world:

Donq ne saurions nous arrester cette vie sur le plinthe de quelque solide et cubique seurté? Il faudroit (cróy je) retrencher l'esle du Tems, duquel l'invisible, mais l'insensible fuite, entreine continuellement toute notre assurance.[2]

Perhaps at this point Tyard gives place to the Solitaire, greeting his visitors

[1] DT, 1556, pp. 1–3.   [2] Ibid., p. 3.

avec la plus joyeuse chere que je pouvois former: laquelle je n'acom-
pagnois, toutefois, de face si riante, qu'à mon obget la melancolie, la
solitude, et telles tenebres, ne vinssent en propos. . . .[1]

But in this Discourse it is harder than ever to separate him from
his hero, and his loss of faith would seem to be real. The whole
Discourse can be read as an account of his struggle to regain it, to
determine what stability it is possible to attain. He seeks reassu-
rance at first in natural beauty, 'un mien jardin, de si commode
plant, que le non trop affecté agencement, mais aussi la non trop
negligente culture, pouvoit assez nous donner de plaisir';[1] in his
social duties, 'le respet lequel la presence des personnes qui escoutoient, nous commanda d'avoir';[2] and in intellectual activities, 'le
souvenir prompt, le penser certein, et l'imaginaire espoir'.[3] But
his disturbance and depression reflect themselves in the subjects of
conversation.

He does not press his scepticism to the point of atheism; but his
doubts are up to date and far-reaching. We obtain no help from
authority, it seems, about the nature of time: 'Les Anciens . . . assez
vainement se sont opiniatrez. . . .'[1] There is no consensus of opinion
about the reckoning of time, 'la diversité des Ans: desquelz l'estendue nous sembloit avoir esté mesuree ores courte, ores brieve, selon
les diverses nacions . . . '.[4] This applies even to Biblical chronology:
'la vie des Peres, escrite par le Theographe Moyse, sembleroit monstreuse au parangon de notre Tems.'[2] Nature itself is irregular:
the length of a day varies in different countries, the length of a
natural hour varies in a single day, and the 'variable inconstance'[5]
of the stars' movements is such that the Solitaire fears that no one
arrangement of them will ever be repeated. 'Hoo (soupiráy je)
combien me plait ce mot d'Euripide . . . la vie n'est point vie mais
calamité.'[6]

If the account of the *Discours du temps* is founded on fact, it was
Tyard's friends who helped him, particularly Scève, since 'Hieromnime' only speaks twice in the version of 1556. 'Parlons piément...',[2] says Hieromnime; and Scève, 'il n'est defendu de recon-
noitre...',[7] 'il n'a esté impossible de considerer...'.[8] They recall

---

[1] Ibid., p. 4.   [2] Ibid., p. 10.
[3] Ibid., p. 5.
[4] Ibid., p. 10; either *courte* or *brieve* seems a slip for *longue*.
[5] Ibid., p. 63.   [6] Ibid., p. 80.
[7] Ibid., p. 12.   [8] Ibid., p. 66.

him to the generally accepted authorities and traditions, they lecture to him out of Giraldi; but it is not to crush him with dogmatism, but to encourage him with reliable history. It is at least fact that the ancients did believe this or that or the other; the Julian calendar may be trusted for all practical purposes—there is

une faute, mais de petite importance, bien qu'elle merite chatiment: comme quelques doctes de ce Tems ont remontré. Toutefois la derniere reformacion de l'An Rommein est sans contredit la meilleure.[1]

Beyond these truths they admit that there are others which approach or pass the limits of reason: 'certeines veritez sont de tant profonde suget, que pour estre de dificile acces, ceus qui sont ennuyez de tant obscure speculacion, les tiennent à mensonges'.[2] Such truths must be accepted with fideistic resignation: 'Parlons piément: et croyons . . . .'

One aspect of the problem of certainty is explored in more detail. Apropos of lucky and unlucky days, the conversation becomes virtually an analysis of what is and what is not 'superstition'. The Solitaire's reaction against what he formerly held 'vray ou bon' extends to mythology (the 'bien folle supersticion'[3] attending on the Athenian mysteries), astrology (the 'grand secret' or 'sotte supersticion d'Albumazar'),[4] and numerology ('les supersticieuses raisons recitees par Hesiode en ses jours et euvres').[5] Scève agrees with him; only the keeping of the Sabbath escapes:

O que Hesiode (dit HIEROMNIME) avoit bien fueilleté les livres de Moyse, envelopant si cautement les secrets de la creacion, et le repos de Dieu souz le repli de ses fables.
Je croy bien (respondí je) qu'il n'estoit sans Theologie . . . .[6]

Here and here only appears the 'témoignage de Platon',[7] and it is dismissed perfunctorily if not contemptuously: 'les raisons Musicales feront place à autre opinion . . . .'[8]

Where the Solitaire is still troubled by coincidences and climacterics, 'J'ay . . . pris garde au jour natal, le plus souvent insine de quelque heur, ou malheur d'importance',[9] 'et petit à petit nous aproche l'An Climacteric, qui finira le jour de notre vie',[1] it is

---

[1] DT, 1556, p. 79.
[2] Ibid., p. 65.
[3] Ibid., p. 45.
[4] Ibid., p. 28.
[5] Ibid., p. 26.
[6] Ibid., p. 27.
[7] Ibid., pp. 26–27.
[8] Ibid., p. 33.
[9] Ibid., pp. 23–24.

Scève who brings common sense to bear. We know from Galen that critical days and celestial influences exist,[1] but the Solitaire's examples may mean anything:

> Ainsi . . . trouverions nous chacun jour de l'annee heureus et malheureus si nous considerions les accidens avenuz.[2]
>
> Quant encores . . . les ans Climacteriques seroient fataus, leur fatalité me semble si bien diversifiee, que le plus prochein ne nous ote l'espoir d'en joindre encor un autre . . .[3]

Scève's conclusion, which to Saulnier has the ring of authenticity, comes with a sure and calming cadence: 'j'estime la vie m'estre donnee de Dieu, comme un depost en garde . . .'.[4]

In the next year *L'Univers* too suggests that since 1555 Tyard had passed through a crisis of doubt and a process of re-education. No change of attitude in the later editions of the *Discours philosophiques* is so great as the change of attitude between the *Solitaires* and the scientific Discourses. *L'Univers* shows from its first page a certainty that it is possible, at least in the 'sciences', to attain 'vraye connoissance':

> Pource qu'il me semble, l'homme ne pouvoir souhaiter, ny recevoir plus grand bien, que la vraye connoissance des choses, je juge la condicion de celui qui coule sa vie avec les sciences, comme en l'exercice pour lequel l'homme est bien expressement nay, et duquel sur tous les animaus il est doué uniquement, heureuse et desirable.[5]

At the same time it shows as much selective and critical power as Tyard was ever to possess. Where his instinct was to believe what was said about the tarantula, it is to disbelieve what is said about the salamander; and, though he still believes more than he disbelieves, the decision has become more conscious. Above all, he goes more often to other sources than to Platonic ones, and two favourite Neoplatonic themes have disappeared entirely from his work: the theme of divine frenzy and that of love.

Was Tyard caught in 1556 by the rising tide of scepticism? It will be remembered that this is the one time between 1537 and 1570 at which it is practically certain that he visited Paris. Busson dates from 1553 the growth of the cultured layman's awareness of free-thinking; but it seems to have been especially around 1556 that it shook the Neoplatonic circles which would be most

---

[1] Ibid., p. 30. [2] Ibid., p. 25. [3] Ibid., p. 79.
[4] Ibid., p. 80. [5] U, 1557, p. 5.

congenial to Tyard. In 1556 Le Caron's *Ronsard* seems to reflect some difference of opinion in the Pléiade about the real existence of *furor poeticus*. Guy Le Fèvre de la Boderie says in 1570:

Il y a plus de quinze ans passez, qu'à mon grand regret j'ay esté fait certain, que sous semblance humaine il se trouvoit de tels monstrueus esprits, qui osoyent pleinement denier et Dieu et sa Providence, et tenoyent pour resolu entre eus que toutes choses alloyent à l'adventure.[1]

His age shows that he cannot be referring to a time much before 1555; he seems to have been born in 1540 or 1541. In 1557 Guy de Bruès found it necessary to publish *Dialogues . . . contre les nouveaux academiciens, que tout ne consiste point en opinion*. His opening defence of human authority reminds one of Tyard's recent attack on it:

Quand je considere l'inconstante entresuitte des choses humaines, je ne puis ce me semble assez honorer la memoire de ceux, qui ont mis peine de subvenir par leurs escris à la grande imbecillité des hommes . . .[2]

and his sceptic, like Tyard, is impressed by the deficiencies of the senses and the inconstancy of nature.

Those Neoplatonists who did not move so far towards scepticism began at this time, nevertheless, to retreat from some of their extreme positions. Medical commentators, instead of explaining the *furores*, tended to explain them away; other writers, as Raymond has shown, took the course of equating all but one with divine inspiration in the purely Christian sense. As for the erotic frenzy, the inmost circle of the Pléiade had already abandoned their half-belief in it, as in the whole system of Petrarchist courtship and Platonic love; and their disciples would soon follow the changing fashion. Perhaps Tyard shared in this intellectual movement; yet, knowing his methods of composition, we should expect to find direct borrowings from sceptical sources, rather than sceptical comments on borrowings from Giraldi. The change which we find in his very processes of thought suggests that he had received an emotional shock, that something happened to him in 1556 which struck harder and deeper than any earlier contact.

Is the key to be found in his allusion to the sneers of one's 'voisins et compagnons' at 'ce qu'en nous pensons estre estimable'?

[1] G. Le Fèvre de la Boderie, *L'Encyclie des secrets de l'éternité*, Antwerp, 1570, 'Advertissement au lecteur'.

[2] G. de Bruès, op. cit., Paris, 1557, 'Preface de l'auteur'.

Does this conceal a real incident, possibly the end of his relations with Pasithée? and did those relations mean more to Tyard than we thought? Curiously strong support for this suggestion is provided by his 'Elegie à Pierre de Ronsard', first published in the *Recueil de nouvelles œuvres poëtiques* of 1573, but difficult to date exactly. The setting is rural with no glimpse of Paris; the style is the simpler one adopted by the Pléiade from about 1553, with the title which for them announced the use of such a style, and with no echo of the Retz *salon*. Tyard refers to Ronsard and himself as 'young', and wishes Ronsard success not only with Jeanne, Marguerite, and Cassandre, but with Marie, whom he is supposed to have first met in April 1555. That date is only a *terminus a quo*; Ronsard ceased to mention Jeanne in 1555, but he had ceased to mention Marguerite in 1550, and Cassandre and Marie were still in his thoughts in 1573.[1] This is all that can be said with certainty; but a subjective impression is that Tyard is writing more naturally, more precisely, more vigorously, and more unevenly than ever before, that the picture he gives of his past occupations squares exactly with what is known of him up to 1555, and that the picture of his state of mind is exactly what would seem to have been true of him in, but not before or after, 1556.

Tyard confides to Ronsard the effects of a separation which appears due to causes beyond his control:

> Oy de mille travaux, de differente sorte,
> Ceux lesquels, eslongné de Pasithé je porte. . . .

His sufferings are Petrarchist, including an obsession by dreams, but the content of the dreams is not. They are more realistic than Tyard shows himself anywhere else, with the significant exception of the *Homilies* of the eighties, and their symbolism is obvious. Pasithée is seen in the power of

> . . . un adversaire sien
> L'enchainant par le corps: Or, dit il, je te tien
> Pour mieux saouller mon ire, esclave de la peine
> Et ainsi le cruel avecque soy l'entraine,
> Malgré mon vain desir Phantastic, qui poursuit,
> De bras et de pieds mors le Phantasme qui fuit
> Aupres d'un roc, lavé d'une lente riviere,
> Où me renaist encor une autre horreur plus fiere
> D'un Lyon qui la va entiere devorant. . . .

[1] P. Laumonier, *Ronsard poète lyrique*, Paris, 1909, pp. 46–47 and 254–5.

Awakening, Tyard turns to his books, but finds no comfort in
mathematics or music; the *Solitaire second* was published in vain:

> Je voy aux traits parfaits de la Geometrie
> Le parfait de ce beau qui mon Ame ha meurtrie,
> Et l'Art doux, du doux nom des Muses enrichy
> (O que je l'ay en vain d'ignorance affranchy)
> De ma peine long temps à son honneur prestée:
> Pour fruict l'esloignement me rend de Pasithée. . . .

Platonism he also rejects, in a couplet as scathing as anything in the
gaulois tradition:

> Vaut-il pas mieux, lointain de ces humains discours
> Me feindre aveq Platon quelque nueux secours?
> Ou opiniastrant en la vieille querelle,
> Tirer du fond secret la cause naturelle?

—the problem of the 'principe de tout', to be studied in *L'Univers*.

> Non: icy je ne voy que discorde, Amitié,
> Hayne, Accord, balancez en esgalle moitié.
> Là Platon m'advertit de beauté faire estime,
> Ou m'apprend à aimer avecques Diotime:
> Et l'Amour, la beauté, la haine et la laideur,
> Sont l'object trop cogneu de mon triste malheur.

What of divination?

> Dea! que ne m'aidez vous ô couvertes sciences,
> Qui jugez l'advenir sur voz experiences.
> O, vain Judiciaire, ô poudreux Geomant,
> O, Necromant nocturne, ô fraisle Chiromant,
> O, superstitieuse, ô, demonique Escole
> Que vous me decevez d'opinion frivolle. . . .
> Donq, livres, demeurez en proye à l'artaison,
> Puis-que je ne rencontre entre vous guarison . . .
> Et vous qui quelquefois (ô Phebeans Poetes)
> M'avez pleu et receu, que desplaisans vous m'estes!
> Je croy de voz plaisirs tous les chants mensongers. . . .

So did Ronsard and Du Bellay at times; but what anti-Petrarchist
ever proceeded to contemplate suicide?

> Ah! que d'estre affranchi ainsi que fust Caton
> Me semble mieux que vivre, au vouloir de Platon. . . .

Tyard has never reproached Pasithée herself, however; only for a moment has he come near to losing faith in her and in virtue:

> S'elle se faict jamais adorer d'autre vœu,
> S'elle embrase son cueur jamais d'un autre feu,
> Et si tout son vivant ma perte elle ne pleure,
> Je dy qu'onques la foy ça bas ne feist demeure,
> Que l'honneur, la vertu, sont mots simplement vains. . . .

It is against a rival, 'quelque disert trompeur', that his suspicions turn; or, as in the *Erreurs amoureuses*, against

> un vieil resveur,
> Qui luy enaigrissant l'amoureuse saveur,
> Presche de combien d'yeux et de langues semée,
> Au populaire vent volle la renommée . . .
> Hélas! sera sa part d'amitié si petite,
> Que ce grand langageur estaigne mon merite? . . .

'. . . Et piz, que ce qu'en nous pensons estre estimable . . . ilz en rident le front, et froncent le sourcil . . . .' Tyard repents of his pessimism:

> Que sçay-je si le Ciel se monstrera plus doux? . . .
> Que sçay-je, si, quand plus loing de moy on l'esclave,
> Plus en son cueur de moy la figure elle engrave? . . .

One may perhaps recall once more that many years later he also repented 'de ce qu'en sa jeunesse il avoit composé quelques poësies un peu trop amoureuses'.

III · *Reason and Faith*

From the questioning of authority and of certainty in the *Discours du temps* it would have been possible to go on to true rationalism, and for Busson and Lapp this is what Tyard did, or rather what he had done from the start. Busson calls him a 'disciple des Padouans avant Montaigne';[1] Lapp follows Busson's assumption that his fideism was Paduan in origin and much outweighed by his rationalism and experimentalism. But the conclusions seem largely drawn from Tyard's mere awareness of free-thinking arguments and from the freedom of expression allowed to the Curieux, assessed somewhat unfairly. When the remarks of the Curieux are studied

---

[1] *Rationalisme*, 1922, p. 389; 1957, p. 361.

in the context of the *Discours philosophiques*, the impression obtained is that Tyard is aiming not to portray 'quel bouleversement la découverte des systèmes philosophiques des païens jeta dans l'âme de notre Renaissance',[1] still less to propagate it, but to restore order in any *âme bouleversée* among his readers, or even in his own.

It has already been seen both that the Curieux scarcely represents Tyard, and that he defends orthodoxy as often as he attacks it. Close examination of what he and the Solitaire actually say reveals also that their free-thinking itself does not go very far. Busson quotes the not unprejudiced witness Mantice to prove that the attitude of the Curieux would ultimately lead to pyrrhonism and atheism:

Par ce libre esgayement de niemens à tous propos, et de refus des raisons jà receuës, perissent toutes les parties de Philosophie. . . . Dieu (l'infinie majesté et grandeur duquel est incomprehensible) pour n'estre prouvé par assés ferme argument, et apparence de la raison sensible, sera anullé de toute congnoissance. . . .[2]

But the Curieux always argues exactly the opposite:

de la profonde source de Philosophie . . . nous puisons la congnoissance certeine de la Nature des choses, qui nous fait eslever jusques en l'admiration de la Divinité. . . .[3]

Nor does any character hold out long against the rulings of the cleric Hieromnime. There is one occasion only when the latter is flatly contradicted: when the Solitaire has reopened the question of the music of the spheres, Hieromnime is made in 1578 to protest:

Si vous avez (dit Hieromnime) raison de faire doute que les Cieux soyent harmonieusement sonoreux en leurs mouvemens: si suis-je contraint par une souveraine authorité de ne refuser creance à ceste verité, prononcee par le souverain Createur des Cieux mesme . . .[4]

that is, in the Book of Job; but in 1587 the last word is refused to Hieromnime: 'Il n'y a (dit le Curieux) apparence d'aucune verité en ces sons cœlestes . . . .' There is one occasion when the Curieux is prepared to go on arguing:

Si aý je (dit le Curieus) en memoire bon nombre de passages et de l'escriture et des interpretes Anciens, mesmes bien expressement de

[1] *Rationalisme*, 1922, p. 410; 1957, p. 402.
[2] M, 1558, p. 56.   [3] Ibid., p. 7.
[4] DD, 1578, p. 34; cf. DP, 1587, p. 231 v°; Job xxxviii. 7.

Chrysostome et Philon Juif, deus ruisseaus d'eloquence, qui soutiennent apparemment le Ciel, nonostant qu'ils le confessent creé, estre exempt de toute corrupcion . . .[1]

but 'l'heure tarde ne permettoit pas de continuer la parole d'avantage'. The Curieux dissociates himself from a few discussions: of Hebrew religious terminology he says, 'Je n'opiniatrerois beaucoup en telle consideracion',[2] and of the human soul, 'Le respect (s'addressant à Hieromnime) que j'ay à vous et à vostre profession, me doit fermer la bouche et empescher d'en discourir'.[3] But there are many more topics on which all Tyard's characters agree, tacitly or explicitly: even the significance of the rainbow,[4] the lack of significance of comets,[5] or the Divine creation *ex nihilo*:

> Aussi (dit Hieromnime) ceux qui ont prins cognoissance de la verité par l'instruction de Moyse, ne recognoissent qu'un Principe: à sçavoir la Sapience de Dieu en laquelle il a fait Tout de Rien . . . .
>
> Pythagore (reprint le Curieux) semble avoir, entre les Philosophes, le premier halené quelque chose de cela. . . .[6]

At one such moment Busson senses 'l'air goguenard d'un homme à qui on n'en impose pas':[7] 'Il vaut mieus (dit le Curieus) en croire plus, et en disputer moins.'[8] But the Curieux may mean simply what he says.

Tyard does in fact dispute little on the questions which Busson selects as characteristic of Renaissance free-thinking, and those unorthodox ideas which he does reflect would appear to have been old fashioned when he wrote, if not already outdated.

He certainly bears no responsibility for propagating doubt of the existence of God. From about 1560, according to Busson, it became usual for Christian apologists to argue the point; Tyard did not do so till 1578, and then perfunctorily. His arguments are embraced and prejudged by the assumptions of *L'Univers* that theism is natural and innate:

> Si tombe il naturellement en l'homme, quoy qu'on die que ce soit de la nourriture et apprehension de jeunesse, et non de la nature de l'espece humeine, une marque de connoissance de Dieu . . .[9]

[1] U, 1557, p. 156.   [2] Ibid., p. 127.
[3] DP, 1587, p. 289 v°.   [4] DD, 1578, pp. 52 v°–54.
[5] Ibid., pp 49–52.   [6] DP, 1587, p. 235 v°.
[7] *Rationalisme*, 1922, p. 413; 1957, p. 403.   [8] U, 1557, p. 73.
[9] Ibid., p. 125, as emended in the author's corrections.

and those few ancients who denied it did so only 'par transport et depravacion de sens commun, et par opinion opiniatree contre leur premier jugement'.[1] The space given to theistic syllogisms is more than double that given to atheistic ones, and the latter are not unfairly parodied by Montaigne: 'Si Dieu ... est sans corps, il est sans ame, et par consequant sans action; et, s'il a corps, il est perissable. Voyla pas triomfé?'[2] Otherwise, the nearest Tyard comes to considering atheism as a possible hypothesis is in Mantice's tirade, refuted in advance by the Curieux. Both Mantice and the Curieux take theism as their starting-point throughout their dispute, and theistic references form a continuous accompaniment to the Curieux's account of the universe:

L'Arc en Ciel (adjoustay-je) est vrayment une apparence de couleurs faite en une nuee espesse et humide. . . .
Cest arc (dit Hieromnime) est adjousté depuis le deluge, aux meteores par ouvrage divin. . . .
Ce meteore (reprint le Curieux) est vray object de maintes belles considerations.[3]

It would be more to the point to accuse Tyard of encouraging unorthodox belief in a world-soul, a notion often involved in his Platonic and Ciceronian borrowings. But to believe in a world-soul is not to worship it, as the *Homilies* will later make clear:

Ce n'est pas mal faict, que d'imaginer des intelligences cœlestes, et motrices des cieux, et d'en discourir et disputer: mais de les adorer, et leur donner sa foy, je tien que c'est pecher tres-griefvement.[4]

The Curieux carefully distinguishes between even an animate cosmos and its Maker: 'le Monde est animal, ayant ame et entendement, pour avoir esté vrayment fait par la providence de Dieu.'[5] Hieromnime throws more light on the distinction when he praises the Pythagoreans' description of God:

un, non comme quelques uns ont pensé, dehors la fabrique mondeine: mais en icelle tout, en tout ... pere, ame et mouvement de toute chose. . . . Vrayment s'ils ne le confinent trop expressement dedens les fins du Monde, je ne say que nous pourrions aujourd'hui plus proprement dire, pour exprimer ce qu'il faut sentir de la Divinité.[6]

---

[1] U, 1557, p. 131.
[2] *Essais*, ii. 12, ed. Strowski, ii. 266; cf. P. Villey, *Sources et évolution des essais de Montaigne*, Paris, 1908, i. 201.   [3] DD, 1578, pp. 52 v°–54 v°.
[4] *Homilies sur la premiere table du Decalogue*, 1588, p. 92 v°.
[5] DD, 1578, p. 105.   [6] U, 1557, pp. 132–3.

And the Solitaire explicitly denounces pantheism:

l'opinion des Poëtes, qui ont chanté tout estre plein de Jupiter: c'estadire, Dieu estre espanché par tout et particulierement et generalement.
Ce que quelques ridicules et maniacles sectistes de ce tems, ont osé
dogmatiser, mais plus impiement que les Poëtes ethniques n'ont jamais
entendu.[1]

The *Homilies* will explain: 'Dieu est par tout, par presence de
divinité, mais non pas par grace d'habitation.'[2]

Paduan rationalism of the earlier part of the century had busied
itself especially with two subjects which Tyard could not well
neglect, the creation of the world and the immortality of the soul.
But his questionings on each subject are curiously restricted to one
aspect, scientific rather than metaphysical. The Curieux has no
trouble with the concept of Divine creation in itself, as has been
seen, nor with that of Divine providence in it. If one page of his
atheistical arguments points out the difficulty of the idea of providence, four pages of his theistical arguments assert its truth, and
so do many passages of his cosmological survey:

la providence se montre admirablement curieuse conservatrice de
l'Univers: qui desja fust tout embrasé, si le Feu eust eu autant de resis-
tence à se deffendre, qu'il ha d'accion pour offenser.[3]

He does, however, recognize two particular problems: it is hard
to date the creation of the world or to admit any physical cause
which can destroy it, and the classical experts do not agree:

Le doute de la creacion du Monde est de difficile assurance, mesmes
que le tems prefix de son commencement est inapointablement opi-
niatré.... Ce seroit (reprint le Curieus) peu de difficulté que le tems,
si la creacion estoit prouvee, et si les Filozofes avoient bien accordé
de leurs raisons contraires....[4]

Anticipating these problems, the Curieux has earlier let slip his
most heretical remark, on 'la generacion et la corrupcion succe-
dantes l'une à l'autre, delivrant par ce moyen le Monde de tout
finissement, et témoignant assez que jamais il n'eut commencement'.[5] But the philosophers he quotes are no more modern than
Aristotle and Philo Judaeus, and Hieromnime is allotted the last

---

[1] Ibid., p. 125.
[2] *Homilies . . . sur l'Oraison Dominicale*, 1585, p. 22 v°.
[3] U, 1557, p. 66.
[4] Ibid., p. 135.   [5] Ibid., p. 111.

six pages of *L'Univers* to refute them in detail and with feeling, on
both the scientific and the theological levels:

ne nions contre notre religion, ce que par un instinct naturel grand
nombre de Gentils ont crù: voire essayé de prouver autant richement,
que voz Peripatetiques l'ont entreprins conveincre.[1]

The immortality of the soul is asserted in passing by all the
speakers in *L'Univers*: for the Curieux 'l'homme est vivant . . . de
vie divine et eternelle',[2] for the Solitaire 'soutenu d'une Ame
perannelle',[3] while Hieromnime splendidly describes the resur-
rected state, 'notre condicion enrichie de toute suffisance . . . au
renouvellement de celle immortelle et glorieuse vie . . .'.[4] The
earlier editions content themselves with such references and with
what can be gathered from the 'beaus, et eslevez discours Platoniques';[5] only in 1587 does Tyard feel obliged, or qualified, to
make Hieromnime select the 'mieux choisi' theory of the soul's
origin and define the soul itself:

l'ame en essence vivante, simple, incorporelle, invisible à nos yeux cor-
porels, immortelle . . . usant du corps comme de son chariot, s'espanchant en toutes et chacunes parties d'iceluy pour l'animer, voire luy
faire part de son immortalité: Le tout sous le benefice de la grace et
volonté divine. . . .[6]

Already in *L'Univers*, however, there is a discussion of hell where
the point is made 'que mal aisément se peut prouver par raison
naturelle, que les Ames incorporelles soient persecutees en tourment d'un feu corporel'.[7] But the discussion is purely apologetic.
It is Hieromnime who opens it, mentions the objection, and meets
it by a reminder of 'celle infinie puissance, qui ha pù emprisonner
si tenamment l'Ame incorporelle dedens le corps materiel'. He
relies on the authority of the Bible, but is willing to support it
by the *consensus gentium*—'Platon et les siens en font foy'—and by
explanation. The Curieux raises scattered objections—Plato's
and Plutarch's references may be interpolations, suffering surely
implies perishability—only in order that they may be crushed:
Plato's and Plutarch's testimonies, not the only ones, are not essential to the argument; the damned soul 's'aquiert une condicion,
comme on diroit, entre la mortalité, et l'immortalité, demeurant

¹ U, 1557, p. 152.   ² Ibid., p. 117.   ³ Ibid., p. 126.
⁴ Ibid., p. 156.   ⁵ Ibid., p. 114.
⁶ DP, 1587, p. 290.   ⁷ U, 1557, pp. 70–72.

passible... immortelle toutefois ...'. The final comment of the
Curieux, 'Il vaut mieus ... en croire plus, et en disputer moins',
is surely a surrender.

In the Renaissance questioning of theological dogma Tyard
seems even less interested. Not a hint is breathed against the
divinity of Christ, always mentioned with reverence; it is the
Curieux who denounces astrologers as blasphemers:

Considerés je vous prie (poursuyvoit le Curieux esmeu jusques à la
colere) de quelle espece de presomption est leur default de jugement
accompagné: prophaner ainsi les choses saintes, attribuer ... la sainteté
des bien vivans, l'abstraction des Prophetes, la merveille des miracles, la
faulte du peché originel, voire la redemption d'icelui, et l'incarnation du
fils de Dieu, aux rencontres des Astres. Cela est trop horrible: cela est
trop indigne de toute humanité.[1]

The word of the Bible is taken as final, 'témoignage franc de toute
excepcion',[2] though it has to be 'entendue en plusieurs sortes'[3] and
perhaps sometimes only metaphorically:

les Estoiles tomberont du Ciel. Ce qu'aucuns ont jugé pouvoir avenir
par la violence de l'embrasement universel. Mais quelques autres
favorisans l'opinion que vous avez, qu'il soit ridicule de l'ainsi croire,
reçoivent ces paroles tropologiquement, comme l'escriture est pleine de
figures ...[4]

which would also cover the problem of the music of the spheres.
It is not correct that Hieromnime, any more than the Curieux,
ignores the Fall;[5] it explains for him both climatic deterioration[6]
and the shortening of human life,[7] while Mantice carries the train
of thought still farther.[8] The creeds of the Church are also to be
believed 'seurement, sans recherche de plus curieus témoignages'.[9]
In the person of Hieromnime, Tyard can accept even Christian
marvels such as 'l'Eclipse solaire ... du jour que Jesus-Christ
souffrit passion ... estant le Soleil au Mouton, et la Lune en la
Balance',[10] and the 'miraculeux effets'[11] of relics; the Curieux's
evasion of the latter point, 'Aussi ... ne les voulois-je alleguer à ce
propos', may mean only that the subject is irrelevant to the account
he is giving of the natural properties of stones and bones.

[1] M, 1558, p. 48.   [2] U, 1557, p. 88.
[3] DD, 1578, p. 75 v°.   [4] U, 1557, p. 76; cf. Matt. xxiv. 29.
[5] Busson, *Rationalisme*, 1922, p. 414; 1957, p. 405.
[6] U, 1557, p. 105.   [7] DT, 1556, pp. 11–12.
[8] M, 1558, pp. 58–59.   [9] U, 1557, p. 135.
[10] DD, 1578, p. 30.   [11] Ibid., p. 90 v°.

Throughout *Mantice* Tyard shows a quite remarkable ability to shut his eyes, whether unconsciously or deliberately, to the possible implications of some arguments for or against astrology. Euhemerism, the belief that gods are nothing but deified men, could lead to denial of the divinity of Christ and the existence of any God; but the introduction of *Mantice* inveighs against human claims to supernatural rank, power, or prescience just because they infringe the prerogatives of the Christian Trinity:

Thulis ... osa s'enquerir de l'oracle de Serapis, qui ou avant ou apres luy l'auroit outrepassé ou l'outrepasseroit de grandeur. La response fu admirable et telle. . . . Premierement Dieu, apres la Parolle et l'Esprit avec eux.[1]

Either acceptance or rejection of astrology could lead to materialistic determinism; but both the Curieux and Mantice take care to leave Providence free: if the Curieux is right, 'les miracles se rapporteront simplement à la Divinité',[2] while Mantice ripostes with the clockmaker's 'pleine et libre puissance, de demonter, voire briser son horologe'.[3] The defeat of either side could undermine the authority of the Bible, relied on by Renaissance astrologers and their opponents alike; but both the Curieux and Mantice abstain to an unusual extent from using it. This abstinence may not be a modern trait so much as a legacy from Neoplatonism, whose tradition was not to impose either belief or disbelief in astrology, but for once to concede the right of private judgement.

Tyard's real interest would appear to have lain less in the problems raised by contemporary free-thinkers than in those raised by his classical reading, and traced back by Busson to the beginning of the Renaissance and earlier: what is to be made of the ancient pagans' possession of religions, records of miracles, literature which seems to have universal value? Into these problems Tyard goes in detail; but the very fact that he does so indicates the essential distinction which he makes: paganism is open to question and criticism as Christianity is not.

All heathen gods, Tyard says with St. Augustine, are born of poetic fables, priestly impostures, or philosophic guesses at the true God.[4] He has revealed Himself partially through all time:

la substance divine espanchant sa puissance par toutes nations, n'a laissé peuple au monde qui n'ait senty quelque odeur de la divinité. . . .[5]

[1] M, 1573, p. 2.   [2] M, 1558, p. 35.   [3] DP, 1587, p. 186 v°.
[4] U, 1557, pp. 126–7.   [5] DD, 1578, p. 98 v°.

... voyez comme le nom de quatre lettres se rencontre en Dieu, soit par fortune, ou par quelque mistere plus secret. ... Mais de l'Essence de Dieu, combien ont esté les opinions differentes?[1]

He has only now revealed Himself fully: 'la Grace, en l'humanité de la parole Divine ... ha ouvert les yeus humeins'.[2] The miracles claimed by the pagans are either to be rejected as 'contes et menteries inexcusables. Tesmoing le rasoir du Prestre, qui coupa la queux ou pierre aguisoire au rapport de Tite Live',[3] or to be explained away like the 'os du pied droit de Pyrrus Roy d'Epire *qui guerissoit les splenetiques*',[4] but did so only by the 'vertus propres aux pierres, et aux os', whereas the bones of Christian martyrs 'ont fait tant de miraculeux effets, que la Nature et les naturels y perdent le sens et la raison'. Pagan authorities may be doubted, as indeed, theoretically, may all authority short of Divine revelation; the position may be naïve, but Tyard is unabashed. He has based it firmly on his answer to the problem of the relation between faith and reason, the oldest of Busson's crucial questions, and the only one faced repeatedly and systematically by Tyard from 1557 onwards.

The Curieux and Hieromnime open *L'Univers* with what is not quite a dispute but 'un propos, touchant les Mathemates, desquelles Hieromnime ne faisoit grande estime'. But the Curieux's defence of mathematics resolves itself into an indirect eulogy of reason:

Car (disoit il) les Mathemates sont le vray moyen (s'il s'en peut trouver un) pour former quelque certitude aus speculacions Theologiennes, et Naturelles: incerteines pour la continuelle mutacion, et variable inconstance des matieres de cestes: et pour la difficulté, voire incomprehensibilité des autres. Quel autre chemin (je vous prie) plus droit nous meine à la Theologie, que l'Astronomie et ses servantes? vù qu'elles seules en leurs demonstracions, qui ont hors tout doute la raison pour fondement, descouvrent comme vous diriez à nud, la procheineté des immuables, perpetuelles, et impassibles substances: aus mouvantes, temporelles, muables et passibles: et, comme favorisant, pour non dire prévenant, la Theologie, nous eslievent au plus haut degré de perspicacité, enamourant noz ames de la Divine beauté.[5]

[1] U, 1557, pp. 127-8.   [2] Ibid., p. 9.
[3] DD, 1578, p. 51.
[4] Ibid., p. 90 v°; the italicized words are added in the author's corrections; cf. Plutarch, *Pyrrhus*, III. iv.
[5] U, 1557, p. 8.

Once again, however, it is not the rationalist view that the Curieux is setting against the Christian view. It is Neoplatonic doctrine, 'which emphasized mathematics as the key to the secrets of philosophy', that is at odds with the 'prevailing tendency of Aristotelianism to minimize the importance of mathematics in the interpretation of the material world'.[1] The rank given to reason by the Curieux is no more, though no less, than that given to it in the *Solitaire premier*, where it is the state between 'false opinion' and spiritual understanding. The 'uncertain speculations' of which the Curieux speaks are based on 'false opinion'. Nature is too changeful to be correctly observed without the help of mathematical method; reason must supersede mere opinion and form a 'foundation' for the exact sciences. But the 'matters' of theology are 'difficult or even incomprehensible' to human opinion and human reason alike; reason must 'lead' to faith, point out the 'relationship' between the changeable things of earth and the eternal things of heaven, and encourage us to 'love' the latter.

Hieromnime accepts this with a little modification:

Il est vray (repliqua Hieromnime) que deus Simulacres ont esté proposez aus humeins pour les eslever et acheminer à l'invisible et intellectuel. L'un est simulacre de Nature, qui est le Monde: la naturelle espece duquel, montre la grande excellence de l'ouvrier: si obscurement toutefois, que cela ne pouvoit illuminer les yeus des contemplateurs, pource que Nature de soy trop debile, ne suffiroit pour nous faire connoitre le surnaturel, sans le second simulacre: qui est la Grace, en l'humanité de la parole Divine, de laquelle la vraye, bonne, et unique clarté, procedante de la vraye, bonne, et unique source de lumiere, ha ouvert les yeus humeins: et par la vive persuasion de sa doctrine, ha donné aus voyans connoissance de la verité.[2]

The speech is complicated by the notion of the 'deus Simulacres . . . proposez aus humeins. . . . L'un est simulacre de Nature, qui est le Monde. . . . Nature . . . ne suffiroit . . . sans le second simulacre: qui est la Grace. . . .' But the basic idea is orthodox: the world (*natura naturata*) shows forth *Natura naturans*, the creative power of God; the Incarnate Word shows forth His other attributes.

The Curieux does not reject Hieromnime's amendment: religion is enough for the individual; but the sciences are necessary for society.

[1] F. R. Johnson, *Astronomical Thought in Renaissance England*, Baltimore, 1937, pp. 5 and 63.   [2] U, 1557, p. 9.

Bien que la doctrine de la religion (suivit le Curieus) soit suffisante
pour donner contentement à l'esprit pie: si ne puís je confesser que les
sciences honnestes, et liberales disciplines ne soient (outre ce que j'ay
desja dit) necessaires à l'utilité, et tranquilité des hommes: et que d'elles
ne dependent les constitucions de toutes Republiques bien gouvernees.[1]

It was not this that Hieromnime denied; he makes no general
attack on the human reason like that of the *Apologie de Raymond
Sebond*, no suggestion that it is essentially weakened or corrupted.
It is not even the method of the sciences that dissatisfies him; it is
their subject, 'Nature de soy trop debile'. But his attack has obvious implications: if Nature is 'insufficient', so are science and
reason.

Again and again Hieromnime emphasizes that human reason is
limited:

Celle diligence (dit il) est louable, qui se travaille à la preuve et recherche de la verité des choses humeines, desquelles l'humeine raison
peut former certeine et demonstrable doctrine: mais de s'avancer à
debatre par dispute, les choses qui sont reservees à la connoissance de la
pureté divine, et desquelles la foy, assise sur un fondement qu'on ne doit
jamais essayer d'eslocher, nous assure suffisamment: il me semble que
c'est lascher trop de bride à l'humeine curiosité, et qu'il vaudroit mieus
ne laisser esgayer noz entendemens outre les bornes constituees de
Dieu. . . .[2]

God is 'outre l'apprehension de tout entendement humein',[3] the
angels 'esloignent de beaucoup la capacité de nos entendemens',[4]
the empyrean is 'trop resplendissante pour l'humeine raison'.[5]
Even the Curieux recognizes that the stars are 'eslevez sur nous
et sur notre jugement',[6] though he tends rather to take the difficult,
if not the impossible, as a challenge:

Nous ne sommes pas (dit le Curieus) seulement eslongnez du Ciel
par distance et intervalle de lieu, mais beaucoup plus de sens et d'intelligence: tellement que des choses qui y sont, nous ne pouvons que difficilement, pour ne dire plus qu'incerteinement, juger. Toutefois cette
difficulté ne doit nous faire peur, ou retirer de la diligente recherche. . . .[7]

But for the Solitaire, as for Hieromnime, the limitations of reason
appear to be permanent; in respect of the destructibility of the

---

[1] Ibid.   [2] Ibid., pp. 150–1.   [3] Ibid., p. 12.
[4] DP, 1587, p. 284 v°.   [5] U, 1557, p. 16.
[6] Ibid., p. 94.   [7] Ibid., p. 56.

world he concludes 'qu'entreprendre par raison d'en descouvrir la moindre connoissance, c'est oser une chose qui ne sera jamais executee'.[1]

To attempt to go farther is for Tyard a misuse of reason. It is presumptuous 'lascher, trop de bride à l'humeine curiosité'; it is also unnecessary, for 'la foy . . . nous assure suffisamment'. Hieromnime can speak of 'foy, appuyee . . . de la connoissance . . .';[2] but that knowledge of God is 'telle qu'il lui ha pleu l'eslargir à ma capacité', and very different from the findings of natural reason. Montaigne knew this difference:

car la vraye raison et essentielle, de qui nous desrobons le nom à fauces enseignes, elle loge dans le sein de Dieu; c'est là son giste et sa retraite, c'est de là où elle part quand il plaist à Dieu nous en faire voir quelque rayon. . . .[3]

But no doubt Tyard would have found Montaigne's estimate of human reason too low, though Montaigne found Tyard's estimate of its limits too rigid:

C'est une opinion moyenne et douce, que nostre suffisance nous peut conduire jusques à la cognoissance d'aucunes choses, et qu'elle a certaines mesures de puissance, outre lesquelles c'est temerité de l'employer. Cette opinion est plausible et introduicte par gens de composition; mais il est malaisé de donner bornes à nostre esprit: il est curieux et avide. . . .[4]

For Tyard there appears to be nothing arbitrary or unnatural in the conception of a reason functioning reliably within its own limits but unable to pass them; the senses do exactly the same. He is scarcely troubled, as Montaigne is, by 'les fautes et tromperies qu'ils nous font';[5] to him 'la saveur, la couleur, et l'odeur, sont trois sens, de jugement non refusable',[6] and 'le Ciel . . . est vù tant visiblement, que le nier seroit d'entendement stupide'.[7] Where he criticizes the senses it is for their limitations. The *Solitaire second*'s argument over the primacy of sight relies largely on pointing out not the powers but the deficiencies of the senses: if sight cannot penetrate paper, yet sound cannot penetrate water. No sense can appreciate fine distinctions: the ear cannot tell a true semitone from an approximate one; as for the other senses:

Combien peu d'accidens interieurs ou exterieurs faut il, pour empescher que la personne au toucher ne puisse discerner vrayement une

[1] U, 1557, p. 156.   [2] Ibid., p. 131.
[3] *Essais*, ii. 12, ed. Strowski, ii. 282.   [4] Ibid., ii. 308.
[5] Ibid., ii. 354.   [6] U, 1557, p. 93.   [7] Ibid., p. 55.

diference (si elle est de bien peu) entre deus chaleurs procheines? Comment est le gout facilement trompé au chois des viandes, si elles ne sont qu'un bien peu dissemblables? Et des odeurs, avec quelle dificulté peut on juger les procheines diversitez? car de la vuë, il est assez descouvert combien le jugement est decevable, en ce qu'elle mal aisement comprent les aprochantes et petites diferences des couleurs emmellees.[1]

Our eyes tell us that the stars twinkle and that the light of Saturn is dim; this is the point at which reason must step in and remind us that our sight is 'travaillee par la trop vehemente intention de laquelle elle s'estend, jusque à un lieu tant eslongné',[2] and that Saturn is 'plus grand que Mars, Venus, Mercure, ny la Lune: qui nous doit faire croire que noz yeux sont plus incapables de choisir sa lumiere, que lui defaillant en clarté'.[3]

Revelation respects the dominion of reason in reason's own field: to Hieromnime's remark that neither divine nor diabolic power ever revealed the measurements of the sky, the Curieux is allowed to reply, 'Je prendrois pour notre avantage leur recellement, de ce dont veritablement nous estions bien capables'.[4] Pascal will later sum up:

Car, puisque vous m'y obligez, mon Pere, je vous diray que, selon les sentimens de deux des plus grands Docteurs de l'Eglise, S. Augustin et S. Thomas, ces trois principes de nos connoissances, les sens, la raison, et la foy, ont chacun leurs objets separez et leur certitude dans cette étenduë.[5]

We have in all this 'the fideist distinction which sets limits to man's reason';[6] but it is not 'the doctrine of double truth'.[7] There is no trace in Tyard of the Averroist and Paduan principle that things can at one and the same time be philosophically true and theologically false, or vice versa: 'ea esse vera secundum philosophiam, sed non secundum fidem catholicam'.[8] If Cremonini wishes to remain Christian about something which he considers philosophically false, 'il apporte précisions et distinctions subtiles: la théorie de l'éternité du ciel, rentrant dans la philosophie naturelle, n'ébranle pas le dogme de la création, qui est surnaturel. . . .'[9]

[1] SS, 1555, p. 95.   [2] DP, 1587, p. 229 v°.   [3] M, 1558, p. 38.
[4] U, 1557, p. 44.   [5] Lettres provinciales, xviii.
[6] Lapp, Universe, 1950, p. xliv.   [7] Ibid., p. xlv.
[8] Siger of Brabant; cf. H. O. Taylor, The Mediaeval Mind, London, 1911, ii. 431.
[9] J. R. Charbonnel, La Pensée italienne au seizième siècle, Paris, 1919, p. 261.

Galileo, if theology contradicts science, will jettison theology: 'si une affirmation théologique contredit une vérité scientifique, c'est à la seconde, d'après Galilée, qu'il faut se ranger. S'il n'y a pas de conflit, il est légitime de conserver le parallélisme de ces deux plans de certitude.'[1] For Tyard theology always takes precedence; to the end of his life he remained an orthodox Catholic, against whom his enemies could muster no worse accusation than that of Gallicanism.

But, further, for Tyard nothing can be simultaneously in the departments of both philosophy and theology; that is why the *Discours philosophiques* are so often concerned with determining which things are in which department, where the limits of reason lie. Things must be either 'choses humeines, desquelles l'humeine raison peut former certeine et demonstrable doctrine' or 'choses qui sont reservees à la connoissance de la pureté divine, et desquelles la foy . . . nous assure'.[2] If you think a Christian truth philosophically false, that only proves that it is not a proper subject for your philosophizing; if Christianity rejects something which you believe philosophically true, that only proves that your belief is based on a delusion.

For example, the existence of 'l'eternelle prison des malheureus dannez' 'au centre de la terre' is for Tyard a dogma which 'lon ne peut nier piement', and Hieromnime's statement of it[3] is not weakened for him by the fact that it postulates a 'puissance incomprehensible' which 'mal aisément se peut prouver par raison naturelle'; faith is not obliged to prove or to make comprehensible. Since Tyard's system does not discredit reason, you may attempt to support the dogma by rational explanations and arguments; but you must not be surprised or shaken if your arguments fail, for this is not a field in which reason should be working: 'les raisons naturelles me semblent non recevables, quelque montre qu'elles fassent de preuve inexpugnable, pour debatre contre la puissance du Dieu de la Nature mesmes.'[4] It is indeed not unlikely that reason will fail here; it pleases God 'quelquefois de permettre, pour punicion de noz esprits enorguillis, que les raisonnemens sophistiques aveuglent et confondent notre jugement trop curieusement employé'.[5]

[1] Charbonnel, *La Pensée italienne au seizième siècle*, p. 386.
[2] U, 1557, pp. 150–1.   [3] Ibid., pp. 69–71.
[4] Ibid., p. 154.   [5] Ibid., p. 151.

That this was really Tyard's position is conclusively shown by a page[1] added in the second edition of his *Homilies . . . sur la Passion de nostre Sauveur Jesus Christ.* It is a late work in which to look for evidence, but we have seen how little the views of the *Discours philosophiques* of 1587 varied from those of *L'Univers* and *Mantice.* An attack on the German Reformers, *De Instauranda Religione,* launched in 1544 over the signature of Hermas Laetmatius, supplied the passage; Tyard underlined it in his own copy. There are four categories of truths, Hermas told Tyard, and defining the categories by their contents each author makes it clear that they are mutually exclusive.

Les diligens rechercheurs de verité (qui est en nous un accordé consentement de nostre entendement avec l'essence de la chose) l'ont disposee en quatre sortes. A sçavoir, l'une des choses qui sont naturelles, et propres à nostre usage, et lesquelles Dieu souffre estre receuës en nostre cognoissance, combien qu'elles n'attouchent aucunement les poincts de la religion.

On those we have already heard the Curieux.

La seconde, est de certaines choses indifferentes, et desquelles le doute, si elles appartiennent à la religion, ou non, n'est encor resolu.

Borderline cases are safely embraced by that category.

La tierce est de celles, desquelles Dieu ne veut que les mortels s'enquierent, pource que sa Majesté ne veut pas qu'ils en ayent aucune cognoissance.

On those we have heard Hieromnime.

Et de ces trois premieres sortes de verité, la recherche n'est pas necessaire à nostre salut. Aussi n'est-il besoin d'appuyer ou fonder la fermeté de nostre foy, en la consideration de telles veritez: desquelles au contraire il se faut quelquefois donner garde:

Here, departing from his source, Tyard introduces the fideist scepticism which undermines in advance the arguments of its opponents—with an echo of Plato's myth of the Cave:

d'autant que les veritez naturelles ou imaginees ne sont qu'ombres, qui peuvent tromper souvent nos esprits, et les destourner de la purité de la verité divine. Qui est la quatriesme sorte: c'est à dire des choses perpetuelles, lesquelles nous recognoissons estre revelees par permission

[1] *Trois livres d'homilies . . ., 1586, pp. 162–3.*

de la divine volonté: ou de celles qui evidemment, probablement, et necessairement apparoissent estre tirees, ou escoulees, de celles qui nous sont
revelees ainsi divinement. This is much older than Paduanism.

There has always been a
'vein of scepticism implicit in all Platonic thought'[1] which has
always become fideism on its infiltration first into Judaism, then
into Christianity:

Cogitationes enim mortalium timidae, et incertae providentiae
nostrae;
Corpus enim quod corrumpitur adgravat animam, et terrena inha-
bitatio deprimit sensum multa cogitantem.
Et difficile aestimamus quae in terra sunt, et quae in prospectu sunt
invenimus cum labore: quae autem in caelis sunt quis investigabit?
Sensum autem tuum quis sciet, nisi tu dederis sapientiam, et miseris
spiritum sanctum tuum de altissimis?[2]
Nam quia in Dei sapientia non cognovit mundus per sapientiam
Deum: placuit Deo per stultitiam praedicationis salvos facere credentes.[3]

Among the French Neoplatonists of the sixteenth century this
development reproduced itself once more; this became their way
of escape from the sceptical crisis of the mid-fifties. 'On pouvait se
cramponner à la foi', as Villey puts it:

Depuis les Padouans et Pomponazzi, ce fut une attitude courante
pendant tout le siècle que de séparer radicalement les domaines de la
raison et de la foi, de mettre sa foi à l'abri en déclarant à l'avance vaines
les conclusions de la raison quand elle prétendait empiéter sur le do-
maine de la foi. Une vérité philosophique pouvait être une erreur au
point de vue de la théologie; et il était constant que les vérités théolo-
giques fussent méconnues par la philosophie. Simple apparence peut-
être chez quelques-uns et précaution prudente pour cacher la hardiesse
de leur pensée, cette attitude était incontestablement sincère chez la
plupart.[4]

Several of those whom Busson once grouped as the 'apologistes
suspects', who made the first resistance on 'le terrain choisi par
leurs adversaires',[5] were more or less Neoplatonists and more or
less fideists. There were Le Caron, Lostal, and perhaps, at some
moments, Bruès. There were, a little later, Guy Le Fèvre de la

[1] Nesca A. Robb, *Neoplatonism of the Italian Renaissance*, London, 1935,
p. 37.   [2] Wisd. of Sol. ix. 14–17.   [3] 1 Cor. i. 21.
[4] Villey, op. cit., 2nd ed., Paris, 1933, ii. 153.
[5] Busson, *Rationalisme*, 1922, p. 417.

Boderie and Pierre de la Primaudaye. There was Jean des Caurres, an even greater plagiarist than La Primaudaye, whose position was almost exactly that of Tyard; one chapter[1] of the augmented edition of his *Œuvres morales* is nearly word for word from Tyard's *Deux discours*, and another[2] declares itself to be an

> Accord faict avec Platon, qui dit en son Dialogue, intitulé Phaedo, que la verité et pure essence des choses de ce monde ne se peut cognoistre en ceste terre, et que nous ne voyons que l'ombre des choses, laquelle se diversifie en tant de formes, qu'elle empesche de cognoistre la pure verité.... Nul ne peut obtenir ... sauvegarde, sinon de Philosophie, et encore ... tant et si avant que Dieu le permet ou inspire.

In the *Microcosme* of Scève himself Saulnier sees a 'retour à l'affirmation des valeurs souveraines ... abdication d'un certain égoïsme d'esthète ...', 'pensée respectueuse de la doctrine chrétienne ...'.[3]

It is surely under Busson's new heading of 'apologistes mineurs' that Tyard must be classed, if not under the old heading of 'apologistes orthodoxes'. Indeed, his behaviour would be as odd in an orthodox apologist as in a free-thinker—his avoidance of the major problems of rationalism, his missing of the points of the minor problems, his real interest only as they move away from metaphysics towards the natural sciences. It is comprehensible behaviour only in a practising fideist, a not very original thinker who has convinced himself that it is his Christian duty to think as far as possible in watertight compartments. And Tyard's method of constructing these compartments links him yet more closely with the Neoplatonists: it appears to be derived from Giorgio, also the master of La Boderie and La Primaudaye. For Giorgio, as for Tyard, as indeed perhaps for the Wisdom of Solomon used by both, knowledge subject to reason and knowledge subject to faith are sharply distinguished, not by the manner of study but by the matter studied, on which the manner depends:

> Duplex est enim processus: sicut et duplex natura.... Altera sensibilis: de qua est opinabilis ratio: quam scientiam vocant: Altera vero incorrupta natura ... [de qua est] divina scientia....[4]

---

[1] *Œuvres morales*, Paris, 1584, i. 3; cf. DD, 1578, pp. 97–100.
[2] v. 2.
[3] *Maurice Scève*, 1948, i. 569–70 and 379–80.
[4] *De Harmonia Mundi*, I. ii. 14.

IV · *Reason and Authority*

So far we have watched Tyard considering not what mental processes are valid, but which are permissible—a question now dead,
but alive for him. He and his contemporaries grew up within the
framework of civil, clerical, and academic authority; they were
only beginning to learn in what ways it might be queried; a conservative royalist cleric might be expected to recoil from some of
those ways. Tyard's finding, in the terms of the *Homilies*, is that
reason need not be exercised on 'indifferent things', must not be
exercised on Divine secrets, and may only make 'acceptable and
necessary deductions' from Divine revelation. The remaining kind
of knowledge, of 'natural things', is 'unnecessary for salvation' and
'liable to deceive'; but that is just why it must be carefully exa-
mined, since it cannot be tested by 'the propositions of religion',
and yet is needed for daily 'usage'. So it comes about that after
1556 Tyard himself claims to be a rationalist in secular matters,
complaining that

qui suivra l'opinion mieus fondee de raison, que de nom authorisé, sera
dit paradoxiste, et presomptueus, osant s'opposer à l'autorité de long
tems avouee.

Je vous enten bien (repliqua le Curieus souriant) sous ombre que
vous faites profession de ne croire de leger, et de ne donner à l'autorité
qu'autant de foy (dites vous) que la raison lui en pourra permettre: vous
feriez peu de conscience de desdire Ptolomee et ceus qui l'ont suivi.[1]

The addition of 1587, 'parlant des choses naturelles', is consistent
with what appears to have been Tyard's position from 1557 onwards, and therefore surely to be understood in the original text.

But Tyard appears to have had very little conception of true
rationalism. By 1558, and especially by 1578, he shows a good deal
of shrewd common sense: he knows that the

nom de Science . . . ne doit estre receu qu'aux congnoissances acquises
par vives et naturelles demonstrations, assises sur quelques principes et
fondemens veritables, certeins, et tellement congnus, que les nier fust
dementir ses sens et raison naturelle . . .[2]

and that, as regards the possible significance of comets, 'ce n'est à
celuy qui nie de faire preuve, mais à celuy qui afferme'.[3] But he does

---

[1] U, 1557, p. 22; cf. DP, 1587, p. 207 v°.
[2] M, 1558, p. 31.   [3] DD, 1578, p. 50 v°.

not always put this knowledge to use, or surrender the principle of authority; even where he offers himself as a 'paradoxiste, et presomptueus' his conclusion is only the cautious one that Ptolemy 'peut avoir esté deceu' and that 'sans erreur lon ne peut se donner quelque assurance de ces mouvemens de la huitieme sphere . . .'.[1] By far the greater part of *L'Univers* and *Mantice* still consists of direct and open borrowing. According to Tyard's system, of course, in secular matters a pagan authority is no less reliable than a Christian, though no more so. *L'Univers* even defends for a moment an astronomical argument by Epicurus, of whose school the *Solitaire premier* said that 'les noms ne se permettent jamais prononcer sans qualité d'infame impieté'.[2]

Tyard has little natural inclination to pure reasoning, the process of discovering how far his reason can go alone; his characteristic approach is not to take a fact and deduce from it a series of consequences, but to take an opinion and muster for or against it all possible arguments. The universe is spherical;[3] that is proved not only by 'l'experience oculaire des Estoiles', but also by the authority of Ptolemy, and because 'la rondeur est la premiere et plus parfaite forme de tous les corps solides'. He has little natural inclination to pure doubt, the process of emptying his mind of a concept until he has good grounds for accepting it again; it does not enter his head that perhaps the concepts of primacy and perfection had nothing to do with determining the shape of the world. Here and there, indeed, he shows a positive distaste for disbelief: 'c'est peu, de dire que la figure ronde est premiere, si lon ne lui donne nom de perfeccion', and as for the fact that the shape made up of a single line must be older than any other, 'on ne le peut nier sans outrager le sens commun'. There seem to be not only dramatic craftsmanship and theological dogmatism, but real self-revelation in Tyard's outburst under the name of Hieromnime: 'Quant aux Sceptiques qui nient tout, j'en souhaitte la memoire estouffee.'[4]

When Tyard questions a particular authority, it is because another has suggested the question; almost every attack on established tradition turns out to be borrowed, that is, to have at least one authority supporting it. He records no protest against an Aristotelian account of a lie-detecting fountain;[5] but he does protest against Aristotle's statement that certain animals can live in

[1] U, 1557, pp. 21–22.   [2] Ibid., p. 42; SP, 1552, p. 119.
[3] U, 1557, pp. 13–14.   [4] DD, 1578, p. 112 v°.   [5] U, 1557, p. 92.

fire—'Car de la Salemandre j'en mesurerois ma credulité à l'avis de Dioscoride',[1] that is, 'frustra creditum est'. When his source chooses for him between alternative views he often follows its ruling; but sometimes the source, like the *De Placitis Philosophorum*, comes to no conclusion. It then rests with Tyard himself to find a method of choice between authority and authority, each perhaps equipped with rational arguments.

Lapp and Baridon rightly stress the 'experimental method'. But Tyard's notion of 'experiment' or 'experience' is not one to satisfy a modern scientist; it means, as for the century in general, little more than observation as opposed to reasoning. When Tyard cites his own experience, he does so sincerely and precisely: at a given time and place Peletier and he observed that the light of Jupiter was sufficient to cast shadows and pick out printed characters;[2] his colds in the head are affected by the prevailing wind, as Hippocrates teaches;[3] he caught a lizard 'tel que lon descrit la Salemandre'[4] and succeeded in burning it. But he has small idea of standardizing the conditions or isolating the subject of an experiment, or repeating it until probability or certainty is reached. It is Montaigne who puts the awkward questions.[5]

Tyard's reliance on the alleged experience of others leads him into further danger. He claims not only 'l'experience certaine des voyages'[6] to prove that the earth is round, but also 'l'assurance toute esprouvee par ceus qui ont couru diverses Mers, qui confessent la Septentrionelle estre plus haute',[7]—sea-level is not the same everywhere. Apropos of the zodiacal sign Aries, he can tell of another

effet fort insigne, qui est observé: c'est que par experiment prouvé, le Soleil eclipsant en ce Signe, presagit sur les moutons une pestilence, mortelle et dangereuse.[8]

There, indeed, the Curieux may be speaking ironically; but no recognition of it comes from his auditors. Tyard justly gives absolute priority to the everyday experience of everybody: 'Que la Lune soit plus basse que le Soleil, l'Eclipse en fait la preuve.'[9] But here he is not using the experimental method; simply, again, common sense.

---

[1] U, 1557, p. 69; cf. Dioscorides, *Materia Medica*, ii. 67.
[2] U, 1557, p. 35.   [3] Ibid., p. 83.   [4] DD, 1578, p. 44.
[5] *Essais*, ii. 37.   [6] DP, 1587, p. 267.   [7] U, 1557, p. 89.
[8] Ibid., p. 24.   [9] DD, 1578, p. 16 v°.

Common sense tells him when an authority is not good enough to be trusted: poets 'honorent leurs escrits de mensonges',[1] historians 'mettent en œuvre toutes pieces qu'ils pensent devoir estre agreables ou merveilleus au vulgaire',[2] and Troy used to dominate Asia, 'si l'antiquité ne rend cette opinion fabuleuse'.[3] But the testimony of ancient poets is allowed to support received opinions; what Tyard distrusts much more are unsupported and unusual opinions. The sum of all this often leaves him siding simply with the majority. Despite Plato and Aristotle, who placed the spheres of all the five planets above those of the sun and moon, 'la commune apparence, donne à Saturne, Jupiter, et Mars, les trois plus hauts lieus ... pour loger au milieu le Soleil ...'.[4] Despite Copernicus, 'l'opinion plus favorisee, et d'autorité et de raison, est que le Ciel se meut, et la terre demeure ferme et immuable.'[5]

Especially, Tyard seems repelled by opinions which make too much demand on his imagination. The Curieux begins his description of the universe 'en admiracion de tant esmerveillable machine', but his first comment is that Aristotle's theory of its infinity 'semble estrange et difficile à croire'.[6] Some opinions are too complicated: 'Car l'opinion de Callippe ne me semble recevable: par laquelle il asseuroit qu'il y avoit au Ciel cinquante cinq spheres. ...'[7] Others are too simple, like those of the early Greeks who believed in only one element: 'En quoy ils ont tous grossierement discouru. ...'[8] Most of all, Tyard is shocked by the atomic theory of Democritus:

en quel labirint d'opinion entra il, resvant ses Atomes, son Vuide, ou Rien, sa monstreuse infinité, et autres telles sources et principes de son Tout? Vous sembleroient point les Principes d'Empedocle Agrigentin plus recevables, à savoir les quatre Elemens, Feu, Air, Eau, et Terre, avec deus grandes et principales puissances, c'estadire Amour, qui unit et conjoint tout, et Discorde qui divise et despart le mesme? A vray dire toutes ces opinions ont plus de tenebreuse obscurité, que d'apparence veritable.[9]

Tyard finally accepts neither view; but it is revealing that his instinctive preference was for the one familiar not only in medieval science but in Petrarchist literature.

It would seem that his unconscious and undistinguished method

[1] Ibid., p. 50 v⁰.   [2] Ibid., p. 51.   [3] U, 1557, p. 102.
[4] Ibid., p. 30.   [5] Ibid., p. 15.   [6] Ibid., p. 10.
[7] DP, 1587, p. 203 v⁰.   [8] U, 1557, p. 64.   [9] Ibid., p. 61.

of evaluating an opinion is to check it against the great body of beliefs and principles which his century inherited from the Middle Ages. An opinion is 'antique' if older than they, unusual if it contrasts with them, 'monstrous' if it entails disbelief in them—and preferable in proportion to its agreement with them. Tyard is invoking the principle of the Great Chain of Being when he proves from the perfection of roundness that the universe is round; the principle of primacy when he says it is 'moins croyable'[1] that men could live without fire than without air; the principle of plenitude when he says that it is 'plus croyable que ce Monde inferieur doive perir et s'anuller du tout, qu'estimer la moindre espece pouvoir se perdre demeurans les Elemens entiers'.[2] The dignity of the celestial bodies must not be impugned:

> Car le penser seroit autant profane et fol, de celui qui croiroit les corps celestes pouvoir choir, que peu recevable l'opinion d'un autre, qui donne pour raison de telle apparence, la comparaison des Estoiles à une mesche de lampe. . . .[3]

Trop mieus me plait de confesser le Ciel parfait en sa ronde perfeccion, sans partie affectee à particuliere disposicion: immuable de sa substance, et exempt d'aucune nouveauté de corrupcion ou generacion. . . .[4]

These are some of Tyard's 'principes et fondemens veritables'. Febvre has argued against the possibility of anyone's abandoning them systematically in the time of Rabelais:

> ses négations n'auraient pu être, tout au plus, que des opinions — des façons de penser et de sentir paradoxales que rien ne venait appuyer du dehors, étayer réellement, substantiellement, ni dans la science ni dans la philosophie de son temps.[5]

Certainly Tyard, with his ready acceptance of guiding influences, his years of training in Neoplatonic credulity, his technique of composition by borrowing, and his power of appreciating both sides of a question, was far from Baudelaire's and Busson's type of the 'Rebelle', whose 'rejet du christianisme est le résultat d'une fermentation spontanée et interne, d'une défiance congénitale à l'endroit du surnaturel, qui se refuse à croire ce qui la dépasse'.[6] He came, as a matter of principle, to a Neoplatonic form of scepticism; he came, as a logical consequence, to a position where he

[1] U, 1557, p. 73.   [2] M, 1558, p. 24.   [3] U, 1557, p. 75.
[4] Ibid., pp. 59–60.   [5] L. Febvre, *L'Incroyance au seizième siècle*, p. 498.
[6] Busson, *Rationalisme*, 1957, p. 12.

had to exercise his reason; but his subconscious preferences seem still to have been for conservatism and fideism, secular as well as religious.

This is illustrated by one more of his favourite approaches to the choice between divergent opinions: before rejecting one, he does all he can to reconcile them. Hieromnime draws attention to his talent for this, in the matter of identifying the river Pison: 'voilà, Solitaire . . . une des matieres propres aux remarques que vous faites sur les bons autheurs anciens, et je vous laisse ceste conciliation. . . .'[1] Aristotle seems to contradict himself about whether animals can live in fire; but perhaps he was distinguishing between the pure celestial element and the impure terrestrial one.[2] Aristotle and Seneca disagree over the cause of earthquakes; but Tyard contrives to take from them just what is common to both.[3] As for Martianus Capella, Tyard will do anything short of disputing his identification of the constellation of Berenice's Hair:

et ne me puis persuader, que les images du Ciel n'ayent esté par les anciens diversement nommees: autrement il se trouveroit des fautes inexcusables en quelques endrois des bons Auteurs. . . .

Je me suis essayé (reprint le Curieus) d'excuser ce passage mais outre ce que vous dites je n'y voy moyen, sinon tordant le texte ou le disant corrompu.[4]

When all else fails, Tyard shows in a remarkable degree the Renaissance ability to suspend judgement. It is not modern doubt, deliberate refusal to believe either one side or the other. At heart Tyard is of the generation described by Febvre, with its 'goût égal pour les opinions les plus contradictoires', satisfied with 'situations troubles, ambiguës, peu définies, qui nous semblent absurdes et nous irriteraient',[5] and vaguely prepared to believe both sides. The *Solitaire premier* accepts a theory of multiple truths, multiple meanings of symbols; the *Solitaire second* is a monument of belief that music can be both a divine frenzy and an art with a history. Even in the scientific Discourses Tyard retains his capacity for not making up his mind. Without expressing any preference, he gives two different etymologies of the Hebrew word for 'sky',[6] Plato's assertion and Aristotle's denial that the sky is

[1] DP, 1587, p. 277. [2] U, 1557, p. 69.
[3] Ibid., p. 110; cf. *Metaphys*. ii. 7; *Nat. Quaest*. vi. 20 ff.
[4] U, 1557, p. 29, as emended in the author's corrections.
[5] L. Febvre, op. cit., pp. 450 and 474. [6] DP, 1587, pp. 231 and 260.

animate.[1] After all authorities and arguments have been quoted, the Curieux still qualifies his praise of the 'demonstrations' and 'observations' of Copernicus with the remark that his 'disposition' may or may not be true and it does not matter anyway:

> Toutefois vraye ou non que soit sa disposicion, la connoissance de l'estre de la Terre telle que nous la pouvons avoir, n'en est aucunement troublee. . . .[2]

Montaigne draws the same conclusion: 'Que prendrons nous de là, sinon qu'il ne nous doit chaloir le quel ce soit des deus?'[3] Tyard takes the earth as immobile two lines later, and everywhere else in *L'Univers* and afterwards, even in the *Homilies* of 1588: 'la terre demeure ferme, au milieu et centre de tout le Monde, n'estant soustenue d'aucune chose, que de la volonté divine . . . .'[4]

It is interesting and characteristic that so many of the problems studied at length by Tyard concern astronomy. It would presumably fascinate him as a Neoplatonist; much of his apparent daring, denying the material existence of epicycles,[5] and giving a fair and even friendly hearing to Copernicus, is Neoplatonic rather than rationalist.[6] But Tyard may also be haunted by the fact that the field of astronomy lies just at the limits of the fields of sense and of reason. Another of the *Homilies* shows clearly that for him the distinction between the natural and the supernatural was not necessarily a distinction between the material and the spiritual. There are three regions of heaven, all material, though we can only in spirit appreciate the existence of the third, throne and habitation of God:

> Aussi le faut il chercher en lieu conditionné de plus pure substance et qualité, que celuy qui est logis du corporel. Il faut bien se hausser plus haut, il faut abandonner intellectuellement la terre, monter à tire d'aile spirituelle outre les estages de l'air, passer toute la region elementaire, s'avancer outre les sieges des planettes, et des autres estoiles superieures, pour arriver à ceste sublime substance, infinie, qui est le siege de l'Eternité. . . . Mais celle partie plus haute, qui est eternel siege de Dieu eternel, outrepasse nos sens, et ne tombe sous aucune distinction de nos discours humains. . . .[7]

---

[1] U, 1557, p. 56. [2] Ibid., p. 100.
[3] *Essais*, ii. 12, ed. Strowski, ii. 322.
[4] *Homilies sur la premiere table du Decalogue*, 1588, p. 30 v°.
[5] U, 1557, pp. 31–33. [6] F. R. Johnson, op. cit., pp. 94–95.
[7] *Homilies . . . sur l'Oraison Dominicale*, 1585, p. 21.

This is not mere metaphor, as Hieromnime and the Curieux have agreed:

> . . . les Mathematiciens, coutumiers de n'ateindre plus haut qu'à ce que les aesles de leurs demonstracions les peuvent eslever, se sont esblouis à la clarté trop resplendissante pour l'humeine raison: mais ceus, qui poussez d'une plus haute contemplacion, ne sont si tenamment arrestez aus matieres, qu'ils n'en admirent et (pour n'oser dire plus) tachent de connoitre la cause, tant que peut leur pouvoir: ont estimé sur la neuvieme Sphere, estre non seulement un Ciel dixieme, surnommé Cristalin: mais encores un onzieme, appellé Empyree, comme vous diriez ignee: non proprement pour aucune qualité chaleureuse, mais à cause de l'indicible splendeur dont il est illustré, comme siege destiné pour l'eternelle demeure de Dieu. . . .[1]

The sublunary region is the province of natural science; that is why Tyard can follow Reisch in renouncing all superstition about comets, for they are only exhalations, and 'il ne se peut faire que la matiere des exhalations monte plus haut que sous le Ciel de la Lune'.[2] The incorruptible and eternal empyrean, seat of God and the angels, is the province of theology. But in which category comes the middle region of heaven, the spheres of the planets, sun, and stars, imperishable according to Aristotle, perishable according to Christianity? Here, most of all, Tyard seems torn between the urge of the Curieux to explore all that is permitted to man, and the doubt of Hieromnime whether certain studies are permitted. Hieromnime suggests that perhaps men ought not to try to measure the sky;[3] the Solitaire thinks that perhaps the motion of the eighth sphere is 'incomprehensible aus hommes';[4] all the speakers in the *Discours du temps* finally agree that a really accurate calendar will never be constructed:

> Il faut donc (respondit Sceve) se contenter des corrections approchantes la verité le plus pres que l'on peut en l'an politique, puis qu'il est impossible ou tant difficile de rencontrer une parfaicte et exacte reformation.[5]

Tyard's views on astrology have suffered an odd variety of interpretations. For D. C. Allen, 'the author obviously inclines to the side of Mantice';[6] for Lapp, 'Pontus aligns himself with

[1] U, 1557, pp. 16–17.   [2] DD, 1578, p. 51 v°.   [3] U, 1557, p. 43.
[4] Ibid., p. 22.   [5] DP, 1587, p. 366 v°.
D. C. Allen, *The Star-Crossed Renaissance*, Durham, N.C., 1941, pp. 78–81.

Le Curieux',[1] 'opponent of astrology, clearly the victor'.[2] Tyard's contemporaries were similarly divided: Estienne Tabourot told him, 'Vous n'y avez rien oublié, à mon jugement pour la confuter';[3] the preface to the first edition of *Mantice* says just the opposite. But this is not good evidence: Tyard seems to have been unable even to make up his mind to publish his manuscript. 'L'Imprimeur' relates how he found it

dens un trousseau d'autres œuvres siens laissé, non pour espoir d'en estre si severe censeur, que lon eust à dependre de son opinion, plus que balancer d'une autre, n'en ayant lui mesme voulu plus avant decider que sa fidele et conscientieuse indagation en ha trouvé: et pour cest esgard . . . me suis ingeré de le t'imprimer ainsi à son deceu, comme non deceu que sa generosité ne contendra jamais au contentement de ses plus affectionnés. . . .

Whoever wrote the preface, it was not Tyard himself; not only is its involved style very different from his, but so are its views on astrology, which it defends with assurance: 'de soy elle est tres-veritable, comme partie et principale des Mathematiques entre toutes sciences plus certeines . . . '. Perhaps a work sold better when advertised as a defence; the publisher of the *Artis Divinatricis* called his collection 'encomia et patrocinia', though the last two pamphlets in it were hostile.

Tyard's personal position seems clearly established at the close of the Discourse; the Curieux and Mantice end by appealing to him directly, 'Saurons nous rien de vostre opinion?'[4] and it can be only his two speeches in reply which are to be taken as giving his own conclusions. The Curieux has used authority, reason, and experience to disprove astrology; Mantice has used them all to defend it; and Tyard sees authority and reason on both sides:

ayant veu, et le pour, et le contre, debatu diligemment par plusieurs doctes et graves personnages, tant anciens, que de ce temps: et formant de moymesme divers argumens et pour l'un et pour l'autre, je suis demeuré suspendu entre l'ouy et non. . . .[5]

What he condemns is 'la façon, avec laquelle besongnent tous ceux, que j'ay veuz en ce temps predire et deviner'.[6] He takes from Pico three precise criticisms: current tables of the day-to-day positions

---

[1] Lapp, in *Romanic Review*, 1947.   [2] Id., *Universe*, 1950, p. xxvii.
[3] E. Tabourot, *Les Bigarrures* . . ., Paris, 1585, end.
[4] M, 1558, p. 88.   [5] Ibid., p. 89.   [6] Ibid., p. 90.

of the planets are incorrect;[1] astrologers do not agree on how to construct the celestial Houses;[2] the position of the constellations of the Zodiac has altered since the time of Ptolemy.[3] A fourth objection,[4] also hinted at by Pico, is added in 1587: the number of the stars is infinite or at least not yet certain, and therefore the number of their possible arrangements is infinite or at least incalculable.

Grandement me delecte (repríns je) la consideration des mouvemens celestes utile et necessaire. . . . Mais je ne puis embrasser de bon cueur la Judiciaire, avant que les mouvemens soient bien exactement congnus . . .[5]

and his other objections met. Unlike the Curieux, he believes that the stars have some 'influence'; unlike Mantice, he asserts that how to predict its workings is at present unknown, if not, as the addition of 1587 would imply, unknowable.

Et vous suffise que je sois d'opinion avec vous, que les Astres ne luisent là hault sans nous faire sentir çà bas quelque efficace de leur[s] vives vertus: car au reste, si je ne tien le parti du Curieux, niant entierement l'influence celeste, je m'eslongne de vous: croyant l'Astrologie, de laquelle en ce temps voz devins Prognostiqueurs tirent leurs divinations, estre vaine et d'inutile usage.[6]

This accords with the views expressed in the other scientific Discourses, where the 'influence' of the stars is not denied even by the Curieux, and the Solitaire only objects that 'plusieurs endroits de ceste divinatrice doctrine, sont fondez sur sablon trop mouvant'.[7]

Tyard does also condemn the misuse of astrology; even divination has its appointed limits. One must not use it to probe the Divine secret of when the world will end:

quelques frivoles discours Astronomiques . . . ont enhardy certains pronostiqueurs de predire la fin prochaine du Monde. Mais telles predictions ne sont recevables: ains convaincues de damnable curiosité. . . .[8]

Nor must one be deceived by the 'fureur impudente . . . de certeins imposteurs', 'qui pour estre estimés Divins, promettent de predire et deviner'.[9]

[1] Ibid., p. 90; cf. *Disputationes*, ix. 8.
[2] M, 1558, p. 91; cf. *Disputationes*, ix. 7.
[3] M, 1558, p. 93; cf. *Disputationes*, vi. 15.
[4] DP, 1587, pp. 195 v⁰–196; cf. *Disputationes*, e.g. xi. 2.
[5] M, 1558, pp. 96–97.   [6] Ibid., p. 97.   [7] DD, 1578, p. 51.
[8] DP, 1587, p. 331 v⁰.   [9] M, 1558, p. 2.

Car . . . si en quelque sorte Divination est une verité: celle me semble seulement recevable, qui, affranchie de toute superstition, s'exerce par congnoissance de quelque raison naturelle.[1]

It is purely as a science, a matter for reason, that the Curieux considers astrology and attempts to prove that it is nonsense. The reply of Mantice is interesting: he is prepared to yield a good deal of ground to the Curieux. He admits 'l'apparente force des argumens contraires',[2] 'l'impuissance de pouvoir rendre raison'[2] in respect of some astrological rules, and 'que les derniers, qui en ont discouru, sont froids en argumens'.[3] Instead, with emotional eloquence, he demands an act of faith in earlier astrologers: 'à qui pouvons nous plus fier de raison aux choses non vulgaires, et hautes, qu'à l'autorité d'une personne illustre?'[3] 'Je me resous de croire. . . .'[4] And his reasoning and examples are of the type valid once the act of faith has been made:

les premiers . . . ont esperé leurs successeurs doués de bonté deuë, leur devoir prester en chose tant utile assés de foy, sans en requerir plus scrupuleux tesmoignage. . . .[5]

Ainsi peuvent estre rendues raisons suffisantes des fondemens d'Astrologie, de telle toutefois et tant rare dignité, qu'il est defendu à ceux, qui par capacité de leurs esprits heureusement eslevés s'en sont renduz congnoissans, de la communiquer trop vulgairement. . . .[6]

Mantice is surely trying to bring Tyard back to the Neoplatonic fideism of his early years; perhaps he is even appealing to the Christian fideism which replaced it:

il est croyable que la longue vie des premiers hommes, estendue ordinairement en plusieurs centeines d'années, et le fraiz resentiment, qu'ils avoient encores de la communication dont à la creation ils avoient esté favorisés de la Divinité, prestoit assés belle commodité aux observateurs de tenter par longues experiences, quelz estoient les celestes effectz.[7]

Where the introduction to the Discourse has placed astrology in the first of the Homilies' categories of truth, and the Curieux has placed it not even among 'veritez naturelles' but among 'veritez imaginees', Mantice seems to be trying to place it in the last category, of revealed truth or deductions therefrom, which may employ but may elude reason.

[1] M, 1558, p. 3. [2] Ibid., p. 55.
[3] Ibid., p. 57. [4] Ibid., p. 80.
[5] Ibid., pp. 57–58. [6] Ibid., p. 75. [7] Ibid., p. 58.

Tyard is not satisfied: the proofs of astrology are not 'evident, probable and necessary' enough for him to class it as either natural or revealed truth. One of the two passages he marked in his copy of the *Artis Divinatricis* . . . *encomia*[1] points in the same direction, an admission by Marstallerus:

Difficile est nobis hominibus, veras causas efficientes Astrologiae invenire. Etsi enim testimonia doctiss. virorum, et experientia, si non utilis, tamen frequens et manifesta confirmant esse quandam, eamque certam astrorum vim in haec inferiora, quae possit a peritis mathematicis praedici seu observari, eius tamen . . . verae demonstrationes non possunt in hac ingeniorum imbecillitate adferri.

So astrology presumably goes into the Homilies' category of borderline cases, 'desquelles le doute . . . n'est encore resolu', and Tyard remains 'suspendu entre l'ouy et non: aymant mieux rester encor douteux en subjet tant serieux, que legerement me liguer . . . '.[2]

v · *At the Doors of the Muses*

If the conjectures of this chapter are correct, Tyard's crisis of doubt was a very natural one for a Neoplatonist, especially in the intellectual ferment of the fifteen-fifties; and particularly a docile Neoplatonist, somewhat unimaginative and literal-minded, brought suddenly into contact, by Parisian rationalists or Burgundian gossips, with the fact that his more esoteric beliefs did not work in the outside world. But the *Discours du temps* does not suggest that Tyard's religious faith was affected; and, together with *L'Univers*, it does suggest that it was under Christian and moderate Neoplatonic influence that he emerged from the crisis. Thus he was able to adopt a typical Neoplatonic way out of his intellectual difficulties, not only in *L'Univers* but for the rest of his life. The parallel development in the variants of the Discourses, towards scientific caution and Catholic orthodoxy, only accentuates the distinction which he made between matters of reason and matters of faith.

Apart from this rigid distinction, the crisis of 1556, or a more gradual process, would seem to have completed the broadening of Tyard's mind begun about 1551 by the influence of the encyclopædists. From 1557 onwards Tyard was prepared to present fairly,

[1] P. 20.   [2] M, 1558, p. 89.

if not to accept personally, the ideas of almost any school. The *Discours philosophiques* became a much more liberal compendium than the abortive *Dialogues* of Le Caron or the rather dogmatizing work of Des Caurres and La Primaudaye. Tyard seems even to have felt some charm in unorthodoxy where it stopped short of heresy or scepticism, where it confined itself to suggesting interesting opinions within a framework of sound belief. He draws the line at Epicureanism and at the atomic theory; but, as he lingered over the 'preuves familieres et evidentes'[1] of Aristoxenus, so he dallies later with 'Origene, beaucoup Filozofe',[2] and his sketch of Rabelais hesitates between condemnation and compliment:

> Huius Luciani nostro saeculo Gallicus non ineruditus imitator viguit, qui omnium mores hominum, religionesque cavillari peritissimus, ludos faciens, et delicias, nasoque omnia suspendens, inter sannatores principem locum obtinuit: ipsius proprio cognomine, sacra etiam lingua, id significantissime demonstrante. Is est famosus ille *Rabelez*, qui ab Hebraeis dictionibus, . . . *Rab*, et . . . *lez*, verissime irrisorum principis nomen habuit, quod Gallice dixeris, *un maistre moqueur*.[3]

It is probably this open-mindedness, coupled with a wish to interest all possible readers, which has given a wrong impression to some critics.

For all their universality, the *Discours philosophiques* remained fundamentally a Neoplatonic encyclopædia, which would have a marked appeal to certain groups of Tyard's contemporaries rather than to others. Montaigne evidently perceived that they would be of little use as a rationalist arsenal—'Voyla pas triomfé?'[4]—and there is no evidence that they became one. They would probably offer much more to the other side, and that may be why Mersenne[5] read them, though in the end he took little from them. They would perhaps serve to combat Aristotelian scientists; certainly to elucidate ancient mythology and Renaissance poetry. They would have been most useful in the earliest years of the Pléiade.

The poets of the Pléiade would appreciate the Discourses, as they appreciated the *Erreurs amoureuses*, because so many of their own ideas were reflected there: their Platonism and Petrarchism, their love of classical and scientific erudition, their desire for

---

[1] SS, 1555, p. 43.   [2] U, 1557, p. 155.
[3] *De Recta Nominum Impositione*, 1603, p. 27. The italics are Tyard's.
[4] *Essais*, ii. 12, ed. Strowski, ii. 266.
[5] M. Mersenne, *Quaestiones . . . in Genesim*, Paris, 1623, lvii, 'De Vi Musicae'.

linguistic reform and for the 'marriage of music and poetry'. They may have found the Discourses helpful sources of information— as Ronsard found the *Solitaire second* helpful for his 'Préface au Roy François II'—but probably not often. Ronsard and Du Bellay did not need Tyard to introduce them to Scève or Ficino, to abridge Giraldi or explain Reisch. They went to the originals. As a link between the Pléiade and the School of Lyons, Tyard would indeed have been an 'inutile trait d'union'.[1]

What he supplied, from the moment he welded together the two parts of the *Solitaire premier* with their very different inspirations, was a link between the two parts of the poetic theory of the Pléiade. At that time the Pléiade half-believed that the *furor poeticus* really descended as Ficino described:

Bien te veux-je avertir de chercher la solitude et le silence amy des Muses, qui aussi (affin que ne laisses passer cete fureur divine, qui quelquesfois agite et echaufe les espris poëtiques, et sans la quele ne fault point que nul espere faire chose qui dure) n'ouvrent jamais la porte de leur sacré cabinet, si non à ceux qui hurtent rudement.[2]

La fureur Poëtique procede des Muses (dí je) et est un ravissement de l'ame . . . elle se sent esmue, esguillonnee, et incitee d'exprimer en vers les choses, qu'elle prevoid et contemple.[3]

Simultaneously they believed in the production of literature by conscious and deliberate art:

ces fleurs, et ces fruictz colorez de cete grande eloquence, avecques ces nombres et cete lyaison si artificielle, toutes les quelles choses, non tant de sa propre nature que par artifice, toute Langue a coutume de produyre . . .[4]

'vers compassez en curieuse observance de nombres et de mesures'.[5] The contradiction was generally resolved simply by saying that inspiration made *docte poésie* possible:

> Sans plus ma saincte fureur
> Polira vostre science . . .[6]

Et ne pensez que le Poëte (bien que l'estude ne lui ayt particularisé toutes doctrines) esmu de celle inspiration . . . ne puisse embellir ses vers des plus absconses, et recelees diversitez naturelles, et surnaturelles: car (comme j'ay dit) il est soutenu, et poussé du Dieu.[7]

---

[1] Parturier, *Délie*, 1916, p. xxxix.
[2] Du Bellay, *Deffence et illustration* . . ., ii. 11.
[3] SP, 1552, pp. 42–43.   [4] Du Bellay, op. cit. i. 3.   [5] SP, 1552, p. 38.
[6] Ronsard, 'Ode à Michel de L'Hospital', Epode 12.
[7] SP, 1552, p. 118.

And hard work without inspiration cannot make a poet:

Mais qui voudroit sans la fureur des Muses approcher (comme dit Platon) aux portes poëtiques sous cete esperance que par l'art il pourroit estre bon poëte: icelui certainement seroit imparfait, et sa poësie au regard de celle qui est pleine de fureur, s'évanouïroit.[1]

Aussi n'entreprenne temerairement chacun de hurter aux portes de Poësie: car en vain s'en approche, et fait ses vers miserablement froids celui, auquel les Muses ne font grace de leur fureur. . . .[2]

Pasithée was an unsuccessful poetess, she implies, in comparison with 'quelques damoiselles (car bien que je sois jalouse d'elles, si ne puís je, et ne voudrois celer combien elles sont louables'.[3] But Tyard did not want to insult or discourage her by classing her with the uninspired poetaster. On her behalf, therefore, he faced the problem of the poet who feels moved and excited but who has not learnt to express himself. 'Quelquefois', says Pasithée to the Solitaire,

je me suis plainte à vous de ce, que je sentois en mon esprit une confusion de choses, lesquelles je ne pouvois desgluer l'une de l'autre, et les mettre dehors avec quelque prompte facilité. Toutefois vous m'aviez simplement dit, que l'indisposition de la lecture des livres, et la mauvaise dispensation des heures en estoit cause.

Encor (lui respondí je) n'estoit ma response eslongnee de raison. . . . Gardez vous aussi que le trop de modestie, qui vous fait souvent estendre au mespris de voz graces, . . . n'irrite les Muses, et . . . les esmeue à restraindre celle prodigue liberalité, avec laquelle elles vous font ouverture de leurs cabinets. . . .[4]

If unfamiliarity with study and excessive modesty were holding Pasithée back, evidently hard work and ambition can make a poet. Tyard is prepared, for Pasithée's sake, either to contradict himself and his leaders, or to accept her disquiet and desire, 'unmanageable thoughts' and 'goadings on',[5] as sufficient first signs of inspiration; signs, one might say if it were permissible to adopt Thomist terms, that she has received prevenient grace moving her to seek habitual grace. The *Solitaire second* can speak of her 'doctes et gracieus vers'.[6]

This solution of the problem was of value, not only for would-be

---

[1] Le Caron, op. cit., p. 136. [2] SP, 1552, p. 43.
[3] Ibid., p. 106. [4] Ibid., pp. 92–93.
[5] Wordsworth, *The Prelude or Growth of a Poet's Mind*, i. 139–42.
[6] SS, 1555, p. 154.

poets but for would-be students; Pasithée represented the latter as
much as the former, and Plato and the Solitaire assured her that
what was true of one group was true of the other:

la fureur divine, laquelle les Muses . . . inspirent, fait non seulement le
bon Poëte, mais encores abruve de sa liqueur le Rhapsode, et ceux, qui
l'escoutent reciter les vers.[1]

Tyard's greatest importance, and his special appeal to the Pléiade,
surely lay in that he formed a link between them and those of the
'profane vulgar' who were capable of being educated to appreciate
their work. He did not wholly reject the principle *odi profanum vulgus*;
though he did not demand qualifications in Latin, he expected
the general education that Pasithée had received, and he had no
use for those who did not want to understand:

Je leur respondray (dí je) que l'intention du bon Poëte n'est de non
estre entendu, ni aussi de se baisser, et accommoder à la vilté du vulgaire (duquel ilz sont le chef) pour n'attendre autre jugement de ses
œuvres, que celui, qui naistroit d'une tant lourde congnoissance. Aussi
n'estce en si sterile terroir qu'il desire semer la semence, qui lui rapporte louenge. . . .[2]

But the Solitaire was there to help Pasithée and all those with
'l'esprit doüé de quelque studieuse curiosité'.[3] By enterprise and
hard work, 'vouloir savoir, et puis se delecter en celle volonté: en
apres estre en instante meditation songneux poursuivant de la chose,
qui delecte',[4] they too would attract the Muses to themselves.

It was to such beginners above all that the *Discours philosophiques* were directed. The *Solitaires* would explain the background of
Ronsard's *Odes*; *L'Univers* would elucidate his *Hymnes*, the *Délie*
and the *Microcosme*, the *Encyclie* and the *Premiere sepmaine* . . . .
Tyard always appreciated the position of those who wanted to follow Renaissance thought but who found it difficult, especially
when expressed in Latin. He himself was not a great thinker, and
found some difficulty in grasping complicated or novel concepts;
but his enthusiasm for knowledge, his talent for expression, and
his sympathetic understanding of others were the gifts of a born
teacher. It is not for his originality or judgement that his Discourses should be read; it is more for his powers of selection and

---

[1] SP, 1552, p. 49; cf. Plato, *Ion*, 533–5; Ronsard, 'Ode à Michel de L'Hospital', Strophe 13.   [2] SP, 1552, p. 109.
[3] DD, 1578, p. 86 v°.   [4] SP, 1552, p. 89.

translation, and most of all for his powers of elementary exposition. It was for these powers that his works would be read and appreciated, perhaps by the Pléiade, certainly by his disciples in Burgundy; and, it may well be, by readers dispersed more widely, readers whom the Discourses would help to form into a public, at first for Ronsard, at last for Montaigne. From Tyard's time, and partly as a result of his work, learning in France ceased to be the privilege of a few Latinists; the Muses opened their doors.

BIBLIOGRAPHY

I · WORKS BY TYARD

1. *Erreurs amoureuses* . . . Jean de Tournes, Lyons, 1549. (Later known as *Premier livre des erreurs*.)
2. *Leon Hebrieu de l'amour.* 3 vols. Jean de Tournes, Lyons, 1551. (Translation of Leo Hebraeus, *Dialoghi d'amore.*)
3. *Continuation des erreurs amoureuses* . . . Jean de Tournes, Lyons, 1551. (Includes re-edition of No. 1; second part alternatively known as *Second livre des erreurs.*)
4. Sonnet and Latin verses introducing Benoit Textor, *De la manière de se préserver de la pestilence et d'en guérir.* Jean de Tournes, Lyons, 1551.
5. *Solitaire premier, ou, prose des Muses, et de la fureur poëtique. Plus, quelques vers liriques.* Jean de Tournes, Lyons, 1552.
6. Edition of Jacques de Vintimille, *L'Histoire d'Herodian* . . . G. Roville, Lyons, 1554.
7. *Erreurs amoureuses* . . . Veuve Guillaume le Bret, Paris, 1554. (Reprint of Nos. 1 and 3.)
8. *Erreurs amoureuses, augmentees d'une tierce partie, plus un livre de vers liriques.* Jean de Tournes, Lyons, 1555. (Includes re-edition of Nos. 1 and 3; third part alternatively known as *Troisieme livre des erreurs.*)
9. *Solitaire second, ou prose de la musique.* Jean de Tournes, Lyons, 1555.
10. Sonnet introducing Louise Labé, *Euvres.* Jean de Tournes, Lyons, 1555.
11. *Discours du temps, de l'an, et de ses parties.* Jean de Tournes, Lyons, 1556.
12. *L'Univers, ou, discours des parties, et de la nature du monde.* Jean de Tournes and G. Gazeau, Lyons, 1557.
13. *Mantice ou discours de la verité de divination par astrologie.* Jean de Tournes and G. Gazeau, Lyons, 1558.
14. *Ephemerides Octavae Sphaerae* . . . Jean de Tournes, Lyons, 1562.
15. *De Coelestibus Asterismis Poematium* . . . Galiot du Pré, Paris, 1573. (Composition may date from 1560.)
16. *Mantice ou discours de la verité de divination par astrologie.* Galiot du Pré, Paris, 1573. (Re-edition of No. 13; an undated impression dates from shortly before or after.)
17. *Œuvres poëtiques.* . . . *A sçavoir, trois livres des erreurs amoureuses, un livre de vers liriques. Plus, un recueil de nouvelles œuvres poëtiques.* Galiot du Pré, Paris, 1573. (Includes re-edition of Nos. 1, 3, and 8; last part alternatively known as *Recueil de nouvell' œuvres poëtiques.*)
18. *Solitaire premier, ou dialogue de la fureur poëtique.* Galiot du Pré, Paris, 1575. (Re-edition of No. 5.)

19. *Deux discours de la nature du monde, et de ses parties. A sçavoir, le premier Curieux, traittant des choses materielles: et le second Curieux, des intellectuelles.* Mamert Patisson, Paris, 1578. (Re-edition of No. 12.)

20. *Discours du temps, de l'an, et de ses parties.* Mamert Patisson, Paris, 1578. (Re-edition of No. 11.)

21. *Homilies, ou discours sur l'Oraison Dominicale* . . . . Mamert Patisson, Paris, 1585.

22. Epitaph on Ronsard included in *Les Funebres regretz sur la mort de Pierre de Ronsard.* . . . Gabriel Buon, Paris, 1586.

23. *Homilies, ou contemplations sur la Passion de nostre Sauveur Jesus-christ.* Mamert Patisson, Paris, 1586.

24. *Trois livres d'homilies.* . . . Mamert Patisson, Paris, 1586. (Includes re-edition of Nos. 21 and 23, and a *Troisieme livre . . . sur la dignité de la Croix.*)

25. *De Coelestibus Asterismis Poematium* . . . . Jean Richer, Paris, 1586. (Re-edition of No. 15, together with some Latin pieces in memory of Ronsard.)

26. *Douze fables de fleuves et fontaines.* . . . Jean Richer, Paris, 1586. (Composed about 1556.)

27. *Les Discours philosophiques de Pontus de Tyard . . . Premier Solitaire. Second Solitaire. Mantice. Premier Curieux. Second Curieux. Sceve, ou discours du temps . . .* Abel L'Angelier, Paris, 1587. (Re-edition of Nos. 9, 16, 18, 19, and 20.)

28. *Homilies sur la premiere table du Decalogue.* Claude Chappelet, Paris, 1588.

29. *Tumuli Duo. Primus, D. Margaritae Bussuleae Sanserninae . . . Alter, illustrissimi et generosissimi Heliodori Tyardaei Bissiani.* . . . n.d., n.p. (Includes pieces dated 1592, 1593, and 1594.)

30. *Extrait de la genealogie de Hugues surnommé Capet, roy de France.* . . . Mamert Patisson, Paris, 1594. (Composed about 1580.)

31. Latin epitaph on himself appended to his own will. 1601.

32. *De Recto Nominum Impositione . . . [et] in librum Philonis Judaei de transnominatis annotationes.* . . . J. Roussin, Lyons, 1603. (Composed in 1593 or before.)

33. *Maximes d'estat pour le gouvernement et conservation des empires et royaumes* . . . . *S'ensuivent les advis du diacre Agapet à l'empereur Justinian* . . . . Jean Osmont, Rouen, 1604. (Mégret argues that this is not a first edition.)

34. *Fragmentum Epistolae pii cuiusdam episcopi.* . . . Hanau, 1604. (Composed 1591.)

II · WORKS REFERRING EXTENSIVELY TO TYARD

ALLEN, D. C. *The Star-Crossed Renaissance.* Durham, N.C., 1941.

BAILLET, Adrien. *Jugemens des savans sur les principaux ouvrages des auteurs.* Paris, 1685. Revûs par M. de la Monnoye. Paris, 1725.

BAILLOU, Jean. 'L'Influence de la pensée philosophique de la Renaissance italienne sur la pensée française', *Revue des études italiennes,* i, 1936.

BARIDON, Silvio. *Le Solitaire premier de Pontus de Tyard, édition critique.* Geneva, 1950.

—— *Inventaire de la bibliothèque de Pontus de Tyard.* Geneva, 1950.

—— *Pontus de Tyard (1521–1605).* Milan, n.d. (1950.)

—— Review of LAPP, J. C. *The Universe of Pontus de Tyard. Bibliothèque d'Humanisme et Renaissance,* xii, 1950.

BAUR, Albert. *Maurice Scève et la Renaissance lyonnaise.* Paris, 1906.

BINET, Claude. *Discours de la vie de Pierre de Ronsard.* Paris, 1586. Édition critique par P. Laumonier. Paris, 1909.

BUSSON, Henri. *Les Sources et le développement du rationalisme dans la littérature française de la Renaissance.* Paris, 1922.

—— *Le Rationalisme dans la littérature française de la Renaissance.* Paris, 1957.

CARPENTER, Nan Cooke. 'Spenser and Timotheus: A Musical Gloss on E. K.'s Gloss', *Publications of the Modern Language Association of America,* lxxi, 1956.

—— 'Ronsard's *Préface sur la musique*', *Modern Language Notes,* lxxv, 1960.

CHAMARD, Henri. *Histoire de la Pléiade.* 4 vols. Paris, 1939–40.

CHAMPION, Pierre. 'Henri III et les écrivains de son temps', *Bibliothèque d'Humanisme et Renaissance,* i, 1941.

CLEMENTS, R. J. *Critical Theory and Practice of the Pléiade.* Cambridge, Mass., 1942.

—— (see under MERRILL).

DROUOT, Henri. *Mayenne et la Bourgogne.* Paris, 1937.

DU VERDIER, Antoine. *Bibliothèque.* Lyons, 1585. Nouvelle édition par Rigoley de Juvigny. Paris, 1772.

FESTUGIÈRE, A. J. *La Philosophie de l'amour de Marsile Ficin.* Paris, 1923.

FLAMINI, Francesco. 'Du rôle de Pontus de Tyard dans le pétrarquisme français', *Revue de la Renaissance,* i, 1901.

FOUQUERAY, Henri. *Histoire de la Compagnie de Jésus en France des origines à la suppression,* vol. ii. Paris, 1913.

FRANCHET, Henri. *Le Poète et son œuvre d'après Ronsard.* Paris, 1923.

FRANÇON, Marcel. 'Un Symbole de l'église catholique: "Luna"', *Publications of the Modern Language Association of America,* lx, 1945.

FRÉMY, Édouard. *Origines de l'Académie Française. L'Académie des derniers Valois.* Paris, 1887.

GUÉGAN, B. *Œuvres poétiques complètes de Maurice Scève.* Paris, 1928.

HALL, Kathleen M. 'En quelle année naquit Pontus de Tyard?', *Revue des sciences humaines,* nouvelle série, fasc. 91, 1958.

JACOB, Louis. *De Claris Scriptoribus Cabilonensibus Libri III.* Paris, 1652.

JASINSKI, Max. *Histoire du sonnet en France.* Douai, 1903.

JEANDET, Abel. *Étude sur le seizième siècle. France et Bourgogne. Pontus de Tyard.* Paris, 1860.

—— *Pages inédites d'histoire de Bourgogne au seizième siècle. Fragments des annales de la ville de Verdun-sur-Saône-et-Doubs.* Dijon, 1893.

JOHNSON, S. F. 'Spenser's *Shepherd's Calendar*', *Times Literary Supplement,* 7 Sept. 1960.

KASTNER, L. E. *A History of French Versification.* Oxford, 1903.

LA CROIX DU MAINE, François Grudé de. *Bibliothèque*. Paris, 1584. Nouvelle édition par Rigoley de Juvigny. Paris, 1772.

LAPP, J. C. 'Pontus de Tyard and the Science of his Age', *Romanic Review*, xxxviii, 1947.

—— 'The Identity of Pontus de Tyard's "Curieux"', *Modern Language Notes*, lxii, 1947.

—— 'Three Attitudes toward Astrology: Rabelais, Montaigne, Pontus de Tyard', *Publications of the Modern Language Association of America*, lxiv, 1949.

—— 'Pontus de Tyard and the *Querelle des Femmes*', *Modern Language Notes*, lxiv, 1949.

—— *The Universe of Pontus de Tyard. A Critical Edition of* L'Univers. Ithaca, N.Y., 1950.

LAVAUD, Jacques. *Un Poète de cour: Philippe Desportes*. Paris, 1936.

LEX, Léonce. 'A propos de la naissance de Pontus de Tyard', *Annales de l'Académie de Mâcon*, troisième série, xx, 1920.

MARIN, F. L. C. *Notice sur la vie, les ouvrages de Pontus de Thiard*. n.p. (Marseilles?), 1786.

MARTINON, Ph. *Les Strophes*. Paris, 1912.

MARTY-LAVEAUX, Ch. *Les Œuvres poétiques de Pontus de Tyard*. Paris, 1875.

—— *La Langue de la Pléiade*. 2 vols. Paris, 1896–8.

MÉGRET, Jacques. 'Une traduction inconnue de Pontus de Thyard', *Bulletin du Bibliophile*, 1931.

MERRILL, R. V. 'Platonism in Pontus de Tyard's *Erreurs amoureuses*', *Modern Philology*, xxxv, 1937.

—— 'Three Sonnets of the Sun', ibid. xxxvi, 1938.

—— (with CLEMENTS, R. J.). *Platonism in French Renaissance Poetry*. New York, 1957.

MORÇAY, Raoul. *La Renaissance*. Paris, 1933.

MORPHOS, P. P. *Les Dialogues de Guy de Brués*. Baltimore, 1953.

NOLHAC, P. de. *Pour le quatrième centenaire de Pontus de Tyard—Pontus de Tyard et Pierre de Ronsard*. Dijon, n.d. (1921.)

PARTURIER, Eugène. *Maurice Scève: Délie, object de plus haulte vertu: édition critique*. Paris, 1916.

PASQUIER, Estienne. *Recherches de la France*. Vol. iv, Paris, 1596. Vol. vi, Paris, 1607. Vol. vii, Paris, 1621.

PATTERSON, W. F. *Three Centuries of French Poetic Theory*. Ann Arbor, 1935.

PERRY, Claude. *Histoire de la ville de Chalon-sur-Saône*. Chalon-sur-Saône, 1659.

RAYMOND, Marcel. *L'Influence de Ronsard*. Paris, 1927.

ROUCHON, Ulysse. 'Un Camarade de Ronsard. Pontus de Tyard', *Journal des débats politiques et littéraires*, 25 Sept. 1924.

ROY-CHEVRIER, J. 'Chalon métallique: description, étude et reproduction de jetons, médailles, plombs et méreaux de Saône-et-Loire antérieurs à 1789', *Mémoires de la Société d'Histoire et d'Archéologie de Chalon-sur-Saône*, xvi (deuxième série, viii), 1919.

Roy-Chevrier, J. 'Les Amours de Pontus de Tyard', ibid. xx (deuxième série, x), 1924.

Sainct-Julien de Balleure, Pierre de. *Discours des antiquitez de la ville et cité de Chalon-sur-Saône*. Paris, 1581.

Sainte-Marthe, Scévole de. *Virorum Doctrina Illustrium Elogia*. Poitiers, 1598.

Saulnier, V. L. 'Étude sur Pernette du Guillet', *Bibliothèque d'Humanisme et Renaissance*, iv, 1943.

—— 'Maurice Scève et Pontus de Tyard: Deux notes sur le pétrarquisme de Pontus', *Revue de Littérature Comparée*, xxii, 1948.

—— *Maurice Scève*. 2 vols. Paris, 1948–9.

—— 'Un nouveau billet de Pontus de Tyard', *Bulletin du Bibliophile*, 1951.

—— 'Maurice Scève vu par Pontus de Tyard', *Mélanges d'histoire littéraire offerts à Jean Bonnerot*. Paris, 1954.

Saulx-Tavannes, Guillaume de. *Mémoires des choses advenues en France*. Paris, 1625.

Schmidt, A. M. *La Poésie scientifique en France au seizième siècle*. Paris, 1938.

—— 'Pontus de Tyard et l'amour famélique', *La Table Ronde*, fasc. 97, 1956.

Séché, Léon. 'Un Monument à Pontus de Tyard', *Revue de la Renaissance*, vii, 1906.

Steadman, John M. 'Timotheus in Dryden, E. K., and Gafori', *Times Literary Supplement*, 16 Dec. 1960.

Thorndike, Lynn. *A History of Magic and Experimental Science*, vol. vi. New York, 1941.

Thou, Jacques Auguste de. *Historiarum sui temporis ... Libri CXXXVIII*. Geneva, 1620.

Thyard, Gaspard Pontus de. *Histoire de Pontus de Thyard de Bissy*. Neuchâtel, 1784.

Torri, L. 'Il *Solitaire Second* di Pontus de Tyard', *Rivista Musicale Italiana*, viii, fasc. 4, 1901.

Vaganay, H. 'Quatre noms propres dans la littérature', *Revue de Littérature Comparée*, xv, 1935.

Vianey, J. *Le Pétrarquisme en France au seizième siècle*. Montpellier, 1909.

Walker, D. P. 'Musical Humanism in the Sixteenth and Early Seventeenth Centuries', *Music Review*, i–iii, 1941–2.

—— 'Orpheus the Theologian and Renaissance Platonists', *Journal of the Courtauld and Warburg Institutes*, xvi, 1953.

—— 'The *Prisca Theologia* in France', ibid. xvii, 1954.

—— *Spiritual and Demonic Magic from Ficino to Campanella*. London, 1958.

Weber, Henri. *La Création poétique au seizième siècle en France*. Paris, 1956.

Yates, Frances A. *The French Academies of the Sixteenth Century*. London, 1947.

Young, Margaret L. M. 'Des Autelz and the *Discours philosophiques* of Pontus de Tyard', *Bibliothèque d'Humanisme et Renaissance*, xxii, 1960.

—— *Guillaume des Autelz. A Study of his Life and Works*. Geneva, 1961.

INDEX

PRINTED IN GREAT BRITAIN
AT THE UNIVERSITY PRESS, OXFORD
BY VIVIAN RIDLER
PRINTER TO THE UNIVERSITY